**Parallel)n
Process **
edited by J A KEANE

 In association with UNICOM

Text © Unicom Seminars and Stanley Thornes (Publishers) Ltd 1996

The right of Unicom Seminars and Stanley Thornes (Publishers) Ltd 1996 to be identified as authors of this work has been asserted by them in accordance with the Copyright, Designs and Patents Act 1988.

All rights reserved. No part of this publication may be reproduced or transmitted in any form or by any means, electronic or mechanical, including photocopy, recording or any information storage and retrieval system, without permission in writing from the publisher or under licence from the Copyright Licensing Agency Limited. Further details of such licences (for reprographic reproduction) may be obtained from the Copyright Licensing Agency Limited, of 90 Tottenham Court Road, London W1P 9HE.

The publishers accept no responsibility for any statements or opinions expressed in this work.

First published in 1996 by:
Stanley Thornes (Publishers) Ltd
Ellenborough House
Wellington Street
CHELTENHAM
Glos. GL50 1YW
United Kingdom

96 97 98 99 00 / 10 9 8 7 6 5 4 3 2 1

A catalogue record for this book is available from the British Library.

ISBN 0 7487 2325 0

Printed and bound in Great Britain by the LooseLeaf Company, Wiltshire.

Contents

Preface   i

PART 1   CHARACTERISTICS AND MOTIVATIONS

1. On the Parallel Characteristics of Engineering/Scientific and Commercial Applications   1
   F. Darema
2. Parallel Processing in a Commercial Open Systems Market   31
   F. N. Teskey
3. Parallel Perspectives on Management Information   39
   B. Porter and D. Holle
4. Parallel Processing for Database Applications: the Forthcoming Revolution   47
   J. Spiers

PART 2   ARCHITECTURES

5. Optimizing Parallel Processing in the Commercial Relational Environment   65
   J. Page
6. The EDS Commercial Parallel Processing System   81
   L. Borrmann, F. Hutner, S. R. Leunig, M. Lopez, M. J. Reeve, C. J. Skelton and K. F. Wong
7. IDIOMS: A Database Machine with Distributed Processor Architecture   103
   J. Kerridge
8. Parallel Architectures for Smart Processing Systems   115
   S. H. Lavington and C. J. Wang

PART 3   SOFTWARE TOOLS AND PROGRAMMING MODELS

9. The PVM Concurrent Computing System   133
   V. S. Sunderam
10. Configuration Tools for a Parallel Processing System   151
    M. Ward, J. Hayley and J. Meadows

11 Customizable Resource Management for Parallel Datavase System   167
    K. R. Mayes, J. Bridgland and S. Quick
12 Performance Evaluation of Large Parallel Database Machines: 185
    Techniques and Tools
    I. Jelly, J. Kerridge and C. Bates

PART 4   APPLICATIONS

13 Real Commercial Applications on Parallel Database Systems   203
    C. Upstill, P. Allen, I. Cramb and N. Winterbottom
14 Recursive Query Processing on a Connection Machine   211
    Th. Zurek, E. M. Minty and P. Thanisch
15 Processing Databases of Chemical and Biological Structures   239
    on the Distributed Array Processor
    P. Willett
16 Exploitation of Parallelism in Commercial Systems   255
    J. A. Keane and X. Ye

Preface

Parallel computer systems offer potential advantages in a number of areas, including processing speed, memory and disk capacity, input/output capability, and system availability. The theme of this book is parallel systems as an enabling technology for information processing. The primary focus is on commercial data processing applications, particularly databases. The related area of knowledge-based information processing is discussed. Issues common to commercial applications and engineering and science applications are also considered. The book is divided into four sections: characteristics and motivation, architectures, software tools and programming models, and applications. The majority of chapters have been selected from seminars held between 1992 and 1994. The remaining chapters are invited contributions from workers active in the area of parallel information processing, both in industry and academia.

The first section deals with the characteristics of information processing, and the motivation for using parallel systems in such. Darema considers the different characteristics of commercial applications and engineering and scientific applications. A trend towards the merging of the application areas is identified, and future systems are discussed. Teskey addresses how the benefits of parallel processing can be realized in commercial applications. The conclusion is that it is in the context of open systems that parallel systems will be integrated into existing mainframe environments. Porter and Holle discuss the growing importance of knowledge workers in commercial enterprises. The increased complexity of knowledge required in turn causes a need for more powerful computer systems. Spiers considers the technological reasons behind the increasing significance of parallel machines for database processing. The implementation of the Oracle relational database system on such machines is discussed in detail.

ii PREFACE

The second section deals with both commercially available and experimental parallel architectures. A debate continues as to the most appropriate type of parallel architecture. One issue is will general-purpose architectures or specialized architectures for specific applications be the most successful commercially. Another issue is the support of single-instruction multiple-data (SIMD) processing or the more general multiple-instruction multiple-data (MIMD) processing. Both SIMD and MIMD architectures are presented here, all being targeted at information processing. Page considers the use of parallel processing to exploit very large relational databases. The commercially available MIMD AT&T 3600 is used as an example architecture. Skelton *et al.* consider the experimental MIMD EDS database server. The provision of declarative language is also addressed briefly. The ICL Goldrush system, a derivative of EDS, is commercially available. Kerridge discusses the experimental MIMD IDIOMS database machine. IDIOMS has been designed to target the requirements of a large UK bank. Lavington and Wang address architecture support for knowledge-based information processing. The design of an add-on active memory unit based on SIMD parallelism is discussed. This design has been prototyped.

The third section deals with the provision of software tools and programming models. Suitable programming models are vital to the growth of the parallel processing market. Sunderam discusses the PVM (Parallel Virtual Machine) model. PVM is regarded as a suitable abstraction for both commercial and scientific applications. The next two chapters are concerned with tool support at the level of the operating system. Ward *et al.* consider the design of configuration tools. The focus being the provision of non-stop file access. Availability, fault-tolerance and ease of management are crucial aspects for mission-critical information processing. Mayes *et al.* discuss how databases can be supported by operating systems. The emphasis being customizable resource management to allow precisely the required operating system interface. To convince commercial users' of the utility of parallel systems it is necessary to establish benchmarks that closely simulate 'real' application activity. Jelly *et al.* present a set of tools to measure parallel database performance in banking applications.

The final section of the book brings together the concerns of each of the previous sections in the context of information processing applications. Following on from the previous section, Upstill *et al.* discuss the design of software tool support derived from work for large companies on real database applications. These include tools for performance evaluation. The provision of recursive queries as an extension to the standard relational database model is of increasing importance. Zurek *et al.* discuss recursive query processing on the SIMD Connection Machine. The chapter by Willett concerns the use of the SIMD Distributed Array Processor for processing databases of chemical and biological structures. Keane and Ye consider the implementation of two applications on three MIMD systems. The focus being the appropriateness of the programming models offered by the systems.

Acknowledgements

Thanks to the contributors; to the Department of Computation for the use of its facilities; to colleagues at UMIST and Manchester; to Dhira and Mark at UNICOM; and to John, Maude, Hubert and Kate.

J. A. Keane
(jak@co.umist.ac.uk)
Manchester, April 1995

PART 1

Characteristics and Motivations

1 On the Parallel Characteristics of Engineering/Scientific and Commercial Applications: Differences, Similarities and Future Outlook

*F. Darema**
Computer Sciences Department
IBM T. J. Watson Research Center

1 INTRODUCTION AND OUTLINE

1.1 Past evolution of engineering/scientific and commercial parallel computing

For over a decade now parallelism has been in the forefront as the cost-effective means of attaining high-performance computational capabilities. Although parallelism has not permeated computing as rapidly and widely as it was predicted in the early 1980s, it is nevertheless steadily maturing. At this point there exists a considerable body of work that has addressed and advanced our understanding in the requirements of the applications in terms of parallel computer architectures (processor, memory and remote store), systems' software (OS, computational models, languages, tools), applications software (parallel algorithms and methods), and application subsystems/enablers (file systems, databases).

Although commercial parallel database systems appeared in the market as early as 1983 (Teradata, 1983), parallelism in the application level in particular, has been primarily pursued and exploited for applications in the engineering and scientific fields, as their needs for extremely large computational capabilities have been strongly voiced, for example (NASA, 1993). This is somewhat paradoxical in that many traditional commercial applications, like for example finance or human resources, have sought and used the largest computers (fastest mainframes) in the market, and the computational needs in these disciplines are also projected to increase with the advent of the information age.

---

*Currently:
Mathematical and Physical Sciences Directorate, National Science Foundation, 4201 Wilson Blvd., Arlington, VA 22230, USA.

2 Parallel Information Processing

One of the reasons for the lack of more widespread use of parallelism is that it is still considered to be in the experimental stage, with the consequence that there are many contending and promising directions to parallelism. Progress has focused in enhancing computing capabilities, while enhancing the capabilities for the secondary storage are now beginning to be addressed in parallel computing. Parallel computer robustness and fault tolerance, absolute requirements in commercial organizations' environments, are far from being declared solved problems. Lastly, but maybe even mostly important, is that the software technology is far from being mature, albeit fast progress is being made.

1.2 Convergence, integration, unification

At the same time, with the advent of parallel computing, we are also experiencing other fundamental changes in the design paradigm of the computing systems. In the past hardware has been treated independently from software, engineering/scientific computing has been considered distinct from commercial. Presently we are in an era of unification in several aspects.

For a few years now (Darema, 1988a,b,c; Messina, 1993) there has been an emerging sense that there is a more symbiotic relation between hardware and software; that in fact by driving the hardware and systems' software design from the end-user application point of view, will result in building better systems; 'application-driven system design' has become the motto since the late 1980s.

In the early 1990s we see that a unification along another axis is emerging: the convergence of the engineering/scientific and the commercial computing arenas. This is driven by many factors, that will be discussed later on, among which are: the technological progress in the computing and communications capabilities; and the change in the business model of modern enterprises, from consisting of isolated functional entities, to a model where the functional entities are interoperating. This unification of ES and commercial applications is an important consideration for this chapter, and I will elaborate more on this aspect.

1.3 Specific areas for unified analysis

Based on the existing body of experience, I will discuss in this chapter what I see as the common and as the distinct features and requirements of commercial and engineering/scientific (ES) applications with regards to parallelism. I will address the emerging trends and the converging trends of these two arenas, and discuss how these characteristics affect the required capabilities of computer systems and the supporting software. I will address some specific areas where I feel unified analysis of ES and commercial parallel systems can yield transfer of technology from one domain to the other, or common technological development, and I will discuss the areas where innovation is needed to address the requirements of the emerging applications. In particular I will focus on the following aspects:

- Common analysis of the trade-offs between shared and distributed parallel architectures, and issues of scalability.
- Software support for the parallel execution and parallel I/O of ES and commercial applications.
- Database facilities, and disk and tape storage requirements for ES applications; and database facilities that enable sharing of data between ES and commercial applications.

In the following I will provide an overview of the predominant parallel systems architectures, and I discuss the characteristics of engineering/scientific and commercial applications, in terms of the traditional differences and similarities of these areas, as well as emerging directions. In doing that I'll attempt to identify how hardware and software design can leverage on the experience and knowledge that exists in one area to complement and enhance solutions for both areas.

2   THE PAST AND THE EMERGING NATURE OF ES AND COMMERCIAL APPLICATIONS

Together with the emergence of parallelism, another important development is the changing nature of the ES and commercial applications. Such trends affect the parallel computing requirements of these applications and deserve to be discussed first.

2.1   Engineering/scientific applications

In ES computing the engineer or scientist attempts to understand or predict the behaviour of a physical process or system by creating a theoretical model of that process and by translating the model into a set of mathematical expressions that due, to their complexity, are solved on a computer. Often the application is specialized and tuned to solve a specific problem, e.g. design of an airplane, DNA modelling, motion of the galaxies. The application lifetime typically is of a few years, the application program to be superseded by a newer program where additional model components and better algorithms are implemented. The terms model, application and the computer program are often used interchangeably in the ES computing world and I will also do that here.

The explanatory or predictive capability of the model is enhanced by including as much a detailed description of the physical system as possible. This results in types of computations that are complex, and consequently 'take a lot of computer time' to get an answer. Because of this characteristic of the applications, the focus in ES computing has been to devote as much of the computing resources as possible to the application running, to get these specific results, versus spending computing resources in executing system software. Thus ES applications avoided in the past using software technology, like databases for the administration of the applications' data. In fact traditionally, many such applications are running with 'bare bones' system software support. It is not desirable to involve the OS in the execution of the application. Because such computations take long times, often are run in *batch mode*, and it is important to minimize the turn-around time for that application and that user. Most users in fact prefer to run standalone on the machine and eliminate any OS interference and overheads resulting from task swapping in multi-user, multi-processing environments.

The focus has been in the computations incurred by the application itself, versus the system software. ES computations involve typically operations on floating point numbers; 'a lot of work' is done per piece of data by the application software. Thus in ES computing addressing and enhancing the capabilities of the CPU has been the focus. In the ES arena, considerations of remote memory requirements, like disks and tapes, and I/O to such devices, in the past had been relegated to secondary importance compared to the quest for high CPU performance.

Another reason for the emphasis on computing versus emphasis on I/O capabilities is that, although there are counter examples, typically ES computing has been 'localized': computations done by a scientist or an engineer in an organization typically were not exchanged with others, except possibly for the distilled results. This is changing in several respects: suddenly today's fast CPU machines produce large amounts of data; there is more tendency to keep the raw information, for further or future post-analysis, or for collaborative work; concurrent engineering is the buzzword of the 1990s. Thus there is need to store, retrieve, manage and manipulate these large amounts of data. Closer interaction of theoretical modelling with experiment in engineering and sciences (Darema, 1988b; Humphrey, 1992; Blech, 1990) together with capabilities like interactive steering of the ongoing computation by the modeller or the experimental feedback, impose data management requirements for ES applications. Added to that, the experimental data collected in the engineering scientific world is increasing, because of the evolution in the capabilities of computers. All these evolving trends bring issues of the secondary storage and data management in the forefront for ES computing.

2.2 Commercial applications

Traditional commercial (or business) computing dealt with management of personnel information (or other human resource records), financial accounts, etc; exemplified by applications such as Decision Support, Management Information Systems (MIS) and OnLine Transaction Processing (OLTP). All these applications are dealing primarily with information tracking and exchange. *Query* and *transaction processing* are the generic operations in traditional commercial computing.

Computationally one inspects a piece of information (data), and maybe modifies it, and the process repeats for another set of data. Thus in commercial applications one processes large amounts of data but the application itself does relatively little computation on the data. Managing data, which is enabled by the application subsystem (the database management subsystem) has been a central aspect in commercial computing.

On the other hand, in commercial applications one deals with a lot of data. An important component of the sophisticated application support systems (or sub- systems, or enablers) that have been developed, are the systems to handle the data, like databases and database management systems. These sub-systems for example aid the application to access the appropriate data, keep track of the different versions of the data, ensure authentication of access and maintain the integrity of the data in hardware or software failures. To provide all these functions such application sub-systems consist of a considerable body of software complimenting the application software and consume considerable computing resources. And, in analogy with the ES applications where the OS is not involved in the computations, in commercial computing the OS is not involved in the data management; the DBMS handles the locks (on data) and data management queues rather than relying for such functions on the OS.

In addition to the needs for sophisticated data management capabilities commercial computing environments operate in a mode where many operations are interactive (e.g. bank-teller transactions), potentially multiple users are acting on a given data, share computing resources, and require that the computing resources are 'continually' available. The database subsystem and the operating system must provide such capabilities: maintain the data integrity upon simultaneous accesses; maintain the data integrity and minimize the interruptions when system components, such as disks' 'crash'; and minimize time 'for all users to get their answer'.

Traditionally the vast amounts of data encountered in commercial environments, are stored in inexpensive, secondary storage media like disks and tapes. Access to such secondary storage is much slower than access to main memory or cache, and the mismatch in speed becomes more acute as the processing speed increases. Thus addressing and enhancing I/O capabilities has been an important aim in commercial computing. That includes capabilities of enhancing the bandwidth to secondary storage, as well as developing software which reduces the frequency of access to the secondary store, with techniques that reutilise as much as possible data that are brought in main memory or cache. We will come back to discuss this with respect to parallelism.

Information exchange has been crucial in the commercial world and storage media, like tapes or disks, has been in the past the means for exchanging data with others. The advent of high speed networks is changing that use, but the need for the cheaper secondary storage still remains.

Another aspect that has implications to parallelism of queries and transactions is the following: in the past queries against data was distinct from transactions; that is changing. Transactions are producers of data, queries are consumers of data. If, for example, queries and transactions were made against the same data, typically these were performed on two distinct copies of the data. Today in the fast-moving-pace commercial world, it becomes more and more imperative that queries are done against the up-to-date data, as they are produced by transactions. For some applications, like statistical market analysis queries, accessing a common data set is no problem, but for applications like CAD, it's important to access the up-to-date data instead of an obsolete and possibly incongruous design. This has implications in considerations of locking and versioning of the data, with implications on parallelism, and as such is a technical challenge to be addressed.

Another emerging trend that is seen more and more often in commercial computing is that modelling and simulations, previously techniques of the engineering/scientific world, are permeating the commercial world; for example, numerical simulations for analysis and management of assets, use an increasing amount of the computing resources in banks and financial institutions.

2.3 E/merging applications

Besides an evolutionary change in the nature of ES and commercial applications, there is also a revolutionary change. I will call these 'E/merging' applications because they are novel applications and at the same time fall in line with the merging requirements of ES and commercial applications. Examples to cite here are: Computer Integrated Manufacturing, Data-Mining, Integrated Modelling and Experiment Simulations, Electronic Libraries, (M)Ultimedia, etc.

It was actually back in the 1970s with the emergence of CIM (Computer Integrated Manufacturing) (COPICS, 1979; CIMAPPS, 1993) that attempted to automate the process and control in manufacturing enterprises that introduced the need for integration of the manufacturing operations, from engineering design and manufacturing floor operations, to sales, distribution, financial accounting and human resources computer automation. In that respect CIM brought into the forefront needs of databases that can be accessed by multiple disciplines: the design engineers and the manufacturing operations, as well as the sales and ordering, that is, the commercial end of the enterprise. Since CIM was considered specific to manufacturing enterprises, it was not viewed as a general trend, and the emerging needs are being developed independently by multiple disciplines.

It is, for example, becoming imperative to use complex data-mining queries and simulation to try to improve the performance of commercial organizations, rather than to manage the information following standard processes. This leads away from general purpose query and transaction processing and towards applications that interoperate with other applications in an organization, or with applications in other organizations, and with large computational needs and thus the need to explore and exploit parallelism. It is beginning to be practical to use massive computation for complex data mining queries and transaction processing. For simulations and modelling of commercial processes, many of the parallel programming techniques developed initially for ES use are likely to become important.

There many other examples of the emerging nature of the applications. Such are the Integrated Experiment and Simulation Environments which involve scientific, graphics and data acquisition applications, and database systems to manage data and enable interoperability of several such applications; such integrated applications are considered an important trend in ES environments; (Darema, 1988c; Humphrey, 1992; Blech, 1990) provide examples from fluid dynamics and aerodynamics applications. Medical applications can be foreseen in the future, that combine patient records and medical history with diagnostic scans (like x-rays, MRI, CATscans, etc.), with simultaneous (or on-line) graphical rendering of such scans and the possibility of other simultaneous simulations, such as transport simulations for adjusting the radiation dose or analysing comparable cases. The list of other such future scenarios is only limited by imagination!.

So although until the recent past the two arenas, engineering/scientific and commercial, have been addressed as distinct, the boundaries are disappearing with implications of that in terms of the future hardware and software development. How can we leverage the experiences from the distinct past histories to address the common future needs?[1]

2.4 Data models

An inherent aspect of the applications with respect to the data they deal with, is how the data are organized to be made accessible to an application. This data

---

[1]*'Repeticio est mater studuorum'*, Latin maxim: 'the repetition is the mother of the sciences'.

organization and the means of describing the data, is generically referred to as the data model.

In ES computing, typical structures are variables, representing single value parameters, and arrays which are collections of data that form an ordered sequence. These data are mapped into the computer memory to be accessed during execution of the application program. The data can also be stored in secondary storage (disks or tapes) either for saving the data of a given computation or as scratch space at run-time, if the computer memory capacity is exceeded. For ES applications disk or tape data are stored in the form of records on sequential or random access files. It is the responsibility of the application program to know what each entity represents, and how it is stored, so that the application can access the data in a consistent manner.

While commercial applications deal with data that can be single parameter variables or arrays, there is a level of abstraction that is introduced by the database subsystem, to enable declarative languages (like SQL) to only be concerned about which data one needs to access, rather than how to access these data. Database management systems not only manage and control access to data but also store relationships among various data elements. The earliest systems were based on the hierarchical model where data items (records) were represented in tree structures. IMS is an example of a database system based on the hierarchical model. The hierarchical model enables easy representation of complex relationships among data elements. However, in dealing with commercial application data the hierarchical model suffered from inefficiency and rigidity in modifying the data structures.

The relational database model (Codd, 1971) is a newer form that allows only simple relations, in the form of tables, thus removing the information of complex relation from the database itself, and moves it to the application level. The gain is high efficiency and flexibility in modifying the data structures. The relational model has gained popularity for data management of commercial applications.

The relational models used in commercial applications do not match well the needs of managing ES data that are in the form of, typically large, multidimensional arrays, or other irregular, or hierarchical structures, such as linked lists. Potential possibilities are to use the relational model for tables on pointers to the actual arrays, but such an approach can become cumbersome in accommodating unstructured data sets. Nevertheless, efforts are underway to use relational DBMS for scientific data and define data models (Stonebracker, 1993). Attempts to define data models for scientific data are mostly domain specific (Hunter et al., 1993). Other possibilities pursued are hierarchical database approaches (Chesshire, 1993), and Object-Oriented technology, like Object-Oriented Data Base Management Systems (OODBMS) as exemplified by products like Objectivity's ObjectStore (ObjectStore, 1993), which seem to be gaining appeal in the CAD (Computer Aided Design) arena.

3   HISTORICAL DIFFERENCES BETWEEN ES AND COMMERCIAL USE OF PARALLELISM

Engineering/Scientific applications have exploited parallelism to gain increased computing capabilities. In fact it's this quest for larger CPU power that has spearheaded the parallel computing movement in the recent years. As such, technical computing has ventured to exploit experimental, prototype architectures (Messina, 1993). The parallel machine became the computing vehicle. Users have hand-modified their applications to map the application to the given architecture and according to the capabilities of the experimental environment they had at their disposition. Many users moved their code to any machine available; especially if the computing time was free of charge!

In distinction, commercial parallel processing has been spearheaded by the quest of increased data processing capabilities. However, commercial users have used parallelism either as a means of off-loading prepackaged application support systems (like the database subsystems), or have used the parallel machine for batch processing of multiple (sequential) jobs, but which share resources like the OS functions or the application subsystem. Commercial users need continuous availability (Keane, 1993) and fault tolerance, and would not move readily mission critical applications.

As a result the applications have exploited parallelism differently. The separate paths are manifested in the differing forms of parallel hardware developed, in the reliability and fault tolerance considerations, in distinct parallel processing paradigms, languages and compiler technology, different performance models, and different approaches to the I/O technology.

As a background and basis for our discussion on the outlook for the future, we will survey briefly the parallel hardware and software environment.

4   WHERE DOES THE HARDWARE PROVIDE PARALLELISM?

We approach the discussion of historical differences between ES and commercial parallel hardware organization by briefly reviewing parallel system architectures which have been pursued. Some have been implemented in vendors' announced products, some are prototype research efforts, but for the purposes of this chapter I will not separate these categories. In this survey I will note how the different application purposes tended to drive towards distinct architectures.

4.1 Parallelism at the CPU level

Parallelism can occur in the hardware at basically two levels: at the CPU level, that is multiple processors; and at the remote memory level: disks and tapes. The intermediate levels of memory hierarchy (cache, local and global memory) do not manifest themselves independently of the CPU parallelism and they are considered more in conjunction with the differing parallel CPU architectures.

Parallel (CPU) architectures are being distinguished by the logical and the physical memory organization. Considering the logical memory organization we have architectures that have one or more of the characteristics: shared (or coherent) caches, shared main memory and local memory. Physically the caches are typically distributed to each computing node; if cache coherence is enforced, it is typically maintained by appropriate additional hardware. Local memory is also typically distributed on each processor node. Shared (or global) memory can be either distributed on each processor node, or be common to all processing nodes. The later architecture, with the shared memory physically common to all processors, is an increasingly less popular architecture for reasons of system scalability to more than a few processors. The former is also refered to as 'distributed shared memory' or 'virtual shared memory', and is gaining in popularity amongst parallel memory organizations for ease of programming, and scalability potential. An early example of distributed shared memory machines was the IBM prototype RP3 (Pfister *et al.*, 1985) which implemented a distributed shared memory architecture, with a portion of the distributed memory (logically) shared among the processors, and a portion of (logically and physically) local to each processor. The architecture supported dynamically setting the portion of the local versus the portion of the shared memory; also it supported local processor caches.

The means for interconnecting these processors vary from bus-based networks, to cross-bar switches, to mesh interconnections, variants of meshes (like toruses), and multistage interconnection networks. Issues of scalability for the various architectures will be addressed later in the chapter, in the context of implications to the parallelisation of ES and commercial applications.

4.2 Parallelism at the disk level

For the parallelism in the remote memory level (disks and tapes), the architectural organizations, implemented or proposed, are based on either the shared disk (SD) or the non-shared disk (or 'shared nothing', SN) paradigms (DeWitt and Gray, 1992). Here too the distinction being with respect to the logical organization, the physical organization being either the disks being attached to the processing nodes via some interconnection network, or disks attached to each individual processing node (possibly multiple disks/node). In some respect this is an analogue to the memory organizations I discussed previously, moved one level further from the processor. We will see that this has exactly corresponding implications in the parallelization methods (differences and similarities) for the ES and commercial applications, and considerations such as dynamic scheduling, load balance and parallelization flexibility.

In the SD approach, the storage devices are connected via a switch since each processor must be capable of accessing any of the data; the switch must support high bandwidth communications for accessing the data and for processor to processor communication relating to locking and local cache coherency. The SN approach is easier to implement as each device is attached to and accessed only by it's associated processor. The trade-offs are: flexibility of accessing data and load balancing, versus easy and inexpensive hardware implementations.

No matter what the I/O subsystem architecture is, several general considerations exist. It's important to supply the required bandwidth and capacity needed. Scalability, as the speed of the individual processors, as the number of processors in the parallel system increases, makes it imperative to have an I/O subsystem that is balanced with the computation rates and the communication system bandwidth.

An issue impacting parallelism is the rate of technology improvement in the processing versus the I/O speed. Typical I/O requirements of ES applications are expressed as the F/B ratio (unit of execution in flops/byte of I/O), such ratios vary from 1 to 25 (Pasquale and Polyzos, 1993). Typical I/O requirements in commercial applications are expressed in instructions per byte of I/O, and this ratio in about 5–10 (Pirahesh *et al.*, 1990). As processors become increasingly powerful, the gap between CPU speed and I/O capability of a single device becomes wider. Thus techniques to increase I/O capacity and bandwidth are to use multiple disks, per processing unit, like disk arrays (Patterson *et al.*, 1988). Potentially this can lead to mismatch in the degree of parallelism required by the computation compared to the amount of parallelism needed for the I/O subsystem. Disk striping (Copeland *et al.*, 1988) exploits the multiple disks to alleviate bottlenecks when data are accessed in a parallel execution, without the need to increase task parallelism to match the I/O parallelism. In addition to improve fast access to data, data caching is used for the efficient reuse of data accessed repeatedly. Data caching requires software and hardware assists, and has further implications in regards to parallel access and manipulation of these data.

We will discuss in a subsequent section about I/O architectures that provide reliability and fault tolerance. At at later section I will describe software capabilities to support parallel I/O.

5 WHERE IS THE PARALLELISM IN THE SOFTWARE?

5.1 Programming paradigms

Application level parallelism can be divided into functional parallelism and data parallelism. Functional parallelism seeks to exploit the independence between different computational tasks in the application program, acting either on different data, or the same data but in a pipelined manner, consistent with the execution of the program on a sequential machine ('preserving the sequential consistency'). Data parallelism exploits the independence of alike computational tasks acting on different data; also preserving sequential consistency. In both the functional and data parallel paradigms the sequential consistency is typically achieved by synchronization methods enabled in the software. Examples of functional and data parallelism approaches are found in both the ES applications and commercial database subsystems, as will be discussed below.

Data parallelism is a generalization of the vector computing paradigm where the same instruction is applied to different data; the generalization being that in this case it is the same tasks that are executing concurrently. In fact this has led to two parallel computing paradigms: the SIMD (single-instruction-multiple-data) and MIMD (multiple-instructions-multiple-data). The difference between SIMD and vector is that SIMD is enabled by multiple (general purpose or RISC) processors, vector computing is enabled by specialized vector hardware. In both vector and SIMD architectures and the corresponding programming paradigms, no explicit synchronization is needed. Data-flow architectures have given rise to another parallel programming paradigm, that can be described as enabling functional parallelism with no explicit synchronization necessary, and an additional important difference: in traditional computing paradigms, tasks or instructions are initiated, and act upon data that are present. In the data-flow paradigm it is the presence of the data that activates (triggers) an instruction to execute. To my knowledge no vector or data-flow architectures *per se* have not been exploited by traditional commercial applications, but the logical triggering method has been extensively used in database design. Data-flow parallelism remains an item-of-interest for ES computing, while vector computing has been the popular supercomputing environment for the last 15–20 years.

Though SIMD parallelism has been exploited to some extend in ES and commercial applications, MIMD parallelism either in the form of functional or data parallelism seems to be the most general means for parallel computing for ES and commercial applications. We will concentrate in discussing this form of parallelism which manifests itself in several paradigms:

- In terms of the synchronization methods, it is distinguished into the 'shared memory' (SM) paradigm (with explicit synchronization via

shared memory semaphores) and the 'message passing' (MP) paradigm (synchronization via interprocessor message exchanges). I will discuss later on issues like dynamic versus static partitioning and load balancing, enabled by these two paradigms.
- In terms of the type of process (or processor) scheduling and control flow through the parallel program, there are two paradigms: the fork-join (or master-slave) computational model, and the SPMD (Single-Program-Multiple-Data) model (Darema et al., 1987).

Though the Fork-Join model has been the earlier (and more traditional model) of the two models, the SPMD has gained popularity in ES parallel computing because it allows more efficient implementations. In addition the model imposes fewer requirements on the operating system, and the compiler, and place fewer demands on the parallel program developer. Specifically process cooperation and synchronization are enabled at the application program level, and the OS is not involved in the synchronization; parallel task procedure encapsulation is eliminated together with the ensuing overheads in doing that, as well as such requirements on the program developer or the compiler. The SPMD model simplifies the transition from sequential programming to parallelism, because it requires minimal extensions to the standard sequential languages, simple for the programmer to understand and learn, easy to embody in a compiler, and thus permits expedient parallel program development. Because of it's efficiency the model can support well both coarse and fine grain parallelism. The SPMD model has been used to parallelize ES applications both for 'shared memory' and for 'message passing' paradigms.

In an ES application program there is a consecutive mix of parallel, serial and replicate sections. The replicate sections option is a capability allowed by the SPMD model, and can be used when replicate computation results in more efficient computation than imposing synchronization. The parallel sections are primarily in the form of 'loops', either explicit or implicit. These loops result from the way we have chosen to represent the physical world: mapping observables onto a time-space grid, or by following particle trajectories through a phase-space. Some involve regular computations and their algorithmic complexity can be analytically expressed, and used to determine data or task partitions so as to achieve maximum parallelism, load balancing, etc. Some are irregular and not as trivially data- or task-partitionable. Nevertheless, the SPMD model naturally enables mapping of such applications onto parallel machines. Both parallel computation and parallel I/O can be implemented in a straightforward way. Several programming environments have been developed to support parallel programming for the two major programming languages used in ES computing: FORTRAN and C. More discussion on parallelism and these languages is defered to a later section. Also later I argue that the SPMD model is suitable and can be applied to the parallelisation of commercial applications. Programming environments to enable expressing parallelism are discussed in the next section.

In commercial applications, both in OLTP and decision support systems, parallelism has primarily been exploited in the application subsystem level, that is the database (DB) level (DeWitt and Gray, 1992). Part of the reason for that is than in traditional commercial applications, the bulk of the computing is the database subsystem level, rather that the application invoking the DB subsystem. As decision support systems become more powerful and more complex, and the queries become more expensive, i.e. a few hours of computation, parallelism in this level is increasingly becoming a topic of interest (Steen and de Jong, 1991). Still the predominant amount of 'parallel computing' in the commercial world is the traditional 'batch processing', where 'serial' jobs are run on the parallel hardware sharing operating system and hardware resources. This is an important characteristic in the parallel computing arena as it concerns system software issues, like job scheduling. In commercial systems the measure of performance is throughput, that is: 'process (and complete) as many users' jobs as possible' in a given time interval; speedup, in the manner discussed above for ES applications, is of secondary consideration. Batch parallel processing is used to enhance throughput.

Before I discuss parallelism at the database level further, I want to briefly address parallelism in the commercial application level. Although this parallelism has not been practically pursued, it is unavoidably the next target in parallel commercial computing, so it's worth elaborating here on the approaches that one could pursue. The vast body of commercial applications is written in COBOL and use SQL (database language) statements to access the database information. The fork-join parallelism can be applied to parallelize such applications, and an example of such work is presented in Keane (1993 and Richter (1993), for coarse grain parallelization of COBOL applications. However, the arguments made earlier for the SPMD model apply also here for the parallelization of COBOL applications, in particular for supporting coarse and finer grain parallelism. Such approach is used by Keane (1993). Usually COBOL loops, like 'perform', usually entail a mix of computation and I/O. I/O can be straightforwardly supported with the SPMD model approach (Darema, 1986), which makes the model an excellent candidate for the parallelization of COBOL applications.

Database computations involve queries (inspections of data), or transactions (modifications of data); the data typically reside in remote memory (disk or tape). One way to partition the work involved in a DB operation (query or transaction) is by partitioning the data and applying the same query or transaction to the independent data; this is called 'function shipping', and can be considered like the data partitioning methods in ES. For queries that are long, it is usual that the query is parallelized (parallel query) and multiple processors are used simultaneously; this can also be considered analogous to a combination of the functional decomposition and the data partitioning methods in ES. An alternate method is to send the queries or the transactions to a given processor, and also send to that processor any necessary data that reside on other processor's disks; then these data are sent to the processing node that owns the function; this is called the 'data shipping' method. In this case the processor that will be chosen, is most likely the one which is idle or less loaded, but also maybe whose local memory or disk contains the majority of data affected by the given operation. The cost of shipping the data and load balancing the system are trade-offs. The data shipping method can be considered analogous to the functional decomposition in ES applications. For either function shipping, or data shipping, or parallel queries, performance is optimized by reducing the amount of time that processors wait for data, or reducing the load imbalance ('skew' in the commercial processing parlance), are important considerations, and algorithms have been developed to chose the optimal method.

There is in some respect a dichotomy in the way queries versus transactions are parallelized. Transactions typically exploit fine granularity parallelism (e.g. record level) to maximize the degree of parallelism, while queries seek coarser grain of parallelism, as locking at the record level would degrade performance, as each query typically deals with many records, and conversely, locks kept by long queries will degrade the performance of transactions performing updates on subsets of these data.

There is also some orthogonality between queries and transactions in the respect of the parallel execution constraints such as: minimize turnaround by maximizing use of resources. Maximizing resources means exploiting more processors, which implies increase the number of tasks, but that has the effect of decreasing the data size (number of tuples) that each task acts on, and that implies more execution overhead.

An analogous situation exists in ES computing where the trade-off is between load balancing versus minimizing parallelization and communication overheads. Load balancing implies scheduling computationaly equal size tasks; since it's not always possible to break the computation into equal size tasks, one would then expect that if the tasks are uneven, the skew will be smaller the smaller the tasks themselves are. On the other hand, since there is synchronization or communication at the beginning/end of each task, small tasks imply increased synchronization or communication overhead.

5.2 Programming environments

Currently a number of environments have been developed that implement the '(virtual) shared memory' and 'message passing' programming paradigms.

Such environments have been either developed by research groups or are marketed commercial products.

Several programming environments have been developed based on the SPMD programming paradigm. For the message-passing paradigm examples are: EXPRESS™ (Flower and Kolawa, 1994), PVM (Sunderam *et al.*, 1994), IBM/EUI (IBM, 1993). For shared memory paradigm, examples are LINDA(R) (Carriero *et al.*, 1993), and the complimentary product Paradice™ (Carriero *et al.*, 1993) that enables co-ordinated execution of two different parallel applications accessing the same data. We will refer to the Paradice™ environment again when the issue of data sharing between applications is discussed.

At this point it behoves us to elaborate more on the advantages and disadvantages of shared memory and message passing systems, and likewise the advantages and disadvantages of partitioned versus shared disk systems.

Parallel computing environments that provide a single logical address space (like distributed shared memory or virtual shared memory) allow all the processes co-operating in the execution of the parallel program to see the same data space, and they can read and write on this shared space using simple operations. Unlike in the message passing paradigm, processes do not communicate directly with other processes using (low-level) message passing operations, but they communicate indirectly via the shared data. It is much easier for the user to determine and express parallelism. The mapping of the existing (serial) algorithms on a shared memory machine is natural and straightforward (Darema, 1988a). In distinction parallel mapping of applications in the message passing paradigm, is more laborious and less flexible. The degree of difficulty can range of simply tedious to the need to modify the algorithm or needing to develop a new algorithm. Explicitly partitioning the data and implementing the message passing directives is the minimal effort needed. Message passing communication is expensive so the user must be concerned about (and minimize) the frequency of communication versus computation. This leads to parallelism that needs to be rather coarse-grained, and typically the partitioning of the data is static, and therefore the parallel tasks are also statically partitioned. In distinction the shared memory paradigm allows either coarse or fine grain parallelism, as dictated by the application; the data and task partitioning can be dynamic. Thus in general compared to the the shared memory paradigm, in the message passing paradigm the resulting parallelism flexibility is hindered by static scheduling and partitioning of task, more coarse grain, with lesser flexibility for load balancing.

There is an analogy between the two paradigms ('shared memory' and 'message passing') for the computation and the shared versus non-shared disk approach that concerns database parallelism. In shared disk architectures such as (Shoens, 1986; Mohan *et al.*, 1990), all data residing on disk are visible to each individual process, which can access (and for performance reasons most likely buffer in local caches) the data. That necessitates global locking and protocols to ensure coherency. For performance reasons, the SD architecture has been used to implement inter-transaction parallelism rather than intra-transaction parallelism. In the shared everything approach the memory and the disks are shared among the processors. Though this approach is considered to have scalability problems, load balancing is easier to achieve. Examples of such systems are the IBM/3090 machines. In shared nothing (Stonebracker, 1986), each processor owns part of the data, stored on it's local disks, and only processes running on that processor can access these data. Such an approach is used by the Teradata machine.

Distributed memory message passing systems have become popular for the following reasons: from the hardware point of view they are easier to build; but the strongest argument that has been made in favour, is that scalability to large numbers of processors is easy to obtain with such systems. By scalability I mean that from the hardware point of view and from the software of view, one can build a system whose hardware implementation requirements are independent from the number of processors in the system, and in particular large numbers of processors, of the orders of 1000's, 'massive parallelism'. Likewise the thesis is that, from the software point of view, parallel applications and algorithms can be developed for such systems, such that they are independent of the number of processors in the system and that their performance is predictable across any range of processors. This caveat of scalabilty is not in general borne in practice. This issue is brought up in a memo published by Jack Worlton (1993) that discussed some of the pitfalls of such claims.

The present chapter makes a further claim that the need for parallel systems with 1000's of processors is questionable. The author of the present chapter has conducted an informal survey of the computing capabilities of large computing centers such as those of Supercomputing Centres and National Laboratories. This survey indicates that the computing power in these centres in the range of a 'few hundred' of the typical fast RISC processors available in the market. Having made this observation one might seriously look at parallel architectures, such as the 'virtual shared memory' machines, that are optimized to support a few hundred processors and develop programming environments accordingly for such systems. We have fallen into the pitfall of the message passing paradigm by pursuing architectures scalable to 'massive parallelism', instead of pursuing the shared address space paradigm.

Environments, like LINDA, that make visible to the user a single address space, provide the flexibility of the shared memory programming model, even if in the actual implementation of such a model, they enable 'under the covers' low level message passing primitives, if the system it is running on is a physically distributed memory machine. Thus such environments provide the following benefits: since they are very easy to understand and learn, they

18 Parallel Information Processing

expedite the transition to parallelism; they provide the advantage of dynamic load balance capabilities; they enable users to create portable programs, because the user uses the shared memory paradigm, independently of the underlying architecture.

Up to this point I have addressed parallelism of the computational aspect of the application or of the application support layer, the database system. We will now discuss issues and approaches to parallelism for the I/O management system, as this is an important aspect of the applications' requirements. We will distinguish parallel I/O requirements from mass storage and tertiary storage systems, dealing with large data sets, and tolerating high latencies. I will confine the discussion to the technology that can support high access rates from the secondary storage.

In the ES arena while much effort and progress has been made to enable decomposition and mapping of the application, until recently little effort has been expended to enable efficient I/O implementation on parallel systems. In distinction, in the commercial arena a considerable amount of work has been done, and techniques for data partitioning, scheduling and load balancing have been addressed extensively.

Parallel I/O can be enabled in several ways. One method is to distribute files across multiple disks (file clustering); the rationale is that if these files are accessed at different times by different processors then the I/O bandwidth of the system is increased. This method provides parallelism at the file level and therefore is coarse grain and limited in the degree of parallelism. It is typically supported by a distributed file system manager, like NFS, AFS. Parallel file systems, that distribute a data file across multiple disks either transparently or under user control, provide finer granularity parallelism. As such, blocks of data are distributed across multiple processors, either one block per processor (data striping), or multiple blocks per processor (file declustering). A block (depending on it's byte size) can contain multiple records. The distribution of the blocks can be done either under user control (Feitelson, 1993) or transparently (Pier, 1989; DeBenedictis and DelRosario, 1992). Such techniques have been applied for I/O management of parallel ES applications. For commercial applications disk-stripping improves inter-transaction parallelism, but is also used to support intra-transaction and query parallelism as well.

5.3 Object-oriented technology

One more caveat that it's worth mentioning in discussing the future of parallel software is the role of the Object-Oriented technology. In particular, Object-Oriented programming in the context of the C++ language, and the Object Oriented Databases. The claims are that OO exposes parallelism in a natural way. However it is parallelism at the functional level, which might be limited in terms of scalability of running the application on parallel systems with larger numbers of processors (we consider systems with hundreds of processors, not thousands). On the other hand the belief is that for this decade OO is going to have it's impact by being used in an 'encapsulation mode', that is encasing standard language programs with an OO layer visible to the end-user interface. Such an approach is considered a tactical step towards OO, and is mostly due to the reality that one cannot afford to dispose at once all this *vast* body of software that already exists, in favour of a not completely mature technology. Thus OO implementations are tentative and no major efforts in parallel OO are under way, and thus the discussion above, regarding the parallel versions of the traditional languages, will be relevant for quite a while.

5.4 Data sharing

We discussed earlieron that in the ES arena typically applications deal with data that are in the form of arrays, and that commercial applications rely heavily on systems that deal with relational tables of data and text. As the applications expand from the traditional to the E/merging ones, one thing that becomes prevalent is that now the applications must deal with sharing data between them. The problem that will need to be addressed is how to create data models that are general to represent (inclusively) all the kinds of data structures from arrays, to tables of data and text. As we embark into parallelism it important to address this issue of data sharing, and in this section we will elaborate on the difficulties and possible solutions to this problem.

While environments like Paradise™ enable interoperability between parallel applications, still the aspect of the data models is explicitly handled by the applications themselves, which must be developed with a common coherent model in mind.

It is clear that applications can share data if they are designed to do so from the outset. For applications that have been designed to interoperate and they are built with a common data model and a common database in mind, they can share data easily. It is much more difficult to share data after the fact, when the applications have been designed to use different data models and different databases. Since parallelism involves some reprogramming (or new application development), it's an opportunity to address the data sharing issue in conjunction with parallelism.

Consider the example of CIM, referred to earlier on, where we need to create applications that share data with other applications, e.g. engineering design drawings for a product, bill-of-materials data, used both by the structural and materials design team (application), and the production floor scheduling (application) for the manufacturing of that product, or the customer order and distribution (application), requesting the order and scheduling the delivery of the product. Specifically, consider the example of a CIM application (we'll call it CIM-A) with another application CIM-B, both designed to access a BOM (Bill-of-Materials) database. The logical data-model is the definition of the data that makes up the bill-of-materials (BOM). This definition might contain part-numbers and parts' information, how these parts are related in subassemblies, and other relevant information, like engineering drawings and cost. If the data model is changed, the application logic usually has to be changed. Data models are usually represented by an abstraction technique known as entity/relationship (or E/R). For the purposes of this example, let's assume that CIM-A is designed to access the data via an SQL access interface, but CIM-B which for the purposes of this example is object-oriented based, accesses the data via an OO access interface. In each case the application logic knows how to process the information stored in the database because the programmer had an understanding of the model.

If the model changes, then the application logic has to be changed to accommodate the augmented data model; that is **for each** application that needs to access the given data set. If the applications use an abstraction, like an E/R model and an access interface to access the data, then the entity model has to be changed and the access interface also has to be changed; and that is for each application. In typical real applications (for example, those encountered in CIM) the number of entities in the E/R model is in the hundreds and thousands of entities. If in addition the application needs to access the data remotely, like in a distributed parallel system, then the application has to have a remote access path to the database on the other processor, use the support protocols to access the data, and have implemented mechanisms that optimize performance when accessing and using remote data by employing data locality, caching, etc.

The CIM example illustrates why it is such a difficult problem to to enable data sharing between applications: In general data sharing requires solutions to the problems of:

(1) dissimilar data models,
(2) different data access interfaces, and
(3) remote data access.

The problem of dissimilar data models can only be addressed by architecting a common data model or by providing data conversion utilities. The former approach requires that the logic of existing applications be changed to accommodate the new data definition, while the latter may not work at all if the two models are incompatible. The amount of effort in reworking the applications to support a common data model can be judged by considering the complexity of the existing data models. With data models that involve hundreds and thousands of entities it is clear that it is a quite complex and laborious effort.

The problem of different access interfaces is rooted in the evolving nature of the database technology. As data storage facilities have evolved from files, to hierarchical (IMS) databases, to relational (DB2), to E/R, and to object oriented, so have the access interfaces. Relational databases support SQL set retrieval of table-rows, while OODBs support direct data structure access via methods written in C++.

One can examine several different approaches to sharing data and enable interoperability of applications.

The first approach is to establish a 'universal data model', upon which all applications can be built. First of all this is hard to design on the outset; such a model would be very complex and it is hard to predict all the possible future needs of the model. So the best hope would be to create a data model that would be extensible. Even so, to exploit such a model each applications' logic would have to be changed to accommodate the new universal model, and that most likely be an unaffordable amount of development effort, as it would amount modifying all the existing applications.

A second approach is to create a common data model only for the data that are shared among the applications. This has some of the same difficulties of the universal shared data model, in the sense that still requires establishing a common data model, albeit the problem here is potentially more tractable, as the set of common data is in general smaller. The more difficult problem now becomes to decide which data are shared. The difficulty arises from the fact that while today's applications do not share a given set of data, tomorrow there might be cases where these applications will need to share these data. An excursion through time (past, present and future) can provide plenty of examples from the recent past and the present for such instances: yesterday's medical records contained patient accounting information; today's and tomorrow's medical records combine many diverse data, including tables with the patient name and medical history, but also medical images like x-rays and cat-scans; tomorrow's medical records might add moving images and sound. Such combinations were not conceived until recently. A data model that would have been constructed on the basis that the data are tables, with the patient name and the medical history in the form of decease/date-of-occurence/tests-performed, would be completely inadequate to accommodate, text relating to the diagnosis and the tests, and raw test and diagnostic data as discussed in the examples above.

A third approach is to support pairwise import/export between families of applications, where the applications within a family can use the same data model, but the data models of the different families are different. In this approach the problems of dissimilar data models, dissimilar access interfaces, and remote data access are solved by specially provided converters. A different converter is required for each pairwise conversion. To avoid data replication the conversion needs to be executed in real-time, as part of the application's request for the data, and lasting only during execution time of the requesting application. Permanent data generated from that particular run will also be converted according to the mapping, if they are to be appended to that database.

Each one of these approaches is difficult to implement and has drawbacks. For the time being applications choose the most suitable data storage and management model, depending on the applications' characteristics, such as reference patterns and performance requirements. If applications continue to optimize on the databases best suited to their individual needs, and as database technology continues to evolve, then it's likely that there will never be a time when there will be a general technology that will ensure interoprativity of applications. I want to re-iterate the opening statement of this section. That is for applications that are developed anew, it is easier to implement data sharing and interoperability, and we should address the problem of data sharing in conjunction with parallelism, instead of independently or relegating it to the future after the parallel applications have been developed.

6 SOME MORE PERTINENT ISSUES

In this section I will discuss some relevant technology areas, language and compiler technology for parallel computing, performance and fault tolerance. To limit the extent of the chapter I have not fully addressed other important issues such as systems management, which deserves addressing as it is an important topic in the operation and use of parallel computing systems. The subject is discussed in another chapter in this book.

6.1 Language and compiler technology

Different programming languages are chosen in ES and commercial applications. The primary language in ES computing is FORTRAN, while in recent years C is also becoming popular. FORTRAN has been the predominant language because the compiler technology that has been developed allows optimizations that can exploit the peak capabilities of the CPU. C is becoming increasingly popular; for a while it was marred by the disadvantage that because of it's pointer structure compiler optimizations for maximum CPU performance were difficult. That point of distinction between FORTRAN and C is disappearing; the new version of the FORTRAN standard supports pointers also!

Nevertheless, because of this past distinction parallel programming, and because of the large amounts of the existing FORTRAN programs, efforts for parallel enhancement to the language, and parallel compilers, have first addressed the world of FORTRAN programming. Primary targets of parallelization in FORTRAN or C programs are the parallel loops. As a developmental process, in the 1980s there were the explicit parallelization efforts. The maturing efforts of parallel FORTRAN standards, like HPF, together with the corresponding compiler development, are driving towards the implicit parallelism capabilities.

Extensions to FORTRAN (and C) have been proposed to enable the user to express parallelism, and/or as directives to the compiler. Although considerable progress has occurred in the compiler technology, especially in the capabilities for FORTRAN compilers to detect (and convert to) parallelism in existing sequential programs, the amount of parallelism enabled by the compiler in a given application is lagging compared to the amount of parallelism that can be enabled by the users (or application developers) who have a good understanding of the underlying application algorithms, and can even modify those to increase or improve the amount of parallelism. This of course has been somewhat of an impediment to parallel computing because it is a big effort to convert to parallel the vast amount of existing serial FORTRAN programs. Nevertheless, hand conversions and the rewriting of codes are the predominant means of exploiting parallel machines in the ES arena. As the parallel extensions to FORTRAN and C become standardized it is expected that it will also make it easier for compilers to optimize programs for a given parallel architecture, so the progress in these two fronts is correlated, and at the same time application algorithm developers are continually making progress in yielding more suitable parallel algorithms.

In commercial applications the predominant languages are COBOL for the application programs, and SQL for the database manipulation. Like the parallel loops in FORTRAN programs, the COBOL 'perform' loops can be the targets of parallelization at the application level. There are no efforts that I am aware of, to automatically detect and parallelize COBOL programs, or to provide parallel extensions to COBOL, like a 'parallel perform' for example. The lack of such motivation can be attributed to the fact that for commercial applications parallelism at the application level is not predominant, and for the foreseeable future will be enabled by the applications' developers. On the other hand, there are some efforts to develop parallel compilers for SQL.

6.2 Performance measures

Different performance measures are being used for applications in the ES and the commercial areas.

In the commercial world computing has traditionally involved manipulation of words and indices, that is an integer data representation. Operations on integers take roughly the same number of cycles as instructions, so the performance requirements are measured in instructions executed (ips = instructions per second). The performance requirements have increased over the years: Kips (1000 ips) have been replaced by Mips (10^6), as the more common measure of performance. In addition in commercial applications 'a small amount of work is done per piece of data' by the application program itself; considerable amount of processing is done in the subsystem and involves manipulation of indices, that is instructions and integer operations. Typically it amounts to inspecting a piece of information, that is a number or a word, generically referred to as 'data', and then maybe modifying that number or word; and this process repeats for another number or word. As a consequence, in a typical commercial application 'one goes through a lot of data'. Since primary memory is expensive, it has been traditional to keep these large amounts of data in the cheaper secondary storage, like disks or tapes. In commercial computing the attention to parallelism has originated for two reasons: obtain 'cheap Mips' by using multiple general purpose microprocessors *and* use parallel I/O and disks to avoid contention in accessing data. Besides cost, the other reason that this storage level is more popular in the commercial arena, is due to the commercial business need to exchange data with others; this was done in the past by physically exchanging disks or tapes, although today such data exchanges are done by electronic data transfer.

In ES the measure of performance pertains the computing aspect, which typically involves operations on floating point numbers. Floating point operations in the past required many more machine cycles to execute than instructions and the measure of performance has been established to be the amount of floating point operations (flops) involved in the computations. In today's machines flops are of the same order of as instructions but the measure 'flops' has remained, with the consequence that the computers are rated with respect to the speed that they perform such operations: Kflops (1000 floating operations per second) of requirements were succeeded by Mflops (10^6 flops), Gflops (10^9 flops), Tflops (10^{12} flops), and now the Pflops (10^{15} flops) are being included in the parlance. CPU parallelism is the means for achieving such capabilities. To achieve the maximum CPU performance, most ES computations access data from the primary memory; data (usually 'scratch' or temporary) that might reside on disks are staged into the primary memory either explicitly by the application program, or transparently by the OS (as in virtual memory systems). Thus together with the higher CPU speeds, the primary memory requirements also increase. Mflops and Gflops are usually accompanied by MB and GB memory requirements; the only limitation for the proportionality factor being constant, for the time being, is only cost. Technology has allowed cheap CPU speed improvements. Primary memory (cache and main memory) is still expensive. The premise still remains that in ES applications 'a lot of work' is done per piece of data, and therefore the immediate need has been to increase the capability of the CPU. Thus for the ES world the focus has been in the parallelism at the CPU level. In the past, in the ES arena, considerations of remote memory requirements, like disks and tapes, had been relegated to secondary importance compared to the quest for high CPU performance. As I discussed earlier on, the emerging data requirements of ES applications bring issues of data management and secondary storage in the forefront.

The quest for higher computing (CPU) capabilities has influenced the measures of parallel systems and applications performance. The objective of any application running on a computer is to achieve maximum execution performance. For parallel computing, measures of performance include the speedup, which is the ratio of the computation rate with p processors to the rate for a single processor; and the efficiency, the speedup divided by p. Ideally the speedup should be linear, and the efficiency a constant, preferably unity. Several considerations enter into parallelizing an application on a parallel system:

(a) minimizing synchronization, which constitutes an overhead absent in uniprocessor execution, and which can cause processors to idle, either awaiting for other processors to complete their assigned tasks or awaiting for data from other processors,

(b) load balancing the computation so that each processor receives equal amounts of work to do, preventing processors from having to wait for the stragglers,

(c) capability to have all the necessary data, as close as possible to each CPU; efficient handling of memory hierarchies, like cache, local, global, and remote memory, maximizes performance.

6.3 Reliability and fault tolerance

Fault tolerance is an important consideration, especially for commercial computing. In the traditional mainframe technology, upon which much of the computing was done, fault tolerance had been adequately addressed and the technology for that had been developed, albeit expensive. Typically it is provided with hardware assists as error detection and correction can be done faster at the hardware level than at the software level.

In the parallel computing world, reliability and fault tolerance also is a requirement, but is considerably more challenging to address, and it is an area where the optimal solutions are being sought. At the hardware level fault detection and tolerance is enabled by redundant components. For fault detection at the computational level, CPU chips, and at the communication level, communication chips, are being duplicated and augmented with error checking circuitry that looks for inconsistencies between the pairs of similar components and takes appropriate action when a fault is detected. In such cases either the entire system shuts down or most likely the faulty component is isolated and the operation of the remaining processors can continue. Redundancy at the network chip level is used to detect network chip faults and when such a fault is detected, the network design allows re-routing of packages to maintain the network integrity. However as we'll discuss later there is still a problem of how to recover the ongoing computations on the faulty nodes.

At the disk level redundantly encoded or mirrored disks can be used to provide fault tolerance. A special case of some interest is that in the partitioned disk case, **twin-tailed** disks are sometimes used not for the sake of increasing the possible parallelism but to ensure that non-volatile disk data is still accessible after a single processor failure. Although one could envision a scheme of 'twin-tailed' CPU's or 'twin-tailed' memories, we are not aware of any implementation of the analogue of allowing a back-up processor (in the distributed memory case) to take over a memory module and continue the processing after a failure of the primary processor using the memory. Processor redundancy is only used as discussed above for error checking. For performance reasons, processor-memory interfaces are not usually designed so as to leave the contents of memory in a recoverable state after a processor failure.

For recovery of the computations on the faulty nodes, several possibilities exist: if the parallel system is used in batch mode, then the single node recovery mode can be effective, including restarting the job.

In the general case a parallel system would be used in some mixed mode with some nodes running 'uni-processor or serial' jobs, and other groups of nodes running parallel jobs. If the system runs a parallel job, that is employing multiple co-operating processors, then when one of the processors in that group has a fault, it becomes a problem of how to enable recovery. Typically, the solution to restart the entire computation is not satisfactory as this is expensive, if, for example, this was a scientific computation that had already consumed several hours computing.

The standard methods of uniprocessor recovery are not sufficient, as one needs to save the inter-related states of all the processors, and not just independent uniprocessor states. In scientific computing, user directed checkpointing is a method has been used in uniprocessor computing, to avoid repeating lengthy computations, and this same approach can be used to recover parallel computations. Periodically, at appropriate stages in the computation the user 'saves' specific data of the computation in disk files. Automating the process is desirable; techniques like the ones used to swap jobs in timesharing environments are under investigation.

Even these methods are not as straightforward. 'Saving' the state of multiple processors requires simultaneous sharing of common resources like network and disks, which incurs potentially considerable additional overhead and peaks in the network traffic and disk I/O. Such peaks of traffic in communications and I/O can be avoided by asynchronously dumping the checkpoint data, but the trade-off here is that additional buffer space would be required. Such performance trade-offs need further study.

While there is redundancy in the CPU hardware, which could be used to execute redundant computation and be switched in when a CPU fault occurs, this is not the way how the CPU redundancy is now used. It is not clear whether techniques like disk mirroring, exploiting redundancy at the disk level, might also become more applicable at the CPU level. Similarly, if one were to apply and replicate our experience in data management and fault tolerance techniques, and apply the same methods with respect to recovery with in-memory data. This would be a case where we could leverage on our experience in commercial computing (I/O fault tolerance) to affect system aspects (CPU) that have been more crucial for engineering/scientific computing.

7 SUMMARY

I have discussed the converging characteristics of of the engineering/scientific and commercial applications and the ensuing possibilities for convergence of the engineering/scientific and commercial computing arenas. Recognition of that positions us in leveraging and correlating the independently developed technology, towards fulfilling the requirements of the applications in the future. In particular, the chapter focuses on aspects of parallel programming environments, and I/O support, and the issue of data models and data sharing.

As we embark in making parallel computing the mainstream computing mode it's important to address the issues of data models and data sharing, and in the context of parallelism, from the onset as not to find ourselves later or 'patching up' mistakes of the past.

In this chapter I have discussed of possible approaches that one can pursue to enable data sharing. The paper makes the point that parallelism for extremely large numbers of processors, might put us in the pitfall of designing and building the wrong systems, and developing the wrong software, and might make the implementation and practical use of parallelism harder than needed and therefore harder to popularize.

8 ACKNOWLEDGEMENTS

During the initial stages of the inception of this paper I had several informational conversations with my colleague Francis Parr regarding commercial database systems and I'd like to gratefully acknowledge here these interactions.

REFERENCES

Blech, R. (1990) Integrating CFD and Experiments, NASA Lewis Report.

Bordawekar, R., del Rosario, J. M. and Choudhary, A. (1993) Design and Evaluation of Primitives for Parallel I/O, *Proceedings of Supercomputing'93*, pp. 452.

Carriero, N. J. et al. (1994) The LINDA alternative to message passing systems, *Parallel Computing*, 20(4), pp. 663.

Chamberlin, D. et al. (1976) SEQUEL 2: A Unified Approach to Data Definition, Manipulation and Control, *IBM J. R&D*, November.

Chesshire, G. (1993) A Hierarchical Database for Scientific Computation, IBM Internal Report, May 18.

Codd, E. (1971) A Data Base Sublanguage Founded on the Relational Calculus, *Proc. 1971 ACM-SIGFIDET Workshop on Data Description, Access and Control*, November.

Copeland, G. et al. (1988) Data Placement in Bubba, *Proceedings of the ACM-SIGMOD Int'l. Conference on Management of Data*.

Darema, F. (1986) I/O Capabilities in the VM/EPEX System, IBM RC 12219, 10/9/86.

Darema, F. (1986a) Parallel Applications Development for Shared Memory Systems, in: (Ed. G. Paul) *Proceedings of the 1986 IBM Europe Institute*, Oberlech, Austria, August, North Holland.

Darema, F. (1986b) Parallel Applications and the Gedanken Laboratory, *Conference of the Society of Engineering Sciences*, Santa Fe, NM, October.

Darema, F. (1986c) Parallel Applications Performance Methodology, *Instrumentation for Future Parallel Computing Systems*, (Eds. M. Simmons, R. Koskela, I. Bucker), ACM Press.

Darema, F., George, D. A., Norton, V. A. and Pfister, G. F. (1988) A Single-Program-Multiple-Data Computational Model for EPEX/FORTRAN, *Parallel Computing*, 7, pp. 11–24.

DeBenedictis, E. and DelRosario, J. M. (1992) nCUBE Parallel I/O Software, *11th Int'l. Conference on Computers and Communications*, pp. 117.

DeWitt, D. and Gray, J. (1992) Parallel Database Systems: The Future of High Performance Data Bases, *Communications of the ACM*, 35(6), pp. 85.

Feitelson, D. G., Corbett, P. F., Johnson Baylor, S. and Hsu, Y. (1993) Satisfying I/O Requirements of Massively Parallel Supercomputers, IBM Research Report RC 19008, 7/15/93.

Flower, J. and Kolawa, A. (1994) EXPRESS is not just a message passing system: Current and future directions in EXPRESS, *Parallel Computing*, 20(4), pp. 597.

Humphrey, J. A. *et al.* (1992) Analysis of viscous dissipation in disk storage systems and similar flow configurations, *Phys. Fluids*, A4(7), pp. 1415.

Hunter, C. *et al.* (1993) Panel on Smart Access to Large Scientific Datasets, *SC93*, pp. 372.

IBM (1979) IBM Product.

IBM (1993) IBM Product, SH26-7228-00.

IBM (1993) IBM Product.

Keane, J. A. *et al.* (1993) Commercial Users' Requirements for Parallel Systems, *Proceedings of the DAGS'93 Symposium*, pp. 15.

Messina, P. (1993) The Concurrent Supercomputing Consortium: year 1, *IEEE Parallel and Distributed Technology* 1(1), pp. 9–16, February.

Mohan, C. *et al.* (1990) A Case Study of Problems of Migrating to Distributed Computing: Page Recovery Using Multiple Logs in the Shared Disks Environment, IBM Research Report RJ7343.

NASA (1993) NASA, Numerical Aerodynamics Simulation Program Plan, NASA/Ames Research Center, NP-1000-02-C00.

ObjectStore (1993) ObjectStore™, Objectivity, Technical Overview, Rel. 3.

Pasquale, B. and Polyzos, G. (1993) A Static Analysis of I/O Characteristics of Scientific Applications in a Production Workload, *Proceedings of Supercomputing'93*, pp. 388.

Patterson, D., Gibson, G. and Katz, R. (1988) A Case of Redundant Arrays of Inexpensive Disks, *Proceedings of the ACM-SIGMOD Int'l. Conference on Management of Data*.

Pfister, G. F. *et al.* (1985) The IBM Research Parallel Processor Prototype (RP3): Introduction and Architecture, *Proceedings of the 1985 Int'l. Conference on Parallel Processing*, pp. 766.

Richter, L. (1993) Restructuring COBOL Applications for Coarse Grain Parallelism, *Proceedings CAPPS'93*.

Pierce, P. (1989) A Concurrent File System for a Highly Parallel Mass Storage System, *4th Conference on Hypercube Concurrent Computers and Applications*, pp. 155.

Pirahesh, H. et al. (1990) Parallelism in Relational Data Base Systems: Architectural Issues and Design Issues, *1990 2nd Int'l. Symposium on Database in Parallel and Distributed Systems*, pp. 4.

Shoens, K. (1986) Data Sharing vs. Partitioning for Capacity and Availability, *Database Engineering*, 9.

van Steen, M. R. and de Jong, E. (1991) Designing Highly Parallel Applications Using Databade Programming Concepts, *1st Int'l. Conference on Parallel and Distributed Information Systems*, pp. 38.

Stonebracker, M. (1986) The case of Shared Nothing, *IEEE Database Engineering*, 9(1).

Stonebracker, M., Frew, J. and Dozier, J. (1993) The Sequoia 2000 Architecture and Implementation Strategy, Sequoia 2000 Technical Report 93/23, University of California at Berkeley.

Sunderam, V. S. et al. (1994) The PVM Concurrent Computing System: Evolution, experiences, trends, *Parallel Computing*, 20(4), pp. 531.

Teradata Corp. (1983) DBC/1012 Data Base Computer Concepts and Facilities, Teradata Corp., Los Angeles, CA, 1083.

Womble, D., Greenberg, D., Wheat, S. and Riesen, R. (1993) Beyond Core: Making Parallel Computer I/O Practical, *Proceedings of the DAGS'93 Symposium*, June.

Worlton, J. (1993) The Massively Parallel Bandwagon, *HPCwire*, May 5.

2 Parallel Processing in a Commercial Open Systems Market

F. N. Teskey
IT Strategy & Policy
National Westminster Bank

1 INTRODUCTION

Parallel processing has the ability to make a significant reduction in the IT hardware costs of processing business transactions and at the same time provide a significant increase in the number of transactions that can be processed each second. This is being achieved by linking many commodity processors together and by splitting business functions and database handling into separate parts that can be farmed out to these processors and executed in parallel. This work was developed initially by niche vendors on Unix-based systems, but now has a significant influence on the major vendors.

2 BENEFITS OF PARALLEL PROCESSING

The prime requirements that the business is placing on IT are to:

- reduce the fixed cost base of the IT systems
- improve price/performance and throughput of the IT systems
- improve speed of delivery of new products and applications.

2.1 Fixed cost

In the current recession, the business has reduction in cost as a prime focus. The Bank has identified the need to migrate the technology from a high fixed cost base to a variable cost base. Many of the current user applications are run on central site mainframe systems with high fixed overheads. To reduce costs, consideration should be given to moving some of this processing to lower cost systems. These cost savings will have to be balanced against the cost of migration.

The scalability of parallel processing is one way of enabling the size of the system to be changed to match the requirements of the application. Current mainframes are designed with an upgrade path of about 20:1 from the smallest to the largest configuration. This gives the user some opportunity to acquire a system that is reasonably matched to the requirements, but problems arise if it is difficult to quantify those requirements before a product is launched. Some parallel processing systems can provide a 1000:1 range in processor powers and they have been designed to make it easy to add additional processors as required. Thus it would be possible to develop and implement an application on a small system and schedule upgrades as and when required. This is particularly valuable when the applications are operating at, or near, the top of the mainframe performance range.

2.2 Price/performance

Mainframes are increasing in power at the rate of around 15% per year. Parallel processing systems, which make use of low cost commodity technologies can achieve very significant cost reduction and a more rapid increase in processor power, doubling every 18 months or less.

By exploiting the scalability of parallel processing systems it should be easy to increase the throughput of systems to any required level by adding additional processors. It should be possible to accomplish this in small increments rather than with the major upgrades necessary with conventional mainframes.

2.3 New products and applications

The Bank has a growing requirement for rapid access/update of critical business data from any location (including remote access) at any time. It will demand an entirely flexible and enterprise wide view of the data. This business need pushes us towards the maintenance of a single-image database; that is, a service which for the purposes of access looks like a single store of all Bank data. It also implies that all the data should be equivalently accessible in actual processing terms. There is little point in assuring users that all the data is held within a logical single-image database if there are still arbitrary performance restrictions on accessing some types of data. It is likely that parallel processing systems will be required to support these very large databases.

There are other classes of applications in the Bank that have not been practical to consider through the lack of a suitable or economical hardware base. Applications such as real time analysis of data feeds or assessing the sensitivity of financial models to parameter variations are possible examples which might become viable using the considerable processor power that can be available from parallel processing systems. In the past users have had to wait for the mainframe supplier to make available a system with the required power; the user can now look to new technology, such as parallel processing, to meet the requirement.

3 TYPES OF PARALLEL PROCESSING

We can identified four distinct categories of parallel processing that could be used within the Bank. The significant advantages and issues for each are listed below.

3.1 Multi-threading within single task

This type of architecture is typified by large scale engineering calculations, and is the traditional area where parallel processing provides significant cost advantages. It probably has a limited role within the Bank, except in such areas as real time analysis of data feeds, assessing the sensitivity of financial models to parameter variations, etc. It requires highly skilled programmers to implement successfully.

3.2 Parallel single threaded tasks

This type of architecture is typified by large OLTP applications accessing a single logical and physical database. Traditional large mainframes handle this kind of work effectively, but not economically, and the area where parallel processing has most to contribute would appear to be in increasing the efficiency of the database management. The critical technology is the database software and its interaction with the parallel processor.

3.3 Distributed single threaded tasks

This type of architecture utilizes the disciplines of open distributed processing and two phase commit or transaction replication to enable individual systems in the network to carry out part of the application independently of each other. The advantages tend to be that the individual processing units and software are considerably simpler and more robust than those implied in the earlier environment.

3.4 Independent single threaded tasks

Taking this progression towards its extreme, the last configuration has separate computing systems working largely independently. When there is a need for them to combine data for some purposes they post the data to each other, often using mechanisms that are asynchronous and so do not require the other unit to reply at the same time.

These four configurations represent a steady trend from systems where there is a high degree of data interaction, to systems where this interaction is low. As you move through the configurations simplicity is gained, but the flexibility of the system to provide a coherent view of the data is reduced.

In the past the Bank's technical architecture has tended to large independent systems with asynchronous data interactions, category 4 above. A good example is the number of independent accounting systems that the Bank runs; these pass information to each other and to the Head Office Accounts System when information needs to be collated.

The growing need to provide the business with efficient access to any of its data is pushing us towards a single logical image database. The second and third of the above categories of parallel processing seems the most appropriate way to to meet this requirement; with the second as the more demonstrable today.

4 SYNERGIES WITH OTHER TECHNOLOGIES

Parallel processing has a role to play in meeting the business requirement for a single logical image of its core data, but our present application architecture creates problems for the deployment of parallel processing systems. The architecture is based on monolithic systems, and interaction between systems is limited by the lack of a unified data model. The architecture has evolved more in response to performance demands than to business needs. In addition the services provided by the mainframe computer are complex and expensive and place heavy demands on IT personnel. We must recognize that there is no 'silver bullet', no single technology that can solve all our problems. Any proposal to adopt parallel processing has substantial overlaps with other other technologies. Some of these are outlined below.

4.1 Open systems

The field of parallel processing has provided an excellent example of how rapidly new technologies can be brought to market using open systems. The danger of staying with proprietary parallel processing vendors is that they may fall behind new technological developments in the open systems market; conversely they may introduce new technologies without waiting for the standards to be ratified. The benefits that parallel processing should look for in open systems is the use of standards to promote inter-operability and the commodity market to further improve the price/performance benefits.

4.2 Client/server architectures

One option for a large organisation, such as NatWest, to move towards a client/server architecture is to adopt an architecture where the existing applications on central central mainframes are regarded as application servers in their own right, by encapsulating them so that they can be accessed by a well defined set of remote procedure calls (RPC). We can then develop new applications using these RPCs and independently re-engineer the old applications. The implementation of a distributed computing environment will be a major part in this process. There will be a need to develop infrastructures to manage this distributed architecture in the absence of any full solution from DME.

4.3 4GL

One of the arguments against the widespread adoption of 4GLs has been the high processing load required by such systems. The ability of parallel processing to provide cheap, scalable processing could change that. However the power of 4GLs and parallel processing should not be regarded as a licence for poor design. There is still a need for design methodologies and tools.

Existing 4GLs use SQL to interface to the database. If we are to develop major applications in 4GLs then there will be a need to provide support for TP monitors. It will be necessary for client applications to use both RPCs and SQL to access the database and other system resources.

4.4 Open Distributed Processing

Open distributed processing (ODP) is a further development of the concepts of client/server architectures. The aim of ODP is the full inter-operability of application entities. It brings together the move to distributed computing and the drive to standardize and harmonize computer platforms through the adoption and support of open standards.The distinguishing features of the various forms of distributed processing can be summarized as:

- distributed processing is provided by the ability of computers to interconnect across a network and transfer data

- co-operative processing is provided by the ability of client and server processes to inter-work as components of the same (distributed) application
- open distributed processing (ODP) is provided by the ability of end-users and application components to inter-operate in complex, ad hoc and reliable ways, unaware of the technological details that support their environment.

4.5 Object orientation

Looking to the future, there is scope for very close synergy between parallel processing and object orientation. One of the trends in parallel processing is towards distributed message passing architectures. Existing shared memory methods of programming cannot take full advantage of this, but it should be ideally suited to the message passing style of object orientation. The trend appears to be that the leading DBMS vendors are gradually introducing object oriented functionality at the user level, and at the same time making increasing use of object oriented techniques internally to develop their own applications. These vendors may, therefore, be better placed to take advantage of the synergy between parallel processing and object orientation than the vendors of proprietary database engines.

5 THE WAY FORWARD

The initial deployment of parallel processing should be in the core data layer. If it can be demonstrated that the necessary database performance can be achieved, there is then a subsequent, but relatively simple, issue about whether any of the application layers should also be housed on the same parallel processor. It seems likely that there will be a case for the business integrity applications to be operated on the same machine, both from the point of view of sharing the business rules between applications and also to reduce the network traffic between the integrity applications and the database. There may also be emotional comfort in establishing a remote procedure call interface to the parallel processor that works at the level of these business integrity processes and not at the SQL level, in order to ensure that no one has access to the Bank's data except through the layer that imposes integrity.

There are, however, a number of issues that need to be addressed before we can consider the deployment of parallel processing into live environments.

5.1 Legacy applications and portability

Processes designed and built to run on serial processors, even if they are portable, may suffer severe performance degradation when migrated to parallel processors. If applications need to be tuned to run efficiently in their new processing environment then the viability of portability is in question.

It would seem that effective portability is at present limited to shared memory machines, though Oracle does provide a degree of portability for SQL applications to distributed memory systems.

Migration of applications from our existing TP monitors to TP monitors such as Tuxedo or Top End, that run on a parallel processing platform, may involve considerable work, even if the underlying code is portable.

5.2 Support for packages and tools

There are many software companies selling open systems products that are portable and hardware vendors selling open parallel processing systems, but there is still relatively little open systems software that can take full advantage of open systems parallel processors. The lack of tools is particularly acute in the area of operational management.

5.3 Response time

The performance of the interface between a parallel processor and the rest of the environment could significantly limit the overall performance compared to systems which have been highly tuned to the existing environment.

5.4 Data centre operation

If parallel processing is to extend beyond niche applications into core business applications then it must be capable of operating in a data centre environment along with conventional systems. This raises a whole new set of issues including:

- systems management
- reliability, availability and serviceability
- legacy applications
- 'parallel processing aware' development tools
- connectivity.

6 CONCLUSIONS

The hardware components for commercial exploitation of parallel processing are now in place, though still they have not achieved their full potential in terms of reliability availability and serviceability.

The capability of application development tools to exploit parallel processing hardware lags further behind; the main exception being relational database systems.

But it must be realized that for most commercial IT departments the major investment is in staff skills, next the investment in legacy applications and lastly the hardware. There will be considerable inertia to changing the hardware platform if this involves substantial changes to the skills and application portfolios.

The layered approach of open system standards may be a major enabler of technological change by allowing the underlying platforms to be replaced or upgraded with little or no change to the remaining infrastructure.

Within such an architecture, the deployment of open parallel processing systems should provide:

- flexibility in developing new, cost-effective applications
- interoperability with applications running on existing platforms
- access to the commodity market for IT systems.

ACKNOWLEDGEMENTS

I would like to thank my colleagues in NatWest Group IT, and in particular the members of the Parallel Processing Expert Panel, Richard Bennett, John Hudson, Pete Symonds, Ashleigh Tanner and Geoff Young, for their help in putting together the internal reports which I have used to help prepare this chapter. None the less the views expressed in the chapter are my own and do not necessarily represent the views of NatWest Group IT.

3 Parallel Perspectives on Management Information

B. Porter and D. Holle
White Cross Systems

1 INTRODUCTION

This chapter looks at some of the new areas of business thinking, the key developments in information systems, the implications for databases in commercial use and the opportunity it presents for massively parallel database systems. It also considers what the characteristics of a massively parallel database system need to be in order to serve the needs of commercial database users.

Three important interrelated strands of recent thinking about how companies should organize for competitive effectiveness have gained considerable credence:

- Flexibility in business operations to achieve tighter integration between the company and its markets, better responsiveness to customer needs, and to market changes. Ultimately the company only produces to order exactly what individual customers need through flexible manufacturing techniques, JIT, build to order and so on. The level of flexibility which is achievable has a direct relationship to the quality of information available to business managers.
- How to enable the Knowledge Worker to create new opportunity for the organization in developing competitive edge, identifying and exploiting new niche markets, reducing costs, etc.
- Reengineering the organization (and its information systems) to be process-driven rather than functionally oriented. The aim is to achieve flexibility objectives and quality goals such as customer satisfaction, and simultaneously reduce unnecessary administrative overhead.

The clear implication of these trends in business management thinking is that organizations need to be more information driven. Unfortunately, although the data is captured successfully by operational transaction systems, until recently the hardware and software technologies to extract the full informational value from that data have not existed. With the new user interface software products, such as Windows, and a myriad of user tools which operate within them, there are now ways of rapidly implementing reasonably intuitive front-end applications for end-users. For information users who need the free-form querying capabilities which these front-end products give them, however, conventional database systems are unable to support consistently fast response times against larger relational databases (more than 1,000,000 records). Yet the knowledge worker must have interactive response times to support creative, train-of-thought processes.

This is the opportunity for high performance database servers based upon massively parallel technology.

2 SOME NEW TRENDS IN BUSINESS THINKING

2.1 Flexibility

'The flexibility wars are coming', *Fortune, Sept 92* (Stewart, 1992).

Fortune magazine reported in September 1992 about the Japanese drive to apply 'flexibility' to stay ahead of worldwide competition. 'Flexibility' is information-driven, and it means being able to change fast, keep costs low and respond quickly to customers.

More and more, the key to competitive success lies in the flexibility that fast accurate information makes possible. Whatever the company or the industry, the market leaders of the future will be those who respond most quickly and accurately to changing customer demands.

If a company can target its customers precisely, and supply exactly the product or service they need, it can increase its returns on investment in production and marketing while reducing inventory and speeding up delivery.

Achieving flexibility requires a shift in thinking, from the mass production emphasis on economies of scale, to the more customer-centred approach of tailored production and increased choice.

In manufacturing, the flexibility strategy requires setting up production lines that can switch instantly between many different products, making an almost infinite variety of customized goods at low unit cost. The flexibility philosophy is just as valid for service companies. Whether in retail, insurance, banking or transport, the ability to segment the marketplace and tailor offerings profitably to individual customer needs provides a powerful competitive weapon.

A key ingredient of flexibility is the availability and quality of customer and business information.

At one company, the systems development manager said the goal is 'to maximize the flexibility of the whole company's response to demand'. Vital to this is the collection and use of data – 'with an Orwellian obsessiveness'.

According to *Fortune* magazine, this flexibility has brought to the company advantages such as 'the knowledge of whether or not a new product is successful within two weeks of launch', and 'a reduction of average inventory as a percent of sales for some 560 products, from 9.2% to 8.6%'.

2.2 In support of the knowledge worker

In a recent article in Harvard Business Review, Alan M. Webber (Webber, 1993) draws upon several authoritative sources to argue that a 'new economy' has arrived, in which the most prized asset is knowledge:

> '*The information technology revolution makes knowledge the new competitive resource*'.

He then argues that it is the abilities, skills, productivity and output of the knowledge workers in an organization that will determine its success. The job of a manager, then, is to:

- create an environment that allows knowledge workers to learn ....
- The chief management tool that makes learning happen is conversation ....
- Conversations are the way knowledge workers discover what they know, share it with their colleagues, and in the process create new knowledge for the organization. The panoply of modern information and communications technologies – for example, computers, faxes, e-mail – can help knowledge workers in this process. But all depends on the quality of the conversations that such technologies support.'

Hence the current interest in work-groups and other management practices which are designed to assist constructive dialogue – conversations. Get this right, and the potential is for knowledgeable participants to consistently make contributions to the organization which are far greater than the sum of individual contributions.

A conversation is an interactive dialogue; it requires alternate contributions from two or more people where the gap between contributions is no more than a few seconds. A conversation is difficult to maintain if responses from one participant take 30 minutes! Conversation and the idea that the efficacy of knowledge workers depends upon it makes a good metaphor to illustrate the value of interactive response performance for large database queries.

Knowledge workers are being encouraged to explore data through the introduction of easy to use tools operating in point-and-click, windowing environments. But *ad hoc* complex querying of data is by nature unpredictable, and user productivity can still be stymied by a database system which is unable to respond quickly and stay in sync with the user's train-of-thought.

In more down-to-earth terms, how often is it that any of us have attended a meeting where at some point, probably sooner rather than later, there is a pause because some key fact is missing? It is likely to be a piece of information which theoretically is available from the company's own databases. In practice, of course, there is no time to instruct an SQL programmer to develop the query, no time to have the database administrator ensure that the query can run without affecting the production systems, and no time to schedule the query to run in batch for an overnight answer. So, in order for the meeting to proceed, we have to rely on gut-feel, make an assumption or consider a range of possibilities. Either the meeting is in danger of continuing in misguided fashion, or else a lot of valuable (highly-paid) time is spent evaluating alternative options.

Suppose the fact could be determined from available information there and then, instantly and by somebody in the room? It is obtained without the meeting losing momentum, and then displayed in a manner which is instantly communicative. The meeting could then at least proceed certain in the knowledge of not running down a blind alley.

Further suppose that having obtained the first fact, it sparks ideas to be tested with further facts? Ordinarily, in the interests of time, other avenues which might yield even better ideas could not be explored. But if a rapid dialogue against the available information is possible while the ideas generators (people) are in one place, imagine how much more creative such meetings would be.

The end result is confident, high quality decisions reached quickly and productively. The relative value of the result may make the difference between success and failure for a new product, the difference between positive and negative payback for a marketing campaign, and so on. A parallel database server like White Cross today has the enabling technology to support the means – the ability to maintain a database 'conversation' with the knowledge worker – through which such a result could be achieved.

2.3 Re-engineering

Many leading management consultants believe that the proper application of modern Information Technology is not the mere automation of existing business functions. In an article in *Harvard Business Review* in July-August 1990, Michael Hammer said,

'We should *reengineer* our businesses: use the power of modern information technology to radically redesign our business processes in order to achieve dramatic improvements in their performance' (Hammer, 1990).

He goes on to use the examples of Ford Motor Company and Mutual Benefit Life who each managed to make substantial staff savings and reduce the lead times of particular business processes by reengineering them around the use of shared databases and networks. In each case this was possible to achieve (but probably easier said than done) by using current computer technologies. The requirement would be to support a finite set of predictable actions against the data – create a purchase order, authorize the purchase, generate the purchase order, receive the goods, make the payment, etc.

But Hammer goes on to make two further points:

- Decision points should be where the work is performed. The doers should become self-managing, management hierarchies can be flattened and huge organizational efficiencies can result.
- Information should be captured only once and at the source. Companies should restructure 'stovepipe' functional applications into integrated and interconnected systems.

In some ways this is not new news, but to make these things happen in most organizations is a daunting, perhaps impossible, task. Some have tried and failed – expensively. The essential reason is that conventional base hardware and software technologies are not designed to enable the implementation of informational systems; they do a reasonable job of capturing the data through the processing of simple business transactions, but do not have the flexibility to let the decision maker or knowledge worker request the information in a more freeform manner.

3   IT CHANGES – ENCOURAGING NEW WAYS OF THINKING

So, the key driver for computer systems in the 1990s is better use of information – the continual quest to improve the transformation from data into knowledge. Knowledge about customers, about competitors, about spending trends, about borrowing trends, about the market acceptance of new products, and so on.

Information is presented to the users more and more through graphical interfaces at PCs or desktop workstations. There is a plentiful supply of cheap desktop MIPS. The distribution of corporate computer power is being turned inside out – a migration from central mainframes to networked PCs and servers 'on the rim' of the organization.

With powerful tools and plenty of processing at the desktop, users are beginning to expect corporate information resources to be instantly available at their fingertips with a simple 'point-and-click'. To make this possible, many companies are re-engineering for the integration of their information facilities – building what has been termed the 'Computer Integrated Company' (Johnson and Caroline, 1990). A CIC views data as its primary asset, and has the facilities to extract the maximum return from that asset.

At the same time, the current recession is squeezing the IT manager to reduce processing costs by saving expensive mainframe MIPS only for those production systems that really need them. The new information systems are being 'rightsized' on low cost MIPS on the network.

To give an idea just how quickly companies are projected to install desktop machines, the number of PCs installed in the USA is forecast to grow from about eight million in 1989 to 44 million by 2000. The ratio of PCs to employees in that time will increase from 6% to 32%, or five times as many desktop users demanding ever more sophisticated access to departmental, divisional and corporate data. These will be the same users demanding the freedom to use information quickly and easily to satisfy their customers, to shorten the time to market for their products, to spot a market opportunity and so on. In other words, these are the knowledge workers who will be driven by the imperative for business flexibility that we discussed above.

There are many examples of the new types of application which the leading CIC organizations are now implementing in their drive for better integration, use of information and hence business flexibility. As we talk to White Cross prospects in various parts of the world, we find more and more such as these in all industry sectors. In many cases, the challenge is not so much to build the application, but to integrate a set of resources consisting of suitable user tools, PCs or workstations, the network, and a flexible, powerful database.

With the large range of easy-to-use end-user tools now available to run on low cost desktop machines, there is no lack of choice on the client side of the network.

With the new interface standards such as Microsoft's ODBC, SQL/CLI and RDA between user tools and database now available, integration should also be considerably easier.

The limiting factor for many new applications is the database itself, yet the database server market is set to share a compound growth rate with PCs in client server systems of some 70% compound between 1991 and 1996.

What properties does a database server need to possess to meet the requirements of the new applications?

1. Be interactive to the desktop user even for whole database analyses. Interactive response for whole database analyses in an *ad hoc* environment has to mean scanning millions of rows per second.

2. Promote rapid time to implementation means achieving the performance criteria without requiring complex and conflicting design decisions in the physical database design. Different users require different access paths to the data; in conventional database systems it is very difficult to resolve the resulting design conflicts. Data structured or organized one way to meet one access time target will fail to meet another. The problem becomes impossible in an *ad hoc* enquiry system, by definition, because the accesses are not predictable.
3. Provide equal levels of service to users in terms of response time, data currency and integrity. Today computer users accept many compromises because of technological limitations. They may accept that certain queries can only be run overnight; that queries can only be run on last week's data, and so on. The ideal solution as far as the user is concerned is a single copy of the data for all applications. This is probably still impractical today, but parallel systems hold out the greatest promise of achieving that aim.

Database systems built upon parallel architectures have the ability to make (1) and (2) above achievable today. The key to success, however, is not merely in switching to parallel hardware. The implications for a modern, truly parallel database server are more than that.

With the price of memory declining for some time at 30% per annum, the price/performance of memory today is now considerably better than disk.

Systems can now be populated with large pools of memory to get as much of the activity against the data in memory as possible. It allows us to rethink some basic assumptions about database processing. Conventional database systems do get advantage out of data cached in memory, but to access a row they typically go through a file system layer, then an operating system layer before finding that the data block was actually in memory all along. As a result, the instruction pathlength per row is high – perhaps 1200 instructions per row in a table search for commodity RDBMS'.

By using a different set of design assumptions in the RBMS software about how data in memory is to be accessed, these pathlengths can be reduced by 20 to 30 times. So, by designing to get the most out of RAM and using large amounts of it effectively, the dividends to the user in terms of performance can be large.

Also, effective utilization of parallel hardware requires specialized software designed from the ground up for parallel working. Unlike conventional SMP RDBMS software, which divides up the workload across processors at the SQL level, a parallel database server such as White Cross has 'true parallelism': the ability to run a single query across a large number of processors simultaneously.

This makes it possible to exploit the full power of all the processors against large single decision support (knowledge worker) queries.

Very fast scan speeds minimize the need for indexes to the data. Few or no indexes mean that update transactions can be committed more quickly, and there is less contention for index blocks. By thinking through the file management system carefully in a parallel system, these advantages can be enhanced by eliminating locking contention such that queries scanning the data can get consistent answers without blocking update transactions on the same data. By careful design, the inherent advantages of parallel database systems for concurrent running of transaction processing and free-from querying against the same data will be leveraged to make single database a practicable reality.

The business and IT trends that we have talked about indicate that 80% of all mid-sized computers will be in client–server systems by 1996. New business dynamics and the knowledge worker's voracious appetite for more information on demand is creating a huge demand for very high performance database servers for commercial use. This is the opportunity for truly parallel database servers such as White Cross. Today, for many applications it is already able to offer 100 times upward shifts in performance at price/performance levels which are 100 times better than conventional alternatives.

REFERENCES

Hammer, M. (1990) Reengineering Work: Don't Automate, Obliterate, *Harvard Business Review*, July-August.

Johnson, T. and Chappell, C. (1990) The Computer Integrated Company, Ovum Report, October.

Stewart, T. A. (1992) Brace for Japan's Hot New Strategy, *Fortune*, September 21.

Tan, P. and Lovery, M. (1992) Rightsizing: Strategies, Tools and Markets, Ovum Report, June.

Webber, A. M. (1993) What's So New About The New Economy, *Harvard Business Review*, January-February.

4 Parallel Processing for Database Applications: The Forthcoming Revolution

J. Spiers
Oracle Corporation UK Ltd

1 THE DESKTOP REVOLUTION

In 1981, the first IBM PC offered something like 0.1 MIP (million instructions per second) of computing performance for a cost of $5000. Ten years later, the same $5000 buys 10 MIPs of desktop performance, a staggering 100-fold performance improvement in just 10 years. By 1993, a further 10-fold performance improvement can be anticipated, with a 100 MIP desktop machine costing the same $5000.

Over the same period, the price performance offered by conventional proprietary minicomputer and mainframe environments has improved by something like a factor of 3.

Today the cost of a raw MIP on a mainframe environment costs around $50,000 – a 100-fold discrepancy with the PC platforms. Taking another measure, database performance as measured through industry benchmarks shows a (mere) 20-fold discrepancy.

These are of course very crude measures, but the underlying message is clear – commodity microprocessors offer huge and indeed growing price performance benefits over conventional architectures.

The impact of these trends is visible in every corner of the IT business. From a beginning as a 'personal computer', which was intended to have very little to do with the conventional world of computing, the PC is now fundamental to the strategies of suppliers and users alike.

The PC bought users the chance to seek independence from their IT departments. Lower costs and shorter timescales outweighed the necessity for IT control. Cheaper processing power on the PC brought new applications, easier to use systems, and new development tools with which the conventional mainframe environment simply could not compete.

The result of course was fragmentation and duplication. The new systems were incompatible, not just with the centralized systems, but also with one another. Information, too, was fragmented and duplicated through a wide range of systems. Much data was simply rekeyed into the new environments, and even where file transfer procedures were used, there was no way of ensuring consistency of information across disparate systems.

2 THE RISE OF CLIENT–SERVER COMPUTING

Riding on the back of lower network costs were reborn the needs for integrated information handling. Workgroup solutions required shared information; PC applications needed up-to-date access to real live data from operational systems which were still the domain of the IT department. Through LANs, file servers and database servers, PCs began to reintegrate themselves with corporate systems, shared information and with one another.

And so was borne client-server computing: the logical separation between personal applications on PC and workstation clients, and shared information resources and corporate applications on shared servers. At its best, client–server computing brings the best of both worlds, with each machine type doing what it is best at.

However, the client–server revolution creates new problems of its own. Integration shifts new workloads back to the larger server machines, with their higher relative costs. And the mere availability of access to shared information creates new applications requirements and new workloads, for example in management information systems, workgroup applications and office automation.

3 THE ROLE OF PARALLEL SERVER TECHNOLOGY

Client–server computing will never achieve its potential whilst a wide mismatch of costs remains between the client and server components. Ideally we would like to see costs equalized at each end, so that the decisions on how to distribute workloads between clients and servers can be dictated by logic and not just price.

At the same time, we will require large and scalable servers to accommodate the growing workloads from new applications. In many cases, it will be easier to meet the need for a single, logical integrated information resource, and to manage that resource through centralization rather than through fragmentation.

So the requirement is clear – to build large and indefinitely scalable systems through the use of the same commodity microprocessor technologies which have bought price performance to the desktop. At the same time, we need to provide on these systems much of the sophisticated software environment of conventional multi-user machines – operating system, networking connectivity and data management.

With current technologies at least, these requirements will only be fully met by non-shared memory parallel environments.

4 THE ORACLE PARALLEL SERVER

The Oracle Parallel Server is an implementation of the ORACLE Relational Database Management System for non-shared memory computers. It provides a software environment in which multiple processors can access a single physical database with full data integrity. Most importantly, it shows scalability with near linear growth in transaction throughput as processor nodes are added to the system.

Table 4.1 shows formal audited benchmark results for ORACLE software across a range of platforms. These demonstrate two key performance aspects of the ORACLE Parallel Server:

- large volume transaction throughput, demonstrated at over twice the transaction rate of a conventional mainframe
- low-cost per transaction unit, measured at comparable cost to a commmodity PC, and significantly lower than large and mid-range machines.

TABLE 4.1. Benchmark performance.

Computer	Model	tps	Cost($)	Cost/tps($)
PC	Compaq SystemPro 386	22*	63k	2.6k
PC LAN Server	Compaq Deskpro 486	43	112k	2.6k
Minicomputer	DEC VAX 6000-560	153	2.6m	17k
Unix	Sequent 2000/700	319	2.4m	7.6k
Mini Cluster	4 x VAX 6000-560	425	7.0m	16.5k
Mainframe	Amdahl 5890	416*	18m	45k
Parallel	nCUBE2 nCDB-1000	1073	2.6m	2.5k

Notes: all are TCP-B transactions using ORACLE, except where marked as *, which are TP1 transactions using ORACLE; all benchmarks audited by Codd & Date.

The ORACLE Parallel Server has been, or is being, implemented on a range of commercially available MIMD (multiple instruction, multiple data) parallel platforms, including the Meiko Computing Surface, the Parsys Supernode 1000 Series, the NCUBE 2 Scalar Supercomputer and the NCR 3600 range. In addition, the same architecture is applicable to clustered environments where disks are shared across multiple conventional computers. Oracle is also being implemented on massively parallel machines from Kendall Square Research, though this implementation, which provides simulated shared memory, is not dependent on the Oracle Parallel Server technology.

A description of the standard ORACLE architecture, and features specific to the Parallel Server is provided at Appendix A.

5 APPLICATIONS OF THE ORACLE PARALLEL SERVER

5.1 General

The Parallel Server is particularly suited to applications which involve high workloads that need to be met at minimum cost. Frequently such applications are subject to high or unpredictable growth, and cost-effective scalability is necessary to provide investment protection into the future. Not only are conventional architectures limited in top-end performance, but they can only offer limited upgrade possibilities.

A particular benefit is the ability to create large and resilient centralized systems at lower cost than conventional architectures. Too often, systems have been forced to be decentralized and fragmented into a distributed database solution, even though the underlying requirement may have been for centralization of the information resource.

A further benefit to many users is the ability, for the first time, to create large systems from non-proprietary hardware and software technologies.

The Parallel Server is particularly suited to applications which fit into one of the following general categories:

OLTP with partitioned data – applications that modify mostly disjoint data sets. Each node in the loosely coupled system accesses its own disjoint set of rows within shared tables. An example might be a banking system, where each branch usually accesses its own accounts and only occasionally an account from another branch.

OLTP with random access to a large database – applications with mostly random access to a database significantly larger than the memory caches of the instances accessing the data. Examples might be vehicle licensing or taxation records.

Departmentalized – applications that primarily modify different tables in the same database. An example might be an integrated business system embracing inventory processing, personnel, sales order processing and similar departmental functions. Data sharing between nodes exists, but is limited. Note that centralization into a single database simplifies data sharing and data administration, and can also reduce total system costs through the use of parallel technology

Decision Support – applications handling large volumes of queries, for example a financial services marketing database that is queried intensively, but updated only on a daily basis.

Mixed Workload Environments – applications in an integrated database environment with a mix of different types of workloads, for example real-time transaction updates, batch processing, simple retrievals and complex analysis and reporting. Problems can frequently arise in this environment, particularly when the workload mix fluctuates dynamically resulting in unpredictable performance of individual elements. Parallel server technology can provide a solution by partitioning the workload across nodes of a parallel configuration, so guaranteeing required levels of performance, for example for real-time event capture, whist at the same time retaining the integration through a single database.

Certain types of applications may be better suited to a clustered solution than to a massively parallel system. If data access can only be logically partitioned into a small number of mostly disjoint data sets, then a small number of high-performance nodes may offer better throughput than a larger number of smaller nodes.

A small class of high-throughput applications, characterized by intensive update to small portions of the database ('hot-spots'), may not be well-suited to loosely couple environments since throughput may be limited by the I/O required to transfer data blocks between nodes.

5.2 Applications examples

The Oracle Parallel Server introduces new technologies, both in hardware and software terms, into the mainstream commercial IT arena. Key to the success of any new technology in the commercial marketplace are proven references and applications. Oracle is working closely with a number of 'early adopters' who are evaluating or building new applications based on parallel server technology.

Oracle is also supporting the DTI/SERC Parallel Applications Program, whose aim is to demonstrate the commercial applications of parallel processing, and to build centres of expertise in the required technologies.

Commercial applications of the parallel server technology are typically currently at the feasibility or development stages, and are subject to commercial confidentiality. Certainly, a number of Oracle's partners believe that the early adoption of this technology will offer a significant competitive advantage.

It is, however, possible to outline in general terms some of applications areas where parallel database technology will make its mark. The following examples are not intended to represent a definitive range; rather they cover real-life applications which have already been shown to benefit from the parallel server technology.

5.2.1 Database accelerators

Perhaps the most straightforward area of application is where a parallel server is used to provide added database performance to an existing Oracle system. This typically involves splitting an existing database application by transferring the database workload to a parallel machine. This creates a client–server configuration, with the applications remaining unchanged on the old system (now a client), operating against the database transferred to the parallel machine.

Clearly, the key benefits here are the ability to extend the life of existing systems cost effectively, using low cost hardware and with no applications redevelopment or porting costs.

In some organizations, the growing demands on existing systems have lead to a conflict between OLTP (on-line transaction processing) workload and MIS (Management Information Systems), forcing a split of these two workloads across different systems, with data being duplicated from the OLTP system to meet the MIS requirements. The addition of a database accelerator allows the database workload to be reconsolidated, supporting both activities concurrently, against the same up-to-date data, and with simplified systems administration.

5.2.2 Mainframe alternatives

A third applications area is as a cost-effective and scalable alternative to conventional mainframe solutions, particularly where there is a large scale operational requirement which approaches the capabilities of the largest mainframes available, and a need for centralization of data.

The feasibility of such applications is dependent on:

- demonstrable cost savings,
- proven scalability of the target parallel environment, and
- cost-effective migration of applications from the old to the new environment.

One such trial with a large international corporation involved the transfer of applications running in a Cobol/DB2/IBM mainframe environment to a

Cobol/ORACLE/Unix/Meiko environment. Subsequent benchmarks demonstrated the ability to run batch jobs formerly taking several hours in less than one hour on a configuration with a fraction of the cost.

The wider benefits are not just the cost savings but the ability to accommodate growing workloads and new demands, for example for management information from operational databases, in a scalable manner.

5.2.3 Low-cost on-line transaction processing

Perhaps the most obvious area of application is for high-volume OLTP applications, particularly where high availability and scalability to meet growing workloads are required.

One application is with a telecommunications supplier. The current customer base of 370,000 is growing at a rate of 50–70% per annum. Overall the goal is to create a system capable of supporting 100 users, 100 gigabytes of data and processing 2.4 million transactions per year.

Another application concerns a national retail chain. Accurate merchandizing is key to competitive success, and this depends upon on-line access to detailed up-to-date information. This is to be achieved through a central database which is updated from 150 stores at 15 minute intervals. Anticipated data volumes are 60–100 gigabytes of data on-line, a peak load of 100 transactions per second and a total of 7 million SQL events per day. Key to performance is the ability to support complex query workloads concurrent with updates. Being a low-margin business a further essential is to achieve the required throughput at the lowest possible cost.

5.2.4 Enabling new applications

Increasingly, customers seek wider choice and flexibility in the products they purchase. Unfortunately, the economics of mass production and distribution are dependent on standardized components, and standardized products, with a limited range of variants.

In the holiday industry, low costs are achieved through bulk purchases of travel and accommodation, which are bundled into standard holiday packages. Yet there is a growing requirement for more flexibility, creating custom holidays, based on the same pre-bought ingredients.

The challenge here is the sheer administrative complexity of creating every product on a custom basis, more particularly when it is realized that 'packages' will need to be created in real time, in front of the potential customer.

New applications of this type will become economically viable for the first time through the availability of parallel computing platforms.

5.2.5 Creating large centralized systems

One application at the feasibility stage involves a large centralized database service with up to 25,000 users. Conventional architectures would force this application to be distributed into multiple databases, even though the underlying requirement is for a largely centralized solution. This application has been estimated to require 10 large shared memory Unix systems each with 10 nodes; more importantly, this involves fragmenting the database across 10 machines. Whilst today's RDBMS products can provide high degrees of location independence to users and developers, there are nevertheless cost, performance and more importantly administration overheads in distributing data.

Simulation of this application on a massively parallel platform indicates that the required transaction rate will be met by a machine with less than 50 nodes, well within the capabilities of current technology, at roughly one third of the cost of the distributed alternative. As well as upgradability as may be required as workload expands, this allows a centralized physical database to be retained.

6 FUTURE DIRECTIONS

6.1 The intelligent server

Client–server computing has grown up around the boundary between clients running applications, and servers managing shared information. This boundary reflects the traditional separation of code from data, supported by the availability of widely accepted standards to provide interoperability across the client server interface.

More logically, however, the separation should be between that which is personal to the individual user, and that which is shared. Thus the client would concern itself with purely personal applications, user preferences and presentation issues. Servers would manage shared corporate resources of all types.

This requires database servers to support shared procedures, algorithms and business rules, and also data-driven behaviour through triggers and event alerters. At the same time, databases need to support a richer view of the structure of data to simplify their applications and end-user access.

Whether we think of these directions as leading to semantic databases, intelligent databases, extended relational databases, active databases or object databases the trend is clear. Most fundamentally databases increasingly will serve as repositories not simply for data but also for shared behaviour and 'meaning'. Through this process, client–server computing can achieve its full potential – the best of both worlds of computing.

Through this process of evolution a significant proportion of conventional applications code will need to migrate across the client–server boundary. The effect is to shift significant new workload from clients to servers. The imbalance in cost between PCs and conventional larger systems serves as a huge barrier to this process, which massively parallel servers are uniquely positioned to address.

6.2 Clustered Unix configurations

The same technology that allows multiple processes in a non-shared memory environment to share a single physical database is also applicable to clustered configurations of conventional machines. Digital's VAX Cluster architecture is the most familiar example of this type, and this is already supported by Oracle.

This architecture is now becoming attractive to vendors of top-end Unix systems. Today, such systems are typically based on shared memory configurations (symmetrical multi-processing or SMP), to achieve maximum performance at relatively low costs. However, although they can be extended through techniques such as local memory caches, such systems will always ultimately be limited by the need for globally shared memory accessed through a single shared memory bus.

The most straightforward way around this limit is to create larger systems as clusters of SMP machines, supported by software which can maintain consistency, coherence and scalable performance across non-shared memory architectures. Oracle is working with a number of hardware vendors on the implementation of the Parallel Server on clustered Unix configurations.

6.3 Software enhancements

The first release of the Oracle Parallel Server is focused on supporting high transaction rates through a single database. For most commercial applications, the ability to support the underlying transaction workload is a clear prerequisite to supporting the query-oriented MIS requirement.

A second stage of research and development is now underway concerned with the handling of large complex queries across multiple parallel nodes. As well as better supporting complex query operations in the MIS environment, this will also address applications such as Geographical Information Systems, which are characterized by very complex queries across large but relatively unchanging data sets. It is anticipated that query performance for an isolated complex query can be improved by something in the range of 10–100 times through parallelization techniques.

Further work is concerned with more fully exploiting parallel architectures and their operating systems to provide higher systems and data availability. This will provide software-based fault tolerance to allow the database to automatically recover from node failures, and to dynamically reconfigure and restart in a reduced configuration.

6.4 Performance trends and targets

At the same time, continuing software and hardware developments will provide for even larger configurations at lower costs per unit of throughput. As illustrated at Table 4.2, within the next two years it is anticipated that a maximum throughput of something like 10 times today's figures should be achievable at a total cost of no more than twice of the most cost-effective systems today.

TABLE 4.2. Price/performance trends.

	PC	Mainframe	Parallel Server		
			Today	*1992/1993*	
				Small	*Medium*
Processors	1	5	64	64	512
MIPS	10	200	600	600	5000
Memory	32M	512M	1024M	1-4G	8-32G
I/Os per sec	250	2500	5000		
Transaction Rate	40	500	1000	1000	10000
Cost	$100k	$20M	$2.5M	$1M	$5M
Cost/tps	$2.5k	$40k	$2.5k	$1k	$0.5k

Note: figures are intended to illustrate general trends and are hence approximate.

APPENDIX A – ORACLE PARALLEL SERVER ARCHITECTURE

1   ORACLE'S VERSION 6 ARCHITECTURE AND SHARED MEMORY PLATFORMS

The architecture of ORACLE version 6, the current release for shared memory platforms, is illustrated in Figure 4.A1. This architecture was specifically designed to address the growing requirement to support large scale transaction-oriented workloads. The major objectives are therefore performance, concurrency, high availability, plus the ability to fully exploit shared memory parallel processing systems. Oracle's shared memory symmetrical multi-processing parallel platforms include the IBM 3090, Digital's VAX 6000 and 9000 series, Convex, Pyramid and Sequent Symmetry.

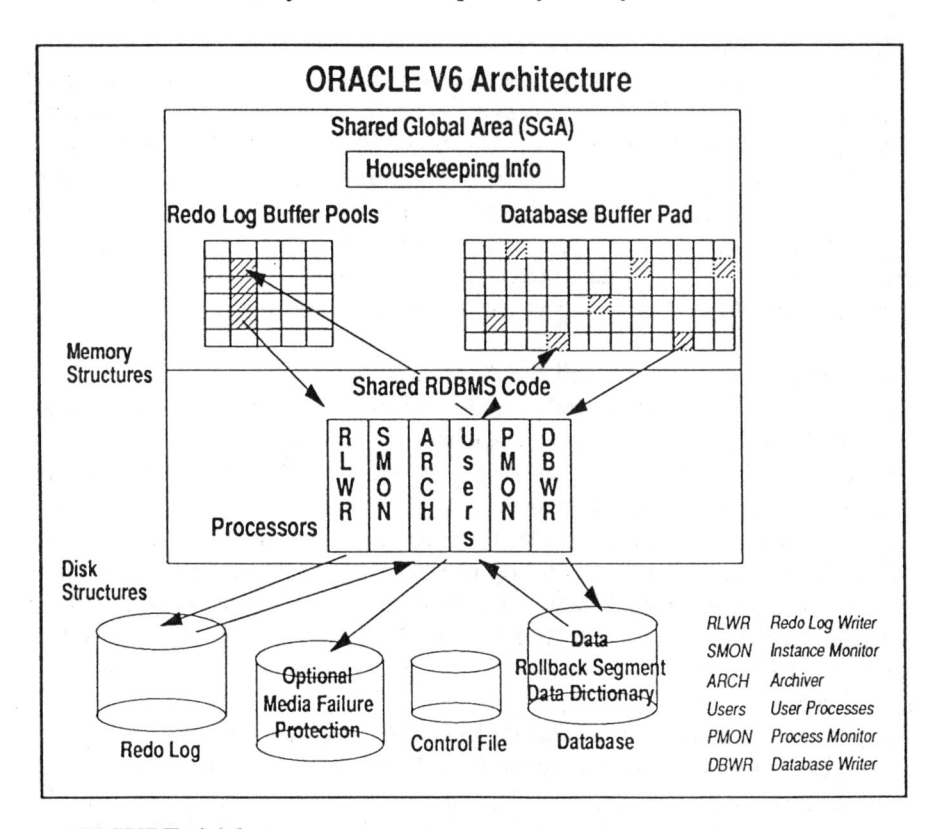

FIGURE 4.A1.

1.1 System global area

The ORACLE version 6 architecture is based around a globally shared memory area accessible to all database processes; this area is known as the System Global Area (SGA).

The SGA is used for buffering disk I/O, to provide a database cache, to maintain details of database locks and to hold queues on shared system resources.

1.2 Parallel processes

The database processing workload is divided amongst a number of processes – the database server processes themselves, of which there is one for each concurrent database connection, and a small number of background processes undertaking the necessarily serial work.

1.2.1 The database server processes

For each concurrent connection to the database, there is a corresponding backend database process; all database processes execute the same code. The backend database process performs the majority of the work involved in processing a database request, including reading data from disk into cache memory where required. This 'process per user' approach fully exploits the parallelism in the incoming workload, with the operating system responsible for scheduling these processes across the available processors. The necessary serialization on physical disk read operations is imposed at the operating system level.

1.2.2 Transaction integrity and the Redo Log

Database update operations need to ensure transaction integrity, such that a set of related updates (a transaction) is applied in full to the database on disk, or (in the event of some error) not applied at all. Only in this way can the integrity of database structures be guaranteed.

As database updates are made, these are initially applied in the database cache. At the same time, a Redo Log record is created consisting of an image of the changed data bytes. The act of committing a transaction involves writing the relevant Redo Log records to disk. The Redo Log itself consists of one or more serial files, and for each such file there is a continuously running Redo Log Writer process (RLWR).

Although the underlying database has not been updated on disk, the system is protected against any failure by the Redo Log entries which have been physically written out to disk prior to signalling completion of the Commit. In the event of failure, the Redo Log contains a record of updates which need to be applied to the database proper to roll it forward to a consistent and up-to-date state.

This 'fast commit' technique is designed to reduce the work to be performed at the commit point to the absolute minimum sufficient amount. The work of physically updating the database on disk, which may involve many I/Os as disk blocks and index entries are reorganized, is deferred such that it can proceed in parallel with other activity.

This technique reduces the volume of disk I/O at the point of a Commit to a single serial write; indeed, the system also takes advantage of writing the

Redo Log records for more than one transaction in a single I/O where possible, a technique known as group commit.

1.2.3 Deferred update

Database updates, which have to date only been applied within the database cache and protected by the Redo Log, need eventually to be physically applied to disk, either to free up space in the cache or to create a synchronization point for housekeeping purposes.

The actual database update operations are performed by a separate task known as the database writer which runs continuously in the background, and which of course can run in parallel with the processing of database requests. In appropriate circumstances, multiple database writer tasks can be used to allow write operations to separate portions of the database to proceed in parallel.

A reduction in total disk write activity is also achieved by virtue of the fact that, where a database record has been changed several times in the buffer cache, then intermediate updates are never physically applied to the database, only recorded in the Redo Log.

1.2.4 Benefits

The effect of this architecture is to exploit to the full the parallelism inherent in the incoming workload. At the same time, the amount of work performed at the Commit point, which is of necessity serial in nature, is reduced to a bare minimum. This not only maximizes the response time to the user but also minimizes the delay to other processes waiting to Commit. By deferring the task of physically updating the database, this work can be executed in parallel with other database activity, by a batch process able to exploit processing capacity not required by higher priority activities.

1.3 Concurrency

The ORACLE architecture also maximizes concurrency by minimizing the impact of database locks.

Data which is to be updated is locked at the most granular level; only the actual records which are subject to change are locked and there is no requirement to escalate locks to the block, table or file level. In addition, index entries are locked individually. The ability to lock at the row level arises as a direct consequence of the deferred update mechanism. In a traditional architecture, the commit process involves physically updating the database on disk, which typically means reorganizing data and index entries at the disk block level, affecting other records held within that block and possibly beyond.

In addition, the ORACLE architecture provides row-level multi-versioning. This provides, automatically and where necessary, multiple versions of the same database row, reflecting its state prior to recent updates. The effect is that processes which are reading from the database can be shown a self-consistent view of data even if that data is being changed at the same time. For this reason, database read activities are guaranteed read-consistency without the need for read locks.

1.4 Other features

The ORACLE version 6 architecture also provides for on-line back-up and recovery. Security backups can be taken whilst the system remains on-line, running in parallel with normal processing. Similarly, in the event of a partial failure, the affected area of the database can be restored in parallel with the continued processing of database activity against the unaffected areas.

A common bottleneck in transaction-based systems is the process of generating unique transaction sequence numbers – order number, invoice number and so on. Conventionally, this requires a database access and update operation. ORACLE provides a memory-based sequence number generation capability to minimize this common point of serialization.

2 ORACLE FOR MASSIVELY PARALLEL SYSTEMS

The ORACLE version 6 architecture described above is dependent on the ability of all processors to access the same memory, the SGA; in hardware terms, the processors are required to share a common memory bus. Ultimately, the performance of the system will be limited by a shared memory bottleneck.

In contrast, traditional loosely coupled hardware architectures, such as the Digital VAXcluster or Tandem systems, are not based around shared memory; each processor has its own local memory and communicates with other processors by passing messages over a common interconnect – a bus or even a LAN. However, this arrangement ultimately leads to an interconnect bottleneck, limited by the fixed bandwidth of the interconnect.

Massively parallel systems eliminate the shared memory bottleneck by employing a distributed memory structure in which each processing node consists of a processor and local memory. The interconnect bottleneck is removed by virtue of an interconnect scheme which not only provides high-speed connections, but which also incrementally scales the total interconnect bandwidth as the number of processors increases.

2.1 Architecture

The Oracle Parallel Server (with version 6.2 of ORACLE) is designed to deliver a broad range of cost-effective performance, up to very high transaction rates of 1000 transactions per second and beyond, on massively parallel platforms and multi-computer cluster configurations.

The architecture used is illustrated in Figure 4.A2. In effect, each processor carrying out database work maintains a buffer cache in its local memory to store the data blocks required by the transactions it executes. Again, background processes executing at each node are responsible for writing Redo log records to disk at the point of commit, and removing data blocks from the cache by physically applying database updates to disk.

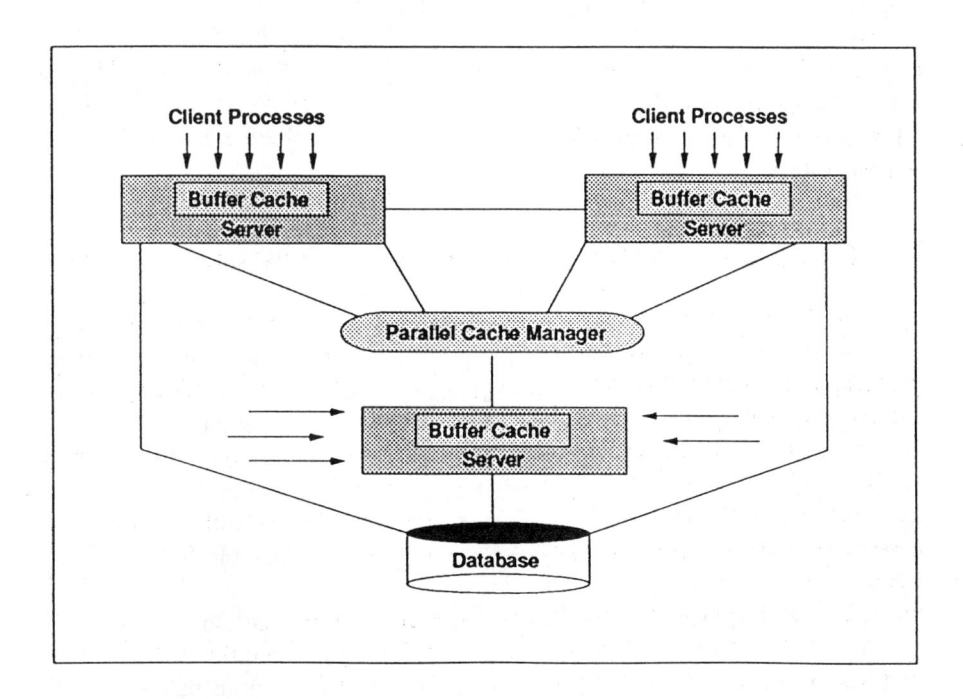

FIGURE 4.A2.

Cache coherency is maintained through the services of the Parallel Cache Manger. When the Parallel Server requires a data block that is not already in local memory, it uses the facilities of the parallel cache manager to determine whether the block is in the memory buffer cache of another node. If it is, the block is physically transferred to the node that needs it; otherwise, the block is obtained from disk storage in the conventional way.

2.2 Concurrency control

A unique feature of ORACLE is its support for unrestricted row level looking; this provides the finest granularity of concurrency control, minimizing contention between transactions, and maximizing the extent to which transactions can be executed in parallel with one another.

The higher the throughput becomes, the more important it is to minimize bottlenecks since the probability of multiple users accessing the same disk block is a direct function of the number of concurrent users. This issue is most critical for index blocks, since not only are index entries accessed most frequently, their small typical size means that a single block may contain perhaps several hundred index records.

Even in the massively parallel environment, full unrestricted row level locking is supported. When a data block is transferred from processor to processor, information on any row level locks held on the data is also passed. Thus multiple transactions executing on different processors can modify different rows in the same data block without ever waiting for each other to release a lock.

Multi-version concurrency control to provide read consistent images is also particularly important in massively parallel environments with their high workload of concurrent read and update transactions. As in the standard version 6 implementation, when a transaction updates a row in a table, a copy of the previous contents of that row can be generated to provide a read consistent image. Moreover, if a data block is transferred to another node, the local copy is retained to allow current query operations to proceed without waiting for the block to be transferred back. Furthermore, additional queries on the same data block may be performed at the same time by other servers once they acquire a copy of that data block in their local memory. Thus multiple operations on the same logical row of data can be processed in parallel without interfering with one another and whilst keeping the number of data blocks transferred between processors to a minimum.

The standard ORACLE version 6 fast commit, group commit and deferred write features minimize disk I/O. In a large massively parallel configuration, with aggregate memory measured perhaps in gigabytes, large databases may indeed be effectively cached entirely in memory; in such cases, only the highly efficient logging information needs to be physically written to disk. Even where the available cache memory is less than the total database size, the most active data is likely to remain permanently in memory.

Massively parallel platforms also require support from new database administration facilities. Each node effectively runs a complete 'instance' of the ORACLE DBMS; in a configuration with perhaps hundreds of nodes it would be inconvenient, to say the least, to require a database administrator to manually start-up, shut down and monitor these instances individually. As a result, new database administration tools are being built to assist in the parallel management of multiple parallel database instances.

5 Optimizing Parallel Processing in the Commercial Relational Environment

J. Page
Executive Architect Consultant
AT&T, G.I.S.

1 INTRODUCTION

A major advantage of the relational approach to data management is that data can be stored in tables that are both simple to understand and unambiguous in content. With data represented in such tables, questions such as who is buying which product or which product is the most popular for a particular class of customer, can be answered through the use of the standard Structured Query Language (SQL). Using this high level language, little knowledge of the physical format of data is required – a huge advantage in the world of end-user computing.

Currently, Relational Database Management Systems (RDBMS) are available on all computing environments from Personal Computers through to the largest Mainframe systems. However, their benefit is perhaps best seen when the relational facility is applied to very large volumes of data; perhaps those typically found in large retail organizations where single tables with over 100 million rows are commonplace.

However, to build a system that can store massive amounts of relationally held data, and to give access to it in an *ad hoc* decision support manner whilst still supporting the normal operational systems that capture the company's data at source, is a huge challenge.

Such a system must be capable of capturing and maintaining data through the use of On-Line Transaction Processing (OLTP), whilst effectively supporting what has now become known as On-Line Complex Processing (OLCP), without forgetting of course the more familiar batch applications. Unfortunately history has already shown that the combination of high *ad hoc* capabilities and high OLTP performance cannot be achieved by conventional computing architecture's within the context of a single database system. However innovative new architecture, can solve both application types at once. This chapter seeks to illustrate such an architecture.

2 SOME RELATIONAL DATABASE SYSTEM ARCHITECTURES

In many ways the birth of the information revolution coincided with that of relational database systems. Chief exponents of the new Relational Theory were primarily Oracle and Ingres in the mini-computer world, and later, DB2 on IBM systems. Oracle and Ingres came to the forefront in the UK in the early 1980s but with very different architectures. Figure 5.1 illustrates the early Ingres architecture. In short, the database management was done by what we can think of as a 'backend' process, whilst the end users application was serviced by a 'frontend' process. Every time a user logged on, perhaps to use Ingres's Query by Forms (QBF) utility as an example, he would create both a dedicated frontend and backend process.

This simple architecture was not that chosen by Oracle. Figure 5.1 also shows that although in the Oracle environment (pre V6 Oracle), whenever a user runs an Oracle application or utility, a dedicated 'frontend' process is created as with Ingres, all such applications from multiple users can utilize a single set of system wide and shared, backend processes. These backend processes manage database writing, before image writing and other system maintenance functions for the database as a whole.

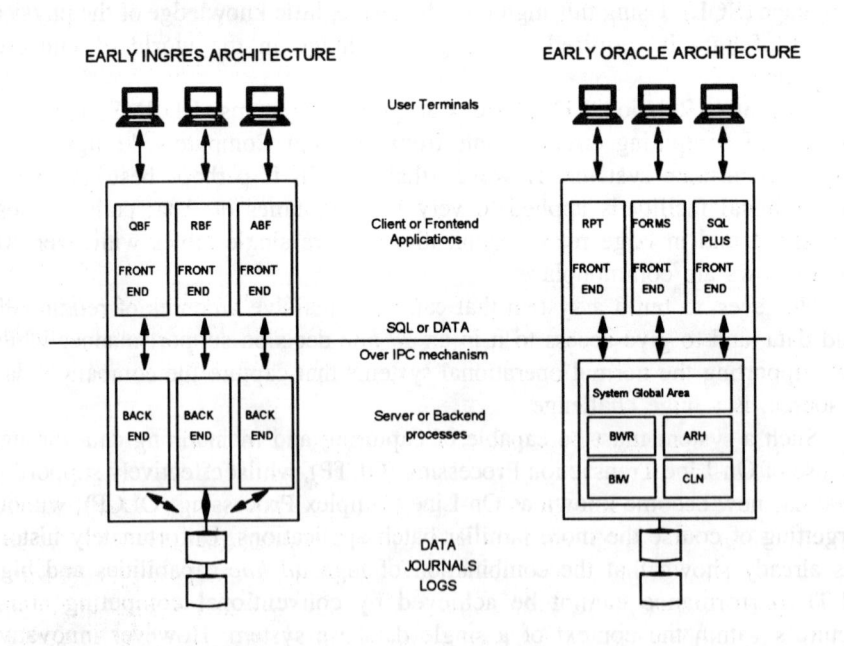

FIGURE 5.1. Early Ingres and Oracle architectures.

Both of these architectures make good use of shared memory facilities and proprietary (to the hardware platform) inter-process-communication mechanisms that are particularly well developed in the minicomputer world. The two architectures, however, both suffer from performance problems when adding many users. Ingres, by creating two processes per user, soon runs out of system resources on the traditional minicomputer systems. The single backend subsystem of Oracle on the other hand, soon becomes a bottleneck with multiple users.

One solution available to both vendors was to separate the frontend and backend processes and place them on different machines. Because the architectures of both so clearly differentiate the frontend and backend functionality, and that communications between these two sets of co-operating processes is merely a matter of ensuring a consistent applications programming interface and otherwise using standard operating system and network facilities. This enables the running of front and backend processes on different hardware platforms connected by standard communications interfaces, with client–server computing utilizing distributed processing in a simple, unsophisticated, but usable manner.

This simple utilization of what can loosely be termed the beginning of parallelism, certainly goes some way towards allowing for a linear increase in users without loosing performance. However there remain two problems:

- Firstly, there is still certain to be contention at data level. The architecture does not allow multiple processors any sophisticated access to the actual data in a concurrent manner.
- Secondly, there is still no way to linearly improve the performance of a single query by utilizing multiple processors, or even in fact, to maintain the performance of a query as data volumes increase. These two problems largely remain unsolved in today's software based database systems. They are instead being solved by specialized hardware implementations and specifically optimized versions of the RDBMS software. It is to the former option, the enabling of high volume and complex relational processing by hardware that is the major thrust of this chapter.

3   THE CASE FOR A DATABASE MACHINE

Referring to our frontend/backend model, we should consider that it is the portability and user friendliness of the frontend application oriented software, that the user base demands in new systems. Portability removes any dependency on hardware, and the ease of use inherent in these systems ensures minimum training requirements and maximum saving on investment.

The technology employed in the backend data oriented process is, however, of very little concern to the user and lends itself very well to the 'black box' approach – an implementation in hardware that is specifically designed to maximize efficiency and cost effectiveness. This works especially well if the 'black box' can handle data at the level of abstraction of the relational model, because this can ensure data portability to other 'black boxes' should need demand.

What other characteristics should this 'black box' have?

Firstly, it should be able to offload as much work as possible from the general purpose host and it must be connectable to many different types of host hardware, each running different flavours of operating system and development software. Connectivity is key.

Secondly of course, it should be able to perform relational database tasks using specific, and optimized hardware and software.

We have lived for the last ten years with the statement that Relational Database Management Systems (RDBMS) are slow, and there has been a great deal of evidence to show that this statement is, by and large, true. For many years RDBMSs such as Ingres, Oracle and even DB2 have failed to compete for the systems that their non-relational cousins such as IMS and IDMS handle so well. Why is this true? Well there are several reasons which include most definitely, the very nature of the RDBMS and the vagaries of the applications that generally access them. In short, they are designed to do different things than their older cousins, and they behave in very different ways. IMS for example, is geared toward short, simple OLTP measured in the hundreds of transactions a second. Their relational cousins on the other hand, are often geared towards serving the *ad hoc* complex relational query, measured in less than one transaction per second.

So is it true to suggesting that there is a need for the coexistence of the transaction oriented network and Codasyl systems, alongside the more data oriented Relational?

The answer to this question today, is absolutely 'NO'. It is now proven that the current existing RDBMSs can handle all types of business transaction if the underlying hardware and operating system can be tailored in a suitable manner.

4 SYSTEM DOWNSIZING

One of the fundamental advantages of the database machine approach is that they can be built to do a specific task utilizing state of the art, non-proprietary and available technologies. Existing machines in all walks of life have successively utilized major advances in chip technology. In the case of Intel for example, using 80286, 80386 and 80486 chips, has yielded MIPs increase of ten fold in less than five years.

However, it's not just in the fast evolution of microprocessors that database machines can benefit. In the same time scale disk technology has improved from the commonly used 500 MBytes fixed disks to 2.6 GByte drives – a further five fold increase in disk capacity with only small modifications to form factors. We find ourselves, therefore, in the luxurious position of being able to utilize large numbers of powerful hardware components to solve our processing problems.

This is good because one thing is clear; the advent of Relational Databases is ensuring that the need for commercial computer power has risen rapidly. For typical marketing applications, where millions of customer records need to be joined to millions of sales records, the power of a single conventional CPU, using software-based RDBMS's such as Ingres, Oracle or DB2, is simply not adequate. For typical on-line systems where hundreds or thousands of users might be making accesses to the same relational data structures concurrently, again the software solutions on their own leave a great deal to be desired.

The challenge, therefore, is to develop a novel architecture specifically to handle this relational processing. Such a system would certainly need to be parallel in nature utilizing many processors, and therefore, the interconnection of the processors is of prime importance.

4.1 Two types of parallelism

There are two very powerful thrusts in the DP world today both of which tend to utilize different types of parallelism.

Firstly, there is the high-end OLTP market being pursued primarily (in the 'open' market) by Oracle with its Parallel Server, and Sybase. Both of these vendors are bringing versions of their RDBMS to market, geared at exploiting specific implementations of parallel architectures aimed at giving transaction per second rates of between 500 and over 1000. At these rates, such systems will run only fairly simple transactions, and will depend on OLTP oriented software facilities some of which may include deferred updates, piggy-backed writes, optimistic locking and sophisticated cache and lock sharing facilities. These will be provided by the RDBMS and platform vendors, and to some extent by independent offerings such as the Tuxedo and Topend UNIX based, transaction monitors.

To succeed in this market, specialized hardware will be needed to enable fast movement of control messages, lock and cache information between processors. The key here will be to allow the utilization of more hardware by enabling users on individual processors to share single images of the database. Such an architecture will mean that to improve the performance of an overburdened single processor, we can simply move some of the 'frontend' processes (equivalent to users) to another processor which can still access the same database – the result, quicker response time (as system resources are freed) and more users.

A generic architecture for such a solution is shown in Figure 5.2. This shows six processors each communicating via a fast bus (the Interprocessor Connect). The two APs in the picture run the user frontend processes and therefore interact directly with the user community. The other four Database Processors as I have called them, run the backend, database services. In this architecture, all data is shared and available to all DPs, which of course necessitates some intelligent, inter-AP locking mechanisms. Because the number of APs and DPs is variable, such a system can support a varying number of users. The thick line shows the path of a query. It is generated by a specific user on a specific AP and is serviced by a database server process which could be running on any of the DPs because each has equal access to the whole database.

In this architecture, the machine illustrated can therefore service four database requests at the same time and the total throughput of the system can be increased by adding more APs and DPs.

The second trend mentioned is a major thrust into the ever expanding world of Decision Support. This area is moving rapidly in three major dimensions:

- Data Volumes
- Number of users
- Complexity of data and query.

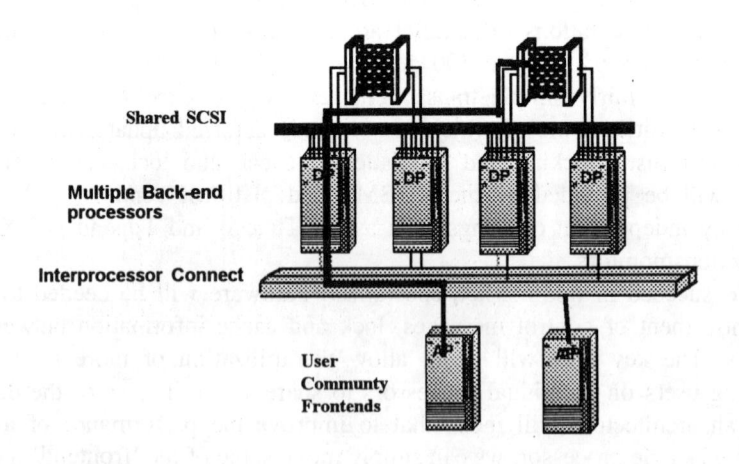

FIGURE 5.2. Support for many separate processes (users).

Parallel Processing in the Commercial Environment 71

This really is the area where RDBMSs come into their own, and the reason that they achieved rapid success over the CODASYL and hierarchical systems. The fundamental nature of decision support is that it tends to be *ad hoc* in nature and has a common requirement of reading and joining many relational tables together prior to aggregation and sorting. Such tasks tend to be very expensive in terms of CPU and I/O and as they increase in their resource requirements, they can only maintain acceptable response times if multiple processors can be utilized to support the same instance of a query.

The solution shown in Figure 5.3 is very different from that is Figure 5.2. Here data is not shared between DPs – each supports its own partition of the total database. If we imagine a Customer table with four million rows, each DP will manage and store one million. Now a complex DSS query originating in an AP is broken down into smaller steps which are each dispatched to the server DPs simultaneously for execution. Let's imagine we simply wanted to count all the rows in the Customer table. The SQL required is:

SELECT COUNT(*) FROM CUST-TAB;

This query will originate in an AP and be dispatched to each server DP who now only has to count one million rows instead of the full four million. The four results generated by each AP are simply added up and presented back to the originating programme. You can see here that performance of a single query is determined by the amount of hardware in a linear fashion.

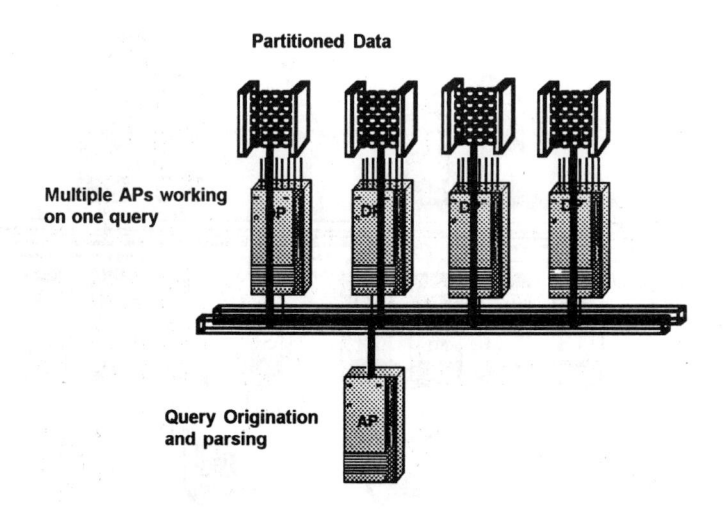

FIGURE 5.3. Many processors applied to the same, single query.

72 Parallel Information Processing

Relational processes are a combination of operations on single tables and operations combining tables (Join, Union, Intersect, Minus). Because there is no absolute need to provide pre-defined access paths into the data, and because to join two data rows demand that they be in the same shared memory, it is likely that any network of processors in a parallel machine, must be capable of supporting movement of relational rows between all processors in the system.

We see, therefore, two very different requirements, and if we look at some of the more advanced computers and software systems available today, we can see that we can easily divide them by their ability to support either large scale decision support systems (DSS) or high volume OLTP. Of course the majority, fall somewhere in between and do neither very well.

4.2 The AT&T 3600

In order to progress further it is necessary to examine the architecture of a specific machine so that we might understand a technology that can enable both types of parallelism in the commercial world of the Relational Database.

The machine depicted in Figure 5.4 is the AT&T3600 parallel processor and I use it because it illustrates some of the features already mentioned very well. Firstly, the machine is a grouping of different types of processor, the number of each being variable and depending only on required system performance. The APs are SMP Unix systems with all the facilities one expects in large scale Unix computers. These systems can run merchant databases such

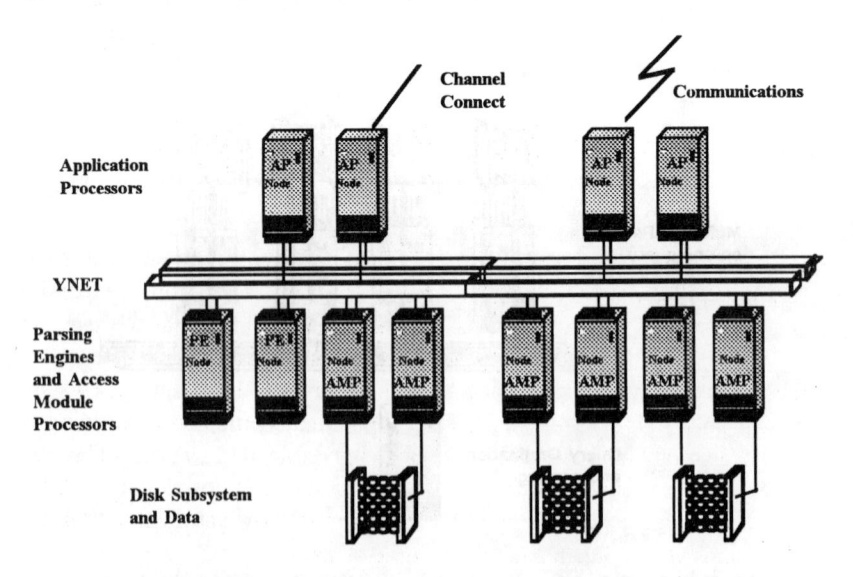

FIGURE 5.4.   The AT&T3600 architecture.

as Oracle and when doing so, presenting architectural possibilities as seen in Figure 5.2. The APs can also host applications that can talk to the processors that are called AMPs. The AMPs are simple processing units that manage relational data held in their own dedicated disk stores (managed by RAID controllers). Each AMP as men- tioned, manages its own discreet partition of data and this subsystem, comprising of many AMPs and an AP running the frontend, works functionally as described in Figure 5.3.

A couple of points worth noting is that for the AMP subsystem, queries are parsed and optimized by a set of dedicated processors – the PEs and the Interconnect is a dual pathed 12 MB bus.

We should be clear now that two of the prime objectives of a parallel system are to be able to deliver the complete power of the system, a combination of multiple processors, to a single 'query', and further, to be able to give access to the same data structures, to many, maybe thousands, of users. For this to be possible using a relational operation, the tables participating in the query must be available to all the processors in the system. On the 3600 each table is hash-distributed to all AMPs, so that each AMP receives an even portion of the rows. This enables a query that requires all rows of a table to be accessed, such as a full table scan, to be processed in parallel by all the AMPs. As shown below, the power of the overall system is thus directly proportional to the number of AMPs in that system.

The simplest way to explain the operation of the AT&T3600 is to follow the route of a query (transaction) from the user running an application on an AP. Let's imagine the query is to retrieve some selected rows from our CUSTOMER table and sort them by CUSTOMER_NO. The SQL might be represented as such:

SELECT * FROM CUSTOMER WHERE CUSTOMER_NAME= 'SMITH' ORDER BY CUSTOMER_NO;

After the query has been generated in the AP environment it is passed to the PE which handles the initial stage of the SQL operation, by parsing the SQL statement to validate that it is a legal statement, and that the user has the access rights to perform the requested action. Assuming a valid statement, the PE then chooses the optimum access path to process the request. This is done using cost based algorithms and a very sophisticated method of holding demographic, statistical data describing underlying table data values. The PE thus breaks down the textual SQL statement into a series of low level 'AMP Steps' that are dispatched to all of the AMPs simultaneously across the YNET.

The steps in this case can be thought of as:

(1) Per AMP: Read all rows from your subset of data where CUSTOMER_NAME = 'SMITH'
(2) Per AMP: Sort them locally
(3) System: Return the rows in CUSTOMER_NO order.

The PE does not, itself, hold any of the relational data, and at this stage must hand the steps of the request to the AMPs for the actual database operations.

The architectural feature which enables the 3600 to combine the power of multiple processors in answering a single SQL query, is the method of distributing data across all the processors. In fact, the data for each relational table in the system is spread equally across all AMP processors and disks, through the use of a special algorithm, and the definition of a 'primary index' for each table. For example, if we decided that the primary index of our CUSTOMER table was to be the unique CUSTOMER_NO attribute, then the hash value of each rows CUSTOMER_NO would be used to indicated the AMP on which this row will be stored or thereafter located. With reasonable choice of primary index, on a ten processor system, each AMP will hold 10% of each and every table.

If we return to our original query, the PE hands each stage (step) of the request to all the AMPs, which can then work independently on their own portions of the data. To summarize the execution of the query, step one will be dispatched to all AMPs and they will each select their qualifying rows into a temporary table. When all AMPs have completed the task, the PE will send the second step, and each AMP will sort its temporary table into the specified sort order. Again when each AMP has completed its local sort, step 3 will be dispatched, and each AMP will pass rows back to the host. It's at this stage that the YNET hardware merges the rows being presented to it by all the AMPs, into the final sort order. This operation is executed at great speed.

In this query, which only used data from a single table, no movement of data is required. However, for complex relational join operations, data movement is often needed and this operation too, is carried out automatically through the Y-Net. Such movement is necessary because in a non-memory sharing system, prior to joining two rows, they must be directly addressable by the same processor, in this case, an AMP.

Let's consider three cases where we join our CUSTOMER table to a SALE table with the following SQL:

SELECT * FROM CUSTOMER,SALE
WHERE CUSTOMER.CUST_NO = SALE.CUST_NO;

The way this query is processed by the 3600, will depend primarily on Primary Index definitions for the CUSTOMER and SALE tables. Figure 5.5 illustrates three different scenarios for the placement of the primary index on each of the two tables.

Case 1: In this example, both table are being joined across their primary indexes. Because the hashing algorithm always produces the same result from the same input, in this case, any row in the CUSTOMER table with a CUSTOMER_NO of 1099 will be 'hashed' to the same AMP as any row in the SALE table who's CUSTOMER_NO is also 1099. Therefore, to join these two rows is a simple task because the rows that must be joined are guaranteed to be already located on the same AMP. AMP local joins are very fast and need no data movement for join preparation.

Case 2: Here matching rows will not necessarily be stored on the same AMP, because the rows in the SALES table that need to be joined to rows in the CUSTOMER table are distributed by the hash value of PRODUCT_NO. To get matching rows on the same AMP, we have two options. Firstly, we can duplicate either of the two tables on every AMP prior to the join, or secondly, we can redistribute the table whose join column is not the Primary Index, on the data values of its join columns. It should be noted that whenever we 'prepare' a table for subsequent joining by way of copying, duplicating or redistributing, we are only taking copies of the base data and it is the optimizer's task to select the smallest amount of data to copied.

UPI = Unique Primary Index
NUPI = Non-Unique Primary Index

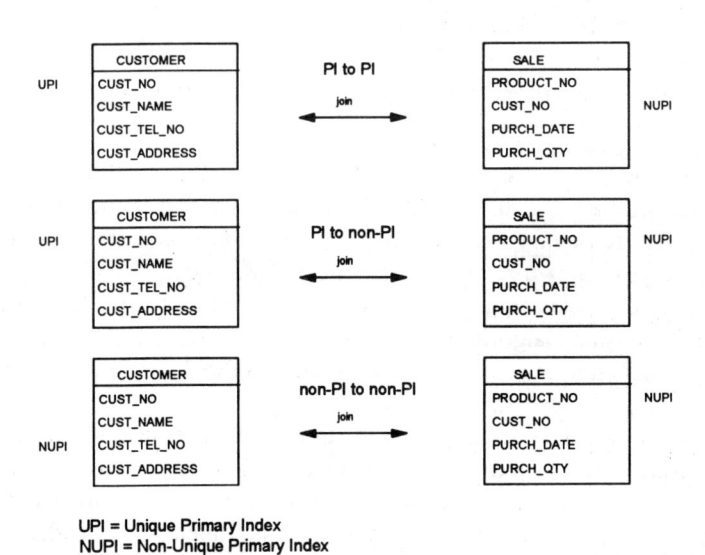

FIGURE 5.5. Three different physical designs.

Case 3: Here is an example where neither join column in the query is the Primary Index of either of the base tables. To resolve this situation, the duplication plan mentioned for Case 2 is still applicable. However as an alternative to Case 2, we can take a copy of the SALES table and hash redistribute it based on the CUSTOMER_NO in each row and at the same time (in parallel) redistribute the CUSTOMER table also on CUSTOMER_NO. This will again bring matching rows to the same AMP.

These distribution scenarios are by no means the only ones available to the 3600. In fact many options are usually available, the cheapest one being selected by a very sophisticated optimizer. We shall return to examine costing later.

The case described above, where the parallel processing capability is brought to bear on a large MIS query, can be distinguished from the case of simple transactions such as those found in high volume On-Line Transaction Processing Systems. Here, access is typically required to single rows (records), accessed by keys (indexes). In this case the requirement is to handle many simple transactions simultaneously, rather than large complex transactions.

5 OLTP PROCESSING

The 3600 architecture is designed to handle multiple simple transactions through the same distribution technique and multiprocessing system as used for the complex transactions. Consider a transaction arising in an on-line AP application, where the original application may well be a C program with embedded SQL. The SQL for such a query might be:

SELECT * FROM CUSTOMER WHERE CUSTOMER_NO = 1009;

As before, the transaction is passed, untranslated, to the PE. During the analysis of the request, the PE will have determined that the request is for a primary index retrieval (if in fact CUSTOMER_NO was defined as the primary index), and generates the appropriate single AMP step.

This step, as before, is sent to the Y-Net, but this time finds its way by utilizing the hashing algorithm, only to the AMP that contains the target row. All other AMPs are unaffected by the transaction and are free to take on other work.

The target AMP is usually able to retrieve the row in a single disk access, or even directly from its data cache memory or RAM. The result row, or rows, are formatted and sent back to the PE and then on to the calling application.

Since each processor in the system is a complete, independent computer system, each is capable of full multiprogramming of tasks and thus able to handle many transactions simultaneously. In this way, the 3600 can be configured to give any required level of transactions per second.

5.1 Data statistics

When a user submits a non-trivial request to the PE and the Optimizer is required to develop an access plan, it does so by rapidly analysing the data demographics of the target tables and determining the most efficient access method. The Optimizer has two ways in which it can analyse the target data demographics. It can utilize pre-generated statistics which have been collected for particular columns or indices. Alternatively, if statistics have not been collected when the Optimizer needs to analyse a column or index distribution, a random AMP is sampled to determine approximate data demographics.

The collection of statistics (via a utility) is generally considered good practice, since it provides the Optimizer with fairly detailed information regarding data demographics and can increase the speed of access plan choice. What happens is that the Optimizer scans the data to be analysed and sorts it into 20 partitions. For each partition it records:

- the number of rows
- the number of unique values
- the most common value
- the maximum value
- the minimum value
- the number of rows with the most common value.

These statistics are used to help the Optimizer guess the cardinality of all result and intermediary tables to be used when answering the query so it might chose the cheapest.

Statistics do, however, have several drawbacks. If statistics become out-of-date due to changing demographics then the Optimizer will generate access plans which may be inefficient. Secondly, the collection of statistics is often time consuming, especially if the target column or index has many distinct values, and the entire table is exclusivly locked during the COLLECT request. Finally, though the Optimizer generally works best when statistics have been collected, it can sometimes generate plans which are less efficient than would have been generated if the statistics had not been present. The Optimizer is, after all, just a program, albeit a very advanced one.

Because choosing the correct execution plan is so vital in these large systems, the system software includes an Explain facility which tries its best to tell the user exactly what low level steps will be generated in the execution of a specific query. Figure 5.6 shows the output of Explain for a simple join.

explain select * from data1,data2 where data1.col1 = data2.col2;

(1) First, we lock JM16.data2 for read, and we lock JM16.data1 for read.
(2) Next, we do an all-AMPs RETRIEVE step from JM16.data2 by way of an all-rows scan with no residual conditions into Spool 2, which is redistributed by hash code to all AMPs. Then we do a SORT to order Spool 2 by row hash. The size of Spool 2 is estimated to be 4 rows. The estimated time for this step is 0.07 seconds.
(3) We do an all-AMPs JOIN step from JM16.data1 by way of a RowHash match scan with no residual conditions, which is joined to Spool 2 (Last Use). JM16.data1 and Spool 2 are joined using a merge join, with a join condition of ('JM16.data1.col1 = Spool_2.col2'). The result goes into Spool 1, which is built locally on the AMPs. The size of Spool 1 is estimated to be 4 rows. The estimated time for this step is 0.13 seconds.
(4) Finally, we send out an END TRANSACTION step to all AMPs involved in processing the request.

We can see therefore that optimizing queries that are complex in nature and utilize multiple processors and data stores is a complex task. In effect, we get performance by splitting up the request and running it on separate pieces of hardware. However, at some stage we need to put the result sets from the many APs back together prior to presentation to the user. Whenever more than one row is returned back to an application/user, a sort is normally required – a job that can be very expensive if data volumes are large. We have already seen that when each AP was simply counting rows, their final answers need to be amalgamated a task done in the 3600 by the YNET hardware which we can

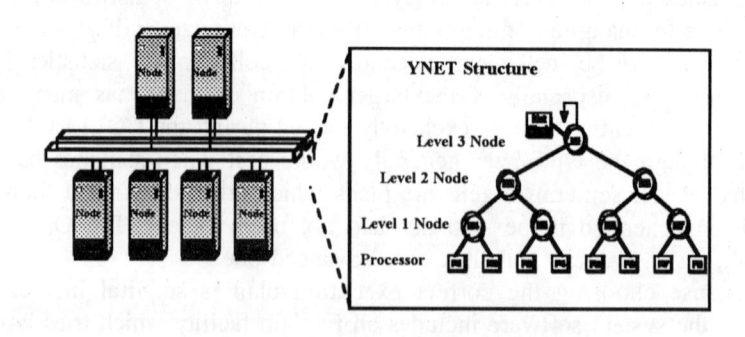

FIGURE 5.6. Interconnect components and architecture.

see below. However, because the YNET is attached to every processor and is hierarchical in nature, it is also ideal for the final sort of resultant data sets. In fact at every node in the tree there is a comparator which can compare character strings allowing only the lower or higher (as specified by the query) to pass. The YNET therefore sorts data rows as they pass through its nodes in a simple tournament sort, and because this is done in hardware, this final sort is done very quickly indeed.

6 CONCLUSION

This chapter has sought to introduce two fundamentally different modes of Parallel Processing in the commercial world of Relational Databases. OLTP requirements are very different form those of DSS, and it is rare that a single machine can cope with both. The AT&T3600 is such a machine and I have illustrated current requirements by explaining the architecture of this machine. Currently, there is still a requirement to run massive DSS separately from massive OLTP, albeit on a single machine. In such a world, query optimization is key and must be performed by a combination of software and hardware.

REFERENCES

Advanced Information Systems 91, 19-21 March 91, Learned Information.

Inmon, W. *Third Wave Processing Database Machines for Decision Support Systems*, QED Information Sciences.

NCR Education Services, *Introduction to the 3600*, CW-0118-9000-1620.

Page, J. (1990) *Relational Databases – Concepts, Selection and Implementation*, Sigma Press.

Reddaway, S. Text Retrieval on the AMT DAP, *Second International Specialist Seminar on The Design and Application of Parallel Digital Processors*, 18-19 April, IEEE Book of Abstracts.

Teradata Systems Manual: Rel 4.1.1/4.1.2: C10-0001-10.

Teradata Reference Manual: Rel 4.1.1/4.1.2: C03-0001-10.

PART 2
Architectures

6 The EDS Commercial Parallel Processing System

[1]L. Borrmann, [1]F. Hutner, [2]S. R. Leunig, [3]M. Lopez, [4]M. J. Reeve, [2]C. J. Skelton, [4]K. F. Wong

[1]Siemens AG, Otto-Hahn-Ring 6, 81730 Munich, Germany
[2]ICL, West Gorton, Manchester M12 5DR, UK
[3]Bull S.A., ZI de Mayencin - 2 rue Vignate, 38610 Geires, France
[4]ECRC, Arabellastr. 17, W8000 Munich 81, Germany

1 INTRODUCTION

Information management systems are encountering performance bottlenecks as applications encompass more users and more of the critical operations. As a consequence, there are growing demands for both performance and system capability in information processing systems. Attempts have been made to increase performance by simply using faster processors. This, however, cannot scale up with the increasing size and complexity of the applications. The prime objective of the EDS (European Declarative System) project is to develop a high performance parallel processing system targerted specifically at commercial information processing based on the results of the EDS project.

EDS is a 57 MECU project supported by the European Commission, DG XIII, under the ESPRIT-II (European Strategic Programme for Research and Development in Information Technology) initiative, and involves collaboration between Bull (France), ECRC (pan-European), ICL (UK), Siemens (Germany) and a number of European industrial and research organizations. EDS will provide a fully integrated parallel platform to meet the increasing performance and programming demands in information technology.

To meet increasing performance demands. Business information processing is one of the target application areas of EDS. Many business applications employ On-Line Transaction Processing (OLTP) technology and demand very high transaction rates to cope with the large number of customers. It is forecast that the transaction rate of a typical OLTP system to grow by a factor of 10 over the next five years. However, based on the current trends, this growth rate will not be matched by the performance growth rate of today's mainframe computers.

In addition, the profile of the transaction load is changing as management support queries and queries over knowledge bases (including rules) are added to the existing, largely clerical workloads. Although very complex queries, e.g.

in knowledge management, will contribute little to throughput demands, medium complex queries, e.g. in on-line decision support systems, will certainly demand significant throughput.

The advanced EDS database server is designed to support a continuum of database applications ranging from OLTP-like (simple) queries to queries of low to medium complexity. It will deliver up to 10 times of the performance of conventional mainframes expected in the mid-90s. In particular, for OLTP applications over 12,000 tps (transaction per second) is predicted (Wong *et al.*, 1992). To achieve this target, parallel technology is extensively used in all levels of the EDS database server. These include the employment of: a distributed memory MIMD architecture for hardware level parallelism, a parallel operating system and a parallel database executive to exploit both inter- and intra-query parallelisms.

To meet greater programming demands. SQL (Structured Query Language) is widely used for database applications and can be found in almost all existing commercial products. Notwithstanding its many desirable high-level program constructs, SQL lacks some advanced functions (e.g. objects with complex structures, multi-statement queries, abstract data types, deductive capability, ... etc.); as a result, the scope of application of conventional relational databases is restricted.

The EDS database system (EDBS), the 'golden-core' of the EDS server, is designed to provide advanced functionalities by incorporating extensions to SQL. The query language under development, ESQL (Extended SQL), is a strict superset of the SQL standard. It is, therefore, upward-compatible for existing database applications. Furthermore, the SQL extensions will make the EDS server also suitable for tomorrow's advanced applications.

To further widen the application spectrum of EDS, two parallel AI programming languages, namely ElipSys (a parallel logic programming language) and parallel EDS Lisp, are supported by the EDS server. Complimentary to ESQL, these languages are designed to solve very complex queries typically found in knowledge based applications.

Section Summary. This chapter presents an overview of the parallel architecture of the EDS advanced database server. The rest of the chapter is organized as follows. In the next three sections, the parallel architectures of of the EDS hardware, operating system and database system are described, respectively. This is followed by a description of the advanced capabilities provided by the database query language ESQL in Section 5. In Section 6, the simulated OLTP performance of the EDS database server is reported. Finally, in Section 7, the conclusion of the chapter is given.

2 THE EDS MACHINE

A major goal of the EDS machine is to provide a high-performance, parallel hardware platform for advanced database applications. A number of design issues were considered in reaching this goal:

- **Scalability.** The EDS machine had to be scalable from a few to several hundreds of processors. Therefore a common bus or a physically shared memory was not viable. For this reason, EDS adopts a distributed memory, MIMD parallel computer architecture.
- **Design effort and price/performance ratio.** Standardized interfaces and off-the-shelf components were used wherever possible during the development. As a result, the EDS machine can be upgraded easily to account for future technology advancements, e.g. the existing main SPARC processor on the Processing Element (PE) module can be replaced by a next generation SPARC processor that can offer higher performance. However, no well suited standard components were available for the interprocessor communication network; so the network switching element and the Network Interface Unit (NIU) to the Processing Element were specially built as semi-custom chips (see next section for the descriptions of the PE and the NIU).

The EDS database server functions as an accelerator for a host computer. The basic building blocks of the EDS machine (Ward *et al.*, 1990) are Processing Elements (PE) where application programs and system software run. By adding PEs a range of machine sizes of increasing performance can be produced. Also, specialized functional elements can be added to the system to perform specific functions, e.g. a Diagnostic Element (DE) that carries out diagnostics, low level debugging and monitoring, a Host Element (HE) that provides the interface to the user and optionally an I/O Element (IOE) that provides local disk access. All elements communicate via the high-bandwidth multistage interconnection network that can accommodate up to 256 of them (PEs and specialized functional elements) in total.

In the following subsections, the functions of the PE, the specialized functional elements and the communication network are described.

2.1 Processing Element (PE)

The PE contains four basic components. The Processing Unit (PU) is the main processor where primarily application programs and the operating system kernel run. It is connected to the Store Unit (SU) via a local bus. The System Support Unit (SSU) is an additional processor that mainly controls communication.

However, these processors can also operate in a symmetrical multiprocessing mode on each single PE, where only the communication control tasks need to be fixed to the SSU and facilitates all other processes can be freely scheduled to any one of the two processors.

The PU and the SSU are both standard RISC processors from the SPARC family delivering about 26 MIPS each. The SSU is tightly coupled to the NIU to allow for very fast control transfer. This also frees the local memory bus from the DMA control traffic. The PU is a complete, commercially available processor module that integrates together an instruction unit, a floating point unit, a cache controller, a memory management unit, and also some cache RAMs. This allows to exchange the PU with newer, faster SPARC processors without any hardware changes. Such compatible, faster processors are currently appearing in the market.

The Store Unit (SU) is a a two-way interleaved dynamic memory with a size of 64 MBytes (extendible up to 4 Gbytes). It has ECC (error checking and correction) logic that can tolerate and correct single bit fails and recognize multi bit fails. The EDS virtual memory scheme is also supported by the SU. There is a tag bit associated with every 128-byte portion of the memory holding information whether this 'sector' is locally valid or not. Thus it is possible to copy only a 128 byte-sector – instead of a whole memory page of 4 kbytes – from a remote node in case of a non-local memory access.

The Network Interface Unit (NIU) provides the interface between the local memory bus and the network. It serves as a DMA (direct memory access) unit under SSU software control. Provided with the necessary parameters (physical address, number of bytes) it arbitrates on the memory bus and transports data from the network to the SU and vice versa performing the necessary data format conversions.

2.2 Specialized functional elements

Besides the PEs, the EDS machine can have varying numbers of specialized functional elements. They form the links to the 'outside' world:

- The Host Element (HE) connects the EDS system to the host computers. A wide range of host machines from ICL, Bull and Siemens will be supported; and HEs are host dependent; the architecture of a HE, therefore, varies between different types of host computers.
- A Diagnostic Element (DE) which provides a routes for initial software loading, alternative access paths to other elements under fault conditions and an engineering tool for fault analysis.
- An Input/Output Element (IOE) which provides additional mass storage devices. This is an optional element. Normally information storage is

provided directly by the SU on the PEs. It should be noted that in the Goldrush product, derived from EDS, attaches disk storage to each PE/CE.

2.3 Communication network

The EDS communication network (Holzner *et al.*, 1990) provides the functionality imposed by the database execution models and achieves high global throughput and low latency to avoid performance degradation due to communication overhead. It is suitable for a wide range of load profiles and distributions which are expected from various workloads. Its topology is a multi-stage interconnection network. The network offers up to 256 full duplex channels with a bandwidth of 20 MBytes/sec in each direction. It is built of VLSI semicustom chips each forming an 8×8 crossbar switch with 32 independent packet buffers. By detailed simulation it was shown that for a full-size network a throughput of more than 3 GBytes/sec can be maintained without saturation.

The EDS network is a packet switched network with variable packet size. A packet consists of 16 header bytes, up to 128 bytes of data, and two more bytes for error detection. The switch operates on the 'virtual cut through' scheme, which adds the advantages of circuit switching to the packet switching mode, i.e. the network has a very low latency as long as the total communication load is low.

At the application layer, the EDS network facilitates inter-PE communication. There are two means in which two PEs can communication: message passing, by explicit transfer of user-specified data from a source PE to a destination PE; and virtual store copying, by accessing virtual shared data which is physically stored on another PE. Message passing is made available to users by a set of operating system primitives. The store copying mechanism is transparent to users and is designed for supporting the virtual shared memory mechanism in the EDS operation system.

3 EMEX – THE EDS OPERATING SYSTEM

The EDS Operating System, EMEX, is the common platform for the EDS parallel database, as well as for two other parallel programming language subsystems supported by the EDS server, namely, ElipSys and EDS Lisp[1]. As such, it is a crucial element of the overall EDS system architecture.

Being an operating system for a parallel machine, EMEX offers novel features to support parallel programming, such as built-in support for virtually shared memory. Additionally, EMEX provides a full Unix SVR4 interface on each node. This was achieved by enriching Chorus/MiX (Chorus Systemes,

1991), a microkernel based implementation of SVR4, by another subsystem for parallel programming support.

The parallel programming interface of EMEX is called *PCL* (Process Control Language). PCL was designed within the EDS project after the requirements imposed by its main 'customers', i.e. the EDS database and programming language sub-systems. Nevertheless PCL is by no means limited to support them only. This was shown in a study which implemented a parallel C++ programming interface (PARC++, an extension of PRESTO) on top of PCL and EMEX.

In the following sections the concept behind PCL and its Chorus based implementation are described. They are followed by the description of the additional operating system facilities supported by EMEX; these facilities include host and file I/O, naming service and dynamic linking and loading.

3.1 Basic concepts of PCL

Besides some minor additional functions, PCL covers three important areas:

- the Process Model
- the Store Model
- the Communication Model.

The Communication Model provides primitives for explicit, synchronous and asynchronous, message passing. These primitives are customized to run on the EDS parallel hardware. The Process and Store Models (Istavrinos *et al.*, 1990) are widely hardware independent and provide abstractions and primitives for process control and memory management. These two are closely related but can be used independently of the Communication Model.

3.2 PCL sub-system implementation

EMEX is based on Chorus. To support the aforesaid PCL operation models, a number of components is added to the standard Chorus system:

- Message Passing Component
- Process Manager
- Memory Manager
- Multiple Mappers
- System Manager.

---

[1]Due to the theme of this chapter, descriptions of ElipSys and EDS Lisp are not given here. Interested readers can refer to Delgado-Rannauro *et al.* (1991) and Hammer *et al.* (1991) for more information about the two systems, respectively.

These components can be added to Chorus in various ways. As mentioned previously, an EMEX mapper is an abstraction of Chorus. Besides a default mapper which is responsible for disk paging, an arbitrary number of mappers can be present in the system. Each memory segment is assigned to a dedicated mapper via a capability which includes the server port address of the mapper. When page faults occur, the kernel will send messages (remote procedure calls) to the responsible mapper using a published and well-defined interface. This interface includes functions like *pullIn()* (get a page of data), *pushOut()* (swap a page of data out), or *getAccess()* (get further access writes, e.g. write access).

The Memory Manager and the Process Manager[2] are supervisor actors which are connected to the system call interface (trap interface) of Chorus. This means that certain system calls generates by a user process will not be handled by the kernel itself, but by the respective manager process. Other than with the mapper interface, no message passing is involved here, but the handler is entered via a direct subroutine call.

The complete set of additional components can be regarded as the PCL sub-system. Effectively, it extends the functions of Chorus by those defined in PCL, similarly to the Unix sub-system of Chorus. The implementation of PCL is thus a good example of how a microkernel can be put into use.

3.3 Additional operating system facilities

In the EDS server, the presence of a Unix sub-system on each PE is optional. The decision to incorporate a Unix sub-system in EDS was influenced by the large number of existing Unix-based applications. The EMEX Unix sub-system will make the EDS server readily usable by such applications.

The support of parallel programs via PCL is independent of Unix. It was thus necessary to provide for certain facilities which are conventionally available in Unix systems without being part of the EMEX kernel. These additional facilities are:

- **Host and file I/O**. The EMEX File Server supports a minimal set of facilities to enable applications running on the EDS machine to interchange data with a remote machine and to create, read, write, and destroy files on a remote Unix file system. This function is built upon the message passing as described above. In general, all I/O except trace messages will be implemented by RPC (Remote Procedure Call).
- **System Manager**. The System Manager provides users with an interface to load EMEX applications and access system information. It uses the File Server for host communication, and the EMEX Loader to load applications. The System Manager also provides for *name binding* in

---

[2]Currently, the process manager is part of the kernel, but this is to be changed to enhance portability.

88 Parallel Information Processing

the distributed environment thus enabling other programs to know about the port Ids of available servers.
- **EMEX Loader and Linker.** This component supports dynamic loading of executable files, as well as dynamic linking to load and exchange code objects at runtime. Load objects are in Unix-compatible format. The mechanisms used are similar to the mechanisms used in SunOS, but with a more powerful programming interface.

4   EDBS – THE PARALLEL EDS DATABASE SYSTEM

The aims of the EDS Database System, EDBS, are firstly to provide an order of magnitude improvement in performance compared to mainframes for commercial OLTP workloads, and secondly to provide advanced functionality (object-oriented and deductive features) to extend database support to a wider range of applications. Moreover, provision of a flexible and extensible database system which can be easily enhanced to provide more advanced facilities over time, is an important design target. In order to achieve these objectives a number of design strategies are being used:

- Exploitation of the parallelism available in the base EDS system. In particular, EMEX has been specially designed to support a high performance parallel database system.
- A large stable RAM is assumed. This will to hold the persistent data, including across system breaks. The prototype EDS hardware will not provide a stable RAM, but the design of the database system assumes its existence.
- The database system will be based on standard relational database technology extended to provide object oriented database and deductive database facilities.
- The programming interface will be via an extended version of the language SQL(ESQL) (Gardarin *et al.*, 1990). In particular the language will provide a rich and extendible type system based on abstract data types (ADTs) where the methods can be defined in various programming languages, complex objects with object sharing by combining the ADTs with object identity, and the equivalent of a DATALOG deductive capability (see Section 5).
- A RISC-like approach is taken in compiling ESQL queries to native machine code.
- The query compiler optimizer been designed to be extensible to allow the system to evolve.

EDBS is split into three main components: the Request Manager (RM) which compiles database commands into native machine code, the Data Manager (DM) which provides the run-time facilities required to execute those commands, and the Object Manager provides the shared object store. In addition to them, interface to the hosts are provided by the Session Manager (SM). The SM provides the mechanism by which an application starts a database session. It creates an instance of each of the the RM and the DM for each database session. The SM-Host communication makes extensive use of standard RPC techniques[3].

In this section the operation principles and the architectures of EDBS are described. The section is structured as follows: first, the operation principles behind EDBS (i.e. the EDBS Execution Model) is described in the next subsection. This is followed by three subsections giving descriptions of the individual EDBS components (i.e. the RM, DM and Object Manager); and at the end of the section some issues relating to integrating between the EDBS and the EDS platform are outlined.

4.1 EDBS parallel execution model

Database relations are declustered (also referred to as horizontal fragmentation) using criteria applied to one or more of their attributes, for example by partioning the relation on ranges of an attribute or by using a hash function. When a relation is declustered, it is partitioned into a number of fragments, each stored on different PE. The set of PEs holding fragments of a relation is the home of that relation. In practice, the number of home PEs for a relation is a function of the relation size and access frequency (Copeland *et al.*, 1 988).

Declustering is the basis for two forms of parallel database execution. By splitting an operation into instances and having each operation instance executing on a home PE, intra-operation parallelism is achieved. Another form of parallelism is achieved by permitting independent operations within a query to be executed simultaneously, where their arguments are declustered onto different homes[4].

In essence, data declustering facilitates the important parallelisation concept of 'performing database operations locally at where the data are'. Operations are sent to the homes of their operands; thus the communication costs can be significantly reduced. Due to the dynamic nature of the data set, it is sometimes necessary to re-decluster a relation in order to increase parallelism. This is more likely (and much simpler) to apply to intermediate relations rather than to permanent base relations.

A third form of parallelism is pipeline (sometimes referred to as streamlining), which exploits temporal parallelism during data transfer between two

---

[3]Work on the Session Manager is trivial; thus, it is not discussed in the chapter.

[4]From a different point of view, an operation which exploits intra-operation parallelism is equivalent to SIMD execution; and a set of operations are performed in MIMD fashion under inter-operation parallelism.

database operations. When a database operation produce some data and these data are consumed by another database operator rather than are materialized, a pipeline (or a stream) can be connected between them for them for data transfer. (The former is the producer and the latter the consumer.) In this case, the consumer operates on data already supplied by the producer in parallel with the producer generating further data.

One of the advances in EDBS has been the development of a cost model (Anfres et al., 1991) which is used to determine the degree of parallelism available in a database and the profile of queries; with this knowledge, the optimal declustering of (i.e. the number of PEs for) a relation can, in turn, be determined. Unfortunately when a permanent relation is created, there is only very little information available and it is insufficient to derive the cost model. As a temporary measure the **CREATE TABLE** command has been extended to allow the user to indicate the degree of fragmentation of the relation, and even the physical PEs to be used for the relation. In the longer term it is envisioned that the database would be periodically re-organized using metrics from the relations and the access patterns in the cost model.

EDBS also supports indexes associated with relations to improve the efficiency of access. These indexes are purely local to the individual relation fragments.

The logical distribution of the temporary data (that is the number of fragments and there association with other relations) is determined at compile time, whilst the run-time system determines the mapping of the fragments to the physical PEs. This gives rise to a better opportunity for load balancing than can be obtained with the permanent relations whose placement is relatively static.

Another attribute of the EDBS execution model is the separation of the control flow from the dataflow operations. This allows the global synchronization necessary for the semantics of a query program to be separated from the purely local low level synchronization that occurs at the level of the local operations. The execution model has also been designed to support the RISC-like approach for query compilation. In this approach the basic database operations of the system are chosen to be a small set of simple operations. The separation of control flow combined with the use of simple operations simplifies the realization of a number of compiler optimization techniques, for example in the area of local data access communication and synchronization overheads can be greatly reduced.

At the implementation level, the distributed store based EDBS execution model maps nicely to the distributed memory EDS machine. Nevertheless, the EDBS execution model is purely a logical one and other alternative implementations are possible. An example of an alternative implementation is the DBS3 parallel database system developed on a Encore MULTIMAX shared store multi-processor (Bergsten et al., 1991).

4.2 RM – The EDBS Query Compiler

The programming interface to EDBS is extended SQL (ESQL), see Section 5. The role of the Request Manager (RM) is ESQL query compilation. Internally, in the RM an ESQL query is processed in various stages. The resulting execution program is based on an intermediate algebraic language, LERA (Language for Extended Relational Algebra) (Chachaty et al., 1992). The LERA program is then executed directly by the Data Manager (DM).

The RM follows a compilation approach with sophisticated query optimization and parallelization processes which work on a representation of the query in terms of LERA. Compared to a relational query optimizer, the EDBS optimizer is complicated by three factors:

- LERA has higher expressive power than relational algebra (ADT functions and predicates, nested operations, fixpoint operations).
- The parallel execution system of the Data Manager (see Section 4) offers a wide range of execution strategies which are difficult to abstract.
- The required ability of efficiently optimizing both repetitive (OLTP) and *ad hoc* (decision support) queries implies that the optimization time, and therefore the optimization algorithm, must itself be controllable.

To cope with the above difficulties, the optimization process is divided into three activities. The query rewriting (logical optimization) activity (Finance et al., 1991) consists of a simplification and partial ordering of LERA operations in order to make the optimization problem tractable. In particular, complex recursive queries are transformed using the Alexander method and a simpler method, based on transitive closure, is used to handle linear recursion. An operation selection activity identifies those operations in the LERA program warranting optimization. For each of them, an operation optimization activity is triggered. The operation optimizer makes use of extended relational query optimization techniques such as join ordring and fixpoint optimization. Furthermore, the design of the optimizer is extendible so that new optimization algorithms and access methods can be easily accommodated. This extendible feature enables the optimizer to cater for a wide range of possible execution strategies. Finally, in order to achieve the performance objectives mentioned above, the cost function used is a combination of response time and total time thus enabling a controllable trade-off between transaction's response time and global throughput. Similarly, the operation optimization algorithms are also controllable so that, when optimization time matters, a trade-off between optimization time and execution time can be achieved.

The execution semantics of an optimized LERA program is a centralized one but the program contains annotations, produced by the optimizer, about distribution decisions indicating where the operations should be executed and about the parallel algorithms that should be used to execute the operations. The paralleliser uses these annotations when translating the LERA program from a centralized semantics to a parallel semantics. To cope with its complexity, the parallelisation process is performed in two phases:

- The Abstract Parallelisation phase generates the programs for the global algorithms associated with the relational operations, produces the communication schemes to facilitate the required data transfer between these operations, and determines a parallel execution schedule.
- The Control Parallelisation phase introduces the control operators (Borla-Salamet *et al.*, 1991) (i.e. synchronization, termination detection, etc.) required to implement the execution schedule.

After parallelization, the LERA program undergoes a code generation phase that produces the executable code to be run in the DM's environment as explained in Section 4[5].

4.3 DM – an environment for parallel database processing

The parallel programs generated by the RM are executed in the run-time environment provided by the Data Manager (DM). The DM consist of four main components:

- **Relational Execution Model.** This component provides the basic operations of the execution model. That is it is a run time library consisting of the relational operations, operations supporting the ADT, objects and rules, and controls operators.
- **Relation Access Manager.** The Relation Access Manager provides a global abstraction of the relations in the database. That is it hides the distributed nature of the relations from the operations in Relational Execution Model. The Relation Access Manager also provides the mechanism for calling the appropriate access methods for the indexes associated with a relation.
- **A Set of Access Methods.** The access methods provide the mechanisms for accessing the tuples of a relation. There will be an access method to implement each index associated with a relation. The indexes are used to provide fast methods for accessing the tuples of a relation. The system has been designed to allow new access methods to be easily 'plugged in' to the DM.

---

[5]It is worth mentioning that there are two code generators in the EDS database systems – one is designed for EDBS (a distributed store based system) and the other for DBS (Bergsten *et al.*, 1991), a shared memory testbed of EDS. Notice that both code-generators accept a common language as input, namely LERA.

- **Basic Relational Execution Model (BREM).** BREM is a parallel program environment which has been designed to provide abstractions tailored for the efficient execution of RM programs. The abstraction provided by BREM gives the upper levels a much simpler environment to implement their parallel programs.

4.4 The Object Manager

The Object Manager provides basic object storage and manipulation facilities required for the support of EDBS. The functions provided by the Object Manager are storage of persistent objects, concurrency control to allow sharing of objects, logging and recovery. The object manager is based on the Arjuna system (Dixon, 1987) with ideas incorporated from the Camelot project and the Choices project.

The object manager has a fairly conventional design and is effectively a set of local object managers, one per PE, which use an optimized 2-phase commit protocol to co-ordinate transactions. Standard 2-phase locking protocol and logging mechanisms are used for concurrency control and recovery.

The performance of the Object Manager has been enhanced by taking advantage of the facilities provided by EMEX and the large RAM store on each PE. In particular, the critical parts of the Object Manager are built with the EMEX kernel and execute in supervisor mode. This avoids context switching when Object Manager operations, such as taking a lock, are performed. Similarly the EMEX mapper (see Section 3) facilities are used in a similar way as Camelot (Spector et al., 1986) to support the Object Manager.

4.5 Integrating the EDBS to the EDS platform

The EDS hardware and operating system have not been designed in isolation, but have been heavily influenced by the requirements of the parallel database system while still providing general purpose computing facilities.

The EDS Machine. In addition to its parallel processing capability the EDS hardware has two main features for the support of EDBS: a high performance message handling system and a large local RAM store (64 Mbytes capacity extendible up to 4 Gbytes per PE). The message handling performance is provided by the interconnection network, which gives a high bandwidth, and the SSU-NIU inter-working pair (see Section 2.1) which gives a high message rate. The large local RAM store improves database performance significantly.

The EMEX Kernel. EMEX has a number of features which have been designed to enhance the performance of EDBS:

- **Message Passing Communication.** The EMEX communication system provides a reliable, ordered stream of data transfer between two interconnected data operators. Moreover the asynchronous send facility enables continuous tuple processing immediately after an intermediate result tuple is sent. This makes data transfer transparent to the EDBS; and as a result, higher concurrency is achieved in the system. This in turn can increase the data processing throughput which is one of the major design targets of the EDS database server.
- **Store Copying.** The EMEX communication system can also transmit data directly from the sender's buffers and delivers them directly into the receiver's buffers. This has several beneficial effects: it removes two data transfers; it avoids the complications of a large kernel buffer pool; and it opens the message passing resources for different jobs, so avoiding interference between different users' work. Furthermore, the use of the SSU-NIU inter-working pair (see Section 2.1) for the message handling significantly reduces the number of context switches in the PU.
- **Threads.** An EMEX thread is a light-weight operating system process and avoids the high overheads of a conventional heavy-weight task or process for small units of work. This is particularly useful in EDBS for supporting the the idea of simple database operations. Simple operations are the basic requirement for achieving the RISC-like approach for compilation and optimization.
- **Scheduling.** EMEX provides preemptive scheduling with priorities between tasks. Time slicing is used between tasks of equal priority. This type of scheduling is vital for any OLTP system which needs to run applications which have different (user) priorities. Threads within a task also have priority based pre-emptive scheduling, but all runnable threads are scheduled before the task suspends itself. This minimizes the number of context switches in contrast with the scheduling systems of the Chorus system where threads are the main unit of scheduling.
- **External Pager Technology.** EMEX provides external pager facilities similar to those of Mach (Spector et al., 1986) and Chorus.
- **Distributed Tasks.** Although it is not necessary for the performance of the system, the distributed task concept provided by EMEX has greatly simplified the initialization of the DM. It allows the EDBS to use a standard dynamic loader instead of developing a complicated multi-processor loaders, found in other multi-processor database systems.

- **Supervisor Subsystems.** Like Chorus, EMEX allows special 'supervisor sub-system' to be built into the nucleus. This is used by the Object Manager to provide trap interface to the critical Object Manager interfaces. This avoids a context switch to enter a protected environment for the Object Manager.

5 ADVANCED FUNCTIONALITY: COMPLEX QUERY HANDLING

The EDS database sub-system, EDBS, is relational in nature, with extensions to support abstract data types (ADTs), objects and deduction capabilities. It therefore implements an extension of SQL called ESQL (Extended Structured Query Language). Database queries in EDBS are specified in ESQL (Gardarin et al., 1990) – a query language designed for traditional data processing applications as well as for non-traditional information processing applications. ESQL is upward compatible with SQL. The SQL extensions are provided with minimal impact to the existing SQL standards; this makes ESQL simple to use by SQL users. In addition, the additional language features in ESQL enable the language to be used for advanced applications such as CIM, CASE and GIS as well as for complex decision support applications.

5.1 Abstract data types and objects

While the relational data model only supports values, ESQL supports both values and objects. A value is an instance of a basic type or of a user-defined ADT while an object associates a unique object identifier to an ADT value (the object's state). An ADT is a new type together with functions applicable to data of that type. Therefore, ESQL data are divided between objects and values, and only objects may be referentially shared using object identity.

To support complex values, ESQL generalizes the notion of domain with generic ADTs which may be combined at multiple levels. Generic ADTs are higher-order constructors that take types as arguments. The generic ADTs are tuple, set, bag, list and vector. By combining objects and generic ADTs, arbitrarily complex objects can be supported.

In the following ESQL type declarations, Person corresponds to an object whose state is a tuple of values. Actor is a subtype of Person thus inheriting its nature (it's an object), structure and applicable functions. Actor is a specialization of Person both from the structural point of view as it has an additional element in the tuple, and from the behavioural point of view as the new function Increase_salary is attached to it. Unlike Person and Actor, which are objects, type Actors represents values whose structure is a set of Actor objects. Similarly to Person and Actor, type Actors is an ADT and therefore it is possible to attach functions, such as Max_salary, to it.

> **TYPE** Person **OBJECT TUPLE OF** (name Char(30), firstname Char(20));
> **TYPE** Actor **SUBTYPE OF** Person **WITH** (salary Numeric);
> **FUNCTION** Increase_salary(Actor, Numeric) **RETURNS** Actor **LANGUAGE C;**
> **TYPE** Actors **SET OF** Actor;
> **FUNCTION** Max_salary(Actors) **RETURNS** Numeric **LANGUAGE C;**

Tables Film and Actor are defined below using these ADTs. Note in particular that attribute actors in table Film and attribute actor in table Actor are both defined on the object type Actors (given that Actors is itself a set of Actor). This allows Actor instances to be shared between these two tables thus reducing data redundancy and enforcing the underlying referential integrity constraint. In EDBS, although objects can be created (within an ESQL procedure) independently from any table, they will not persist unless they are attached to (referenceed by) a table's attribute, i.e. tables are the only persistency roots.

> **CREATE TABLE** Film (filmnum Num, title Char(50), actors Actors, producer Person);
> **CREATE TABLE** Actor (actor Actor, films Films);

In order to query and update the corresponding database, ESQL provides facilities such as the possibility of ADT method calls in SQL statements, the manipulation of shared objects by using a functional notation, and the manipulation of nested objects through nested statements. Data manipulation in ESQL is more regular than in SQL, much in the way of SQL2. The following statement illustrates some of these features. Extract and Getfield are generic functions delivering an object's status, i.e. a value, and a tuple's component respectively. Note that the join condition is expressed using function Contains (another generic function) which delivers 1 as its value if the given set contains the given object.

> **SELECT** Extract(actor)
> **FROM** Film, Actor
> **WHERE** title = 'Pretty Woman'
> **AND** Getfield(actor, salary) = Max_salary(actors)
> **AND** Contains(actors, actor) = 1

5.2 Recursive views and deduction

A deductive capability enables one to abstract in a rule base the common knowledge traditionally embedded with redundancy in application programs. The rule base provides centralized control of knowledge and is primarily useful to infer new facts from the facts stored in the database. ESQL provides this deductive capability as an extension of the SQL view mechanism, including recursive views. This gives to ESQL the power of the DATALOG logic-based language using statements already available in SQL.

As an example, consider the definitions of table Dominates and of view Better_than hereafter. Table Dominates records the fact that in a given film actor1 had a more important role than actor2. The view is recursive and corresponds to a classification (partial order) among the actors. Note that it is almost standard SQL2 except that SQL2 does not allow referencing views in a view definition. The EXCEPT statement is used to eliminate cycles.

    CREATE TABLE Dominates (filmnum Num, actor1 Actor, actor2 Actor)

    VIEW Better_than (actor1, actor2) **AS** (
        SELECT actor1, actor2
        FROM Dominate
    UNION
        SELECT B1.actor1, B2.actor2
        FROM Better_than B1, Better_than B2
        WHERE B2.actor1 = B2.actor1
    EXCEPT
        SELECT B1.actor1, B2.actor2
        FROM Better_than B1, Better_than B2
        WHERE B1.actor2 = B2.actor1
        AND B1.actor1 = B2.actor2)

6 OLTP PERFORMANCE

One of the main application areas for the EDS database server is On-Line Transaction Processing (OLTP). It is targeted to provide a OLTP-transaction rate of 12,000 tps (transaction per second) st 30% machine utilization. This performance target assumes the TPC-B (Gray, 1991) operation conditions. These conditions influence the operation behaviour of the EDS server and thus affect its performance. Noticeably, during the benchmarking period under TPC-B, 90% of the transactions are required to have a residence time of under two seconds

98 Parallel Information Processing

and 85% of them are required to be performed locally (i.e. access to the branch, teller, account and history relations are made on the same home PE).

To ensure that the design of the EDS server can meet the performance targets, its OLTP performance is constantly assessed throughout the development stage. This is performed by using the EDS OLTP behavioural simulation model which is programmed in VHDL (Wong *et al.*, 1992). The simulation model is based on some critical baseline performance parameters. These parameters account for the execution times of machine operations, database processing primitives, network communications and EMEX primitives[6] and are always kept up-todate with the latest measured values.

Recent simulation results show that the EDS server can comfortably meet the 12,000 tps target at 30% load; in fact, the actual OLTP performance at 30% load is simulated to be 16,000 tps. In addition to OLTP performance assessment, the EDS Behavioural simulation model has also been used to study a number of implementation techniques, e.g. parallel logging (Wong *et al.*, 1992).

Simulation is not the only means for performance evaluation of the EDS system. Direct measurements of both hardware and software components are actively underway. Unfortunately, due to commercial reasons, these measurements figures cannot be presented here.

7 CONCLUSION

The design of the EDS database server focused on two main aspects: high performance through different levels of parallelism and advanced database functionalities through the ESQL query language. They have been described in the preceding sections.

Database processing in the EDS server is done with two main goals in mind: first, to achieve high performance in terms of both global throughput and execution time; second, to be able to tune the system to provide this high performance in OLTP environments, in information management environments or in a combination of both. The features of the server that contribute most to the achievement of these goals are as follows.

From the data processing point of view, the EDBS uses the parallel facilities provided by EMEX to exploit both inter- and intra-query parallelism. Furthermore, the ADT and object mechanisms are closely integrated with the relational mechanisms to avoid system oversizing and interaction overheads. This integration is done in such a way that query execution performance in purely relational (standard SQL) applications is not degraded.

Related to parallel data processing and from the system administration point of view, ESQL provides the database administrator with a facility to explicitly cluster or decluster (partition) relations over multiple PEs. Both uniform and

---

[6] A list of performance parameters used in the OLTP simulation can be found in the appendix of Wong *et al.* (1992).

non-uniform data distribution are supported. A number of data placement (e.g. hashed, range, etc.) strategies can be used to achieve non-uniform distribution of data. Data placement is an important technique for system tunning. In addition, relations (de)clustering in EDBS facilitates the implementation of ESQL on a parallel computer.

In addition to ESQL, EDS supports two other parallel programming language system, namely ElipSys (Delgado-Rannauro *et al.*, 1991) and EDS Lisp (Hammer *et al.*, 1991). These languages can broaden the application spectrum of EDS from the existing targets of simple and medium-complex queries to very-complex queries, especially in the areas of decision support and intelligent information systems. Such systems are envisaged to occupy the main workload in future business applications. For this reason, the advanced parallel EDS database server is and will remain a leading edge technology for both present and future business professionals.

7.1 Future work

From a commercial exploitation point of view, EDS has achieved the major objectives set out at the beginning of the project. ICL (UK) has launched its Goldrush commercial scale open system parallel database server. Siemens (Germany) is exploiting the EMEX operating system as well as EDS-Lisp and Bull (France) the parallel advanced database system. Furthermore, from the research point of view, the EDS technology and experience will be continued beyond the ESPRIT-II initiative. The project participants have been exceptionally successful in winning a number of ESPRIT-III research projects based on the EDS results. EDS2 is evaluating the EDS system with commercial scale applications. IDEA is continuing the development of the advanced EDS database system. EPOCH is extending the work on EMEX to develop an operating system for high parallel performance, system management and integrity. APPLAUSE is developing large-scale applications using ElipSys to provide a commercial evaluation of the technology. PYTHAGORAS is a follow-up project based on the EDS performance evaluation activities and is aimed to produce a performance evaluation toolkit for advanced information systems (Wong *et al.*, 1992b). ADA–EDS is migrating the ADABAS database management system to Goldrush.

8 ACKNOWLEDGEMENTS

Thanks are due to the EC for partially funding the EDS project (ESPRIT-II project number EP2025 and EP6057) and to all the researchers and engineers who have contributed to the project.

REFERENCES

Andres, F. et al. (1991) A Multi-Environment Cost Evaluator for Parallel Database Systems, in: *Proc. 2nd Conference on Database Systems for Advanced Applications*, Tokyo.

Bergsten, B. et al. (1991) Prototyping DBS3, a Shared-Memory Parallel Database System, in: *Proc. of 1st International Conference on Parallel and Distributed Information Systems (PDIS91)*, Florida.

Borla-Salamet, P. et al. (1991) Compiling Control into Queries for Parallel Execution Management, in: *Proc. 1st International Conference on Parallel and Distributed Information Systems*, Miami, Florida.

Borrmann, L. et al. (1991) EDS: An Advanced Parallel Database Server, in: *Proc. ESPRIT Conference*.

Chachaty, C. et al. (1992) A Compositional Approach for the Design of a Parallel Query Processing Language, in: *Proc. of 1992 Conference on Parallel Architectures and Languages Europe (PARLE92)*, Paris, pp. 825–840.

Chorus Systemes (1991) CHORUS Kernel v3r4.0, Implementation guide, CS/TR-91-68.

Copeland, G. et al. (1988) Data Placement in Bubba, in: *Proc. ACM SIGMOD Conference, Chicago*, USA, pp. 99-108.

Delgado-Rannauro, S. A. et al. (1991) A Shared Environment Parallel Logic Programming System on Distributed Memory Architectures, in: *Proc. of 2nd European Conference on Distributed Memory Computing*, Munich, Germany, LNCS 487, Springer-Verlag, pp. 371–380.

Dixon, G. N. et al. (1987) Exploiting Type-Inheritance Facilities to Implement Recoverability in Object-Based Systems, in: *Proc. 6th Symp. Reliability in Distributed Software and Database Systems*, pp. 107–114.

Finance, B. et al. (1991) A Rule-Based Query Rewriter in an Extensible DBMS, in: *Proc. IEEE Data Engineering Conference*, Kobe, Japan.

Gardarin, G. et al. (1990) ESQL: An Extended SQL with Object and Deductive Capabilities, in: *Proc. International Conference on Database and Expert System Applications* (Eds. A. M. Tjoa and R. Wagner), Springer-Verlag, Berlin, pp. 299–307.

Hammer, C. et al. (1991) Using a Weak Coherency Model for a Parallel Lisp, in: *Proc. of 2nd European Conference on Distributed Memory Computing*, Munich, Germany, LNCS 487, Springer-Verlag, pp. 42–51.

Holzner, R. et al. (1990) Design and Simulation of a Multistage Interconnection Network, in: *Proc. of the Joint Conference on Vector and Parallel Processing*, Zurich.

Istavrinos, P. et al. (1990) A Process and Memory Model for a Parallel Distributed Memory Machines, in: *Proc. of the Joint Conference on Vector and Parallel Processing*, Zurich.

Spector, S. Z. et al. (1986) The Camelot Project, Database Engineering, 9(4).

Transaction Processing Performance Council (TPC) (1991) TPC Benchmark B, in: *The Benchmark Handbook* (Ed. J. Gray), Morgan Kaufmann, pp. 79–117.

Ward, M. et al. (1990) EDS Hardware Architecture, in: *Proc. CONPAR90 – VAPP IV Joint Conference on Vector and Parallel Processing*, Zurich, pp. 816–827.

Wong, K. F. et al. (1992a) Performance Evaluation of an OLTP Application on the EDS Database Server Using a Behavioural Simulation Model, in: *Data Management and Parallel Processing*, Chapman and Hall.

Wong, K. F. et al. (1992b) Pythagoras: Performance Quality Assessment of Advanced Database Systems, in: *Proc. 6th International Conference on Modelling Techniques and Tools for Computer Performance Evaluation*, Edinburgh.

7 IDIOMS: A Database Machine with Distributed Processor Architecture

J. Kerridge
National Transputer Support Centre

1 INTRODUCTION

The timely availability of management information and facilities to support decision making is vital to the well-being of an organization. Unfortunately, for most organizations such systems are not feasible if they manipulate a large volume of on-line data subject to some form of On-Line Transaction Processing (OLTP). Typically, the system used for OLTP is incapable of supporting the extra processing that is required for MIS and decision support, even if the data were stored in a form which enabled both types of processing. Traditionally, OLTP systems have been developed as a stand-alone, single application, programmed in a 3GL with the highly likely possibility of key time critical components being written in a 2GL. Thus the feasibility of creating *ad hoc* queries on the data is impossible because a program has to be specified, designed, implemented and tested. A process which could take as long as three months to complete.

The advent of relational database technology appeared to offer a solution to the dilemma of answering *ad hoc* queries. Highly structured data could be held in a flat-file or tabular form, and could be queried using the values of columns to access data. It was not necessary to know how the data was stored. It was thus relatively easy to formulate an *ad hoc* query. The only problem was that the processing time, for all but the simplest query, on a small data set was prohibitively long for everyday use. These early systems were improved so that their performance became acceptable.

In the mid-1980s the bench mark wars commenced (Gray, 1991), in which the comparative performance of a number of systems was determined. This lead to even greater performance improvement. However, these improvements were focused on the transaction processing capabilities of the relational database systems. There was no benchmark for query processing that was universally accepted. This was before the setting up of the Transaction Processing Council, and benchmarks such as the Wisconsin benchmark. It could be argued that relational database technology was being developed in a direction that was totally inappropriate in that it was designed for information system use rather than transaction processing. Transaction processing performance was obtained at the expense of having poor query processing performance. The required optimizations for one style of processing are inappropriate for the other.

To overcome these performance limitations a number of different solutions were attempted based on the use of dedicated hardware. The most successful were those of Britten-Lee and Teradata (Su, 1988). Other companies such as Oracle, Ingres and Sybase were adopting a different approach based upon the use of shared memory multi-processors.

The Britten-Lee and Teradata approaches were based upon using dedicated hardware that improved the data access and relational processing part of database manipulation. The user interface was retained on the host mainframe that was originally used to support the database in its entirety. The advantage of off-loading data access is that the customer retains the user interface, which occupies most of the application development time. Thus actual database users do not have to be retrained and existing communication structures can be retained. Thus rather than having to upgrade the central resource a database accelerator is bought. A very real advantage if the mainframe manufacturer has not yet produced the required more powerful machine.

The approach adopted by third party vendors has been to develop their database architecture to execute on shared memory multi-processor systems. The original architectures were developed for single processor systems, and thus a major architectural re-design is not required. In particular, components such as locking for concurrency control do not need to be re-designed. Thus in the short-term, a performance advantage was easily obtained by moving to such share everything multi-processor systems. However, it has become apparent that the load placed upon a shared memory multi-processor by database software is such that it is not usually possible to fully utilize all the processors that could be connected. That is the performance limit of the shared memory had been reached, and the addition of further processors yield no improvement in performance.

It was within this framework that the IDIOMS project (Kerridge, 1991) was proposed to investigate the feasibility of constructing a distributed memory share nothing multi-processor system which could support both OLTP and MIS functionality on the same data set. It was also vital that the scalability of the system should be demonstrated and that it should be designed for large data volumes, at least 10 Gbytes.

2   THE IDIOMS COLLABORATORS

IDIOMS (Intelligent Decision making In On-line Management Systems) is a collaboration between the National Transputer Support Centre (NTSC) in

Sheffield, the Bristol Transputer Centre (BTC), Strand Software Technologies Ltd (SSTL) and TSB Bank plc. The NTSC's role is to develop the database engine which supports both OLTP and MIS processing. The BTC is developing parallel algorithms which allow large volumes of on-line data to be processed using neural network, constraint satisfaction networks and genetic algorithms for decision support. SSTL are providing a parallel environment, called STRAND, which will enable the easy construction of an interface between the MIS and the SQL queries that are required for the database engine. TSB are providing data from both banking and credit-card systems to enable the construction of two demonstrations of the IDIOMS approach. These demonstrations will be using real data from each of the applications to ensure that any comparisons drawn with their existing systems are realistic.

The aim of the IDIOMS project is to build a demonstration of transputer (Inmos, 1987) based hardware to construct a shared nothing distributed memory parallel database machine. Of particular interest to TSB are the aspects of performance in both OLTP and MIS modes separately and combined, and the ease of system scalability.

Currently TSB have one system which provides a repository for the banking data and is accessed solely in OLTP mode, with batch runs overnight. These batch runs generate some statistics, but it is not possible to query the data in an MIS mode. A separate system, based upon a Teradata machine, is used to provide a customer information database. There is some duplication of data between the banking and customer information systems. The credit-card system is kept on a totally separate system, even though many of the customers are common. TSB are atypical of UK banks in that they actually update the banking information on-line, rather than the more usual cheque clearing run overnight. This results from the fact that account holders have passbooks, as well as cheque books and there is a need to be able to update the customer's passbook whilst the customer is being served. If the on-line data could be accessed in an MIS decision support mode, then the TSB would be able to improve both its services and its profitability.

3   OVERVIEW OF THE IDIOMS DESIGN

The block architecture of the IDIOMS machine is shown in Figure 7.1. It shows that the OLTP and MIS functions of the machine are completely separate but that they both have access to the shared data storage. The shared data storage is fundamental to the IDIOMS design and arises from an appreciation of the differing processing characteristics of OLTP and MIS.

An OLTP transaction is generally of short duration and manipulates one or more related records using both read and write operations. An OLTP record is usually accessed via a unique generated key such as account number. It is

106 Parallel Information Processing

therefore normal in an on-line environment to build an index based upon the key to optimize access to the data. Normally the data is organized into one large record so that with one disk access all the possibly relevant information

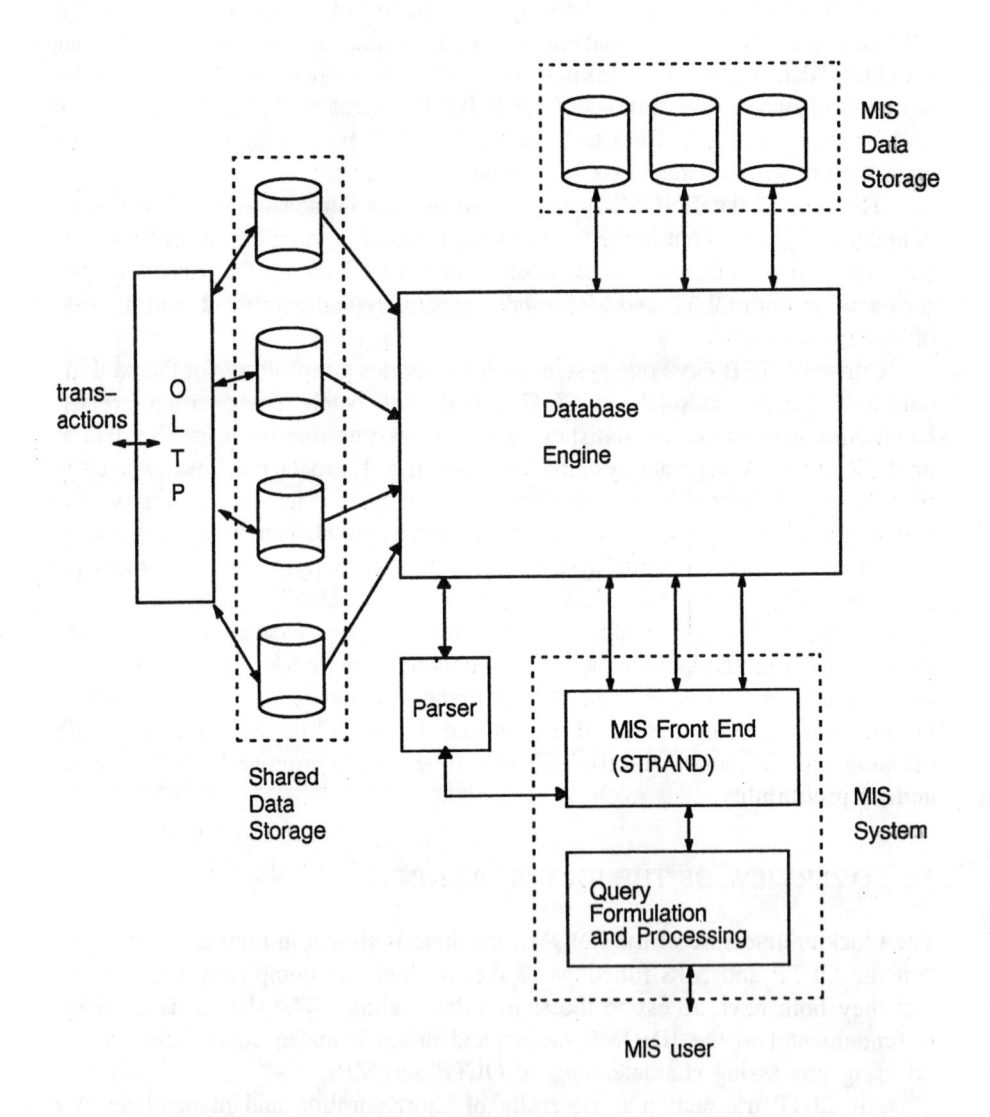

FIGURE. 7.1. IDIOMS basic blook architecture.

IDIOMS: A Database Machine with DPA   107

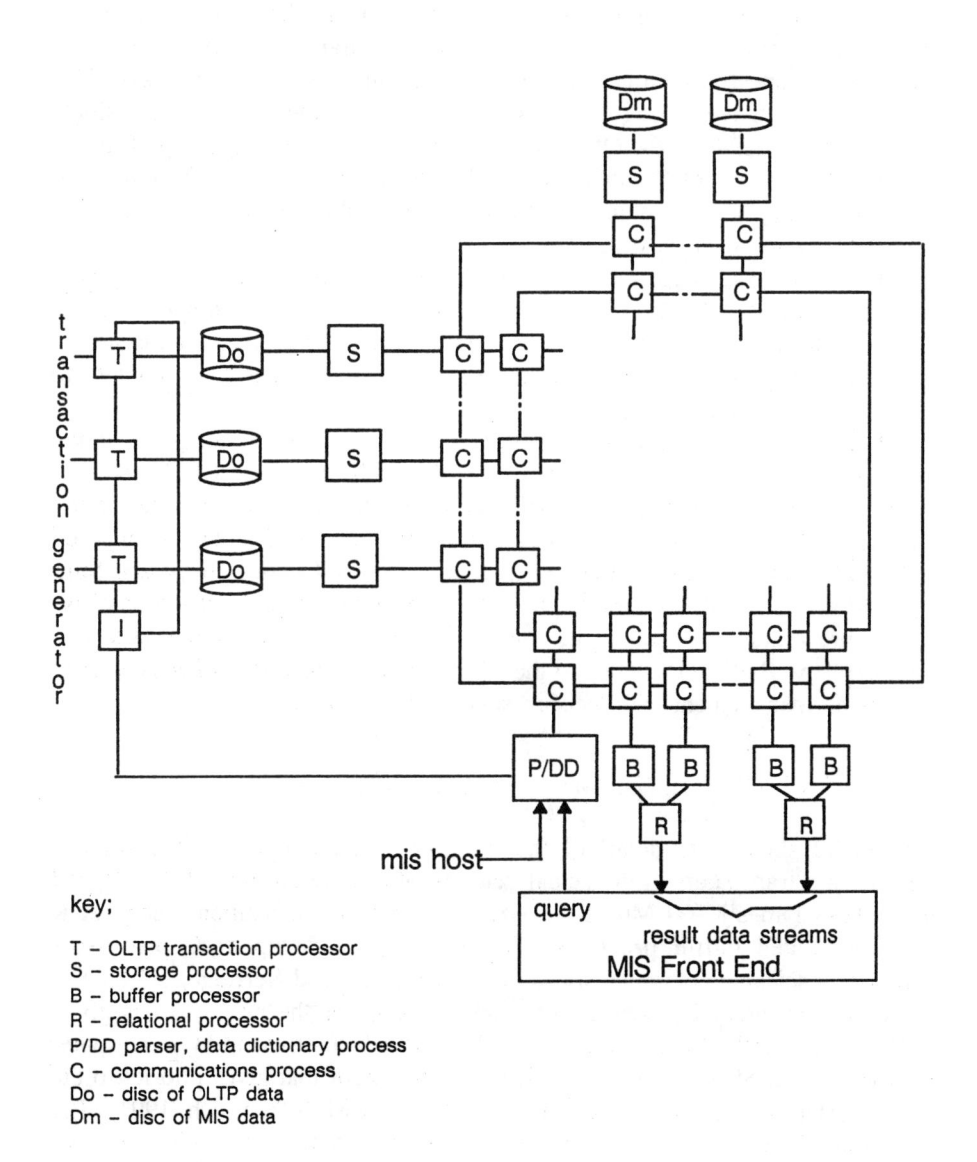

key;

T – OLTP transaction processor
S – storage processor
B – buffer processor
R – relational processor
P/DD parser, data dictionary process
C – communications process
Do – disc of OLTP data
Dm – disc of MIS data

FIGURE 7.2. Basic database engine architecture.

can be fetched regardless of the particular transaction to be undertaken. This is a non-relational way of storing the data, because it is generally not normalized. For example, a bank account record contains sufficient space for as many account movements as appear on a statement. Thus the record contains a repeating group. In the IDIOMS machine we have separated the fixed information concerning an account and the account movements into two tables so that all the movements (up to the length of a statement) occur as a single group in the table. Thus the OLTP system can access the whole group of movements, whereas the MIS can access each row independently. Effectively we have used the grouping column of the movements table to control the physical placement of the data on disk.

The data is range partitioned across the shared disks. The account number is used as the key for range partitioning. This means that transactions for a particular account are directed to the disk upon which the account data is stored. The shared data storage is organized so that access requests from OLTP are given priority over MIS requests.

The MIS makes requests for data from the shared data storage as if the data were stored in relational tables. The MIS only makes SELECT requests upon the shared data storage. The MIS can access the MIS data storage for any type of SQL query and the data is stored as pure relational tables, as opposed to the combined form used in the shared data storage. Queries are passed form the MIS front end to the parser, which determines which parts of the database engine are required to satisfy the query. The resultant data is returned in a number of parallel data streams to the MIS, where the data is further processed to provide management and decision support information.

4 DETAIL OF THE IDIOMS DATABASE ENGINE

Figure 7.2 shows the detail of the database engine. Each of the squares represents a transputer. In the actual demonstrator there are nine disks Do and three disks Dm all 100 Mbytes in size. There are three relational engines R with associated buffer processors B. The rings made up of C processors comprise a scalable communications network (Walter and Kerridge, 1991). The design of the internal processes that make up each of the processors is given in (Kerridge, 1991). Each of the disks is interfaced to the system by a transputer with associated SCSI bus interface. It is this processor that gives priority to the OLTP system using firmware provided on the processor (Transtech, 1991). The processors T receive the transactions to be carried out via a routing network (Thompson and Waithe, 1991). Each of the T processors is capable of carrying out all the transactions. As stated earlier, the data on disks Do is range partitioned, and this ability to carry out all transactions is a necessity. The ring of T and I processors is required to implement transactions which need access to more than one account, where the account information is stored on different disks. This would occur in transactions involving the transfer of funds from one account to another. For the purposes of this demonstration we have assumed that a customer does not have accounts on different disks. Thus the customer information pertaining to several accounts held by the same customer is always on the same disk as is the account information. This is not unreasonable for the purposes of the demonstration as the number of situations where this is not the case in real life is small. The transaction code is written in C encapsulated in an occam harness. The transaction code has been written as a pair of parallel processes, one which requests data from the disk, processes the data, and writes any results back to the disk. The other process accesses the disk, using the key value provided and accesses the disk for the correct record. The layout of data on the disk is held in the data dictionary and is communicated to each of the T processors using the I process at system boot time. The role of the data dictionary will be described later.

The database engine comprises the disks Do and Dm and the processors S, C, B and R. P/DD is the parser/data dictionary processor. Each of the S engines comprises a number of table handler processes running in parallel, one for each table stored on the disks. Each table handler is initialized with details of the table structure and physical disk placement from the dictionary at boot time.

The table handler then contains processes, yet again running in parallel, which undertake the basic manipulations of SQL (SELECT, UPDATE, INSERT and DELETE). These processes are allocated to a particular query on an as-needed basis, by the parser. The basic premise of the database engine is that data filtering (equivalent to the relational select and project operations) is carried out in the table handler associated with the disk. The selected rows are then transferred round the network of C processors to the relational engines (B, R) where two table operations are carried out. In the case of S processors connected as part of the shared data (disks Do) then they are restricted to SELECT operations only. Thus a query being processed by such an S engine can be stopped whilst the disk is accessed by a T processor during an OLTP operation. This does mean that an MIS query will probably see the data in an inconsistent state, but for such processing this is not critical. We are developing concurrency management algorithms that will overcome this problem.

In the demonstrator we chose not to implement any indexes, either primary or secondary on the MIS data. This arises because most of the queries will be based on ranges of values and the natural keys of the data, account and customer numbers will not normally form part of an MIS query. In due course we hope to be able to add indexes in order to measure performance improvement, if any, with indexes. We have implemented a mechanism of scanning the data set, and for the selected tuples doing a memory-based sort so that subsequent join processing can use a sort-merge join. The sorting process can also be used for DISTINCT and GROUP BY operations. We have thus traded run-time performance of a query for the ease of table modification and not having to maintain indexes. Current performance measurements indicate that this is proving not to be desparately expensive because we have subdivided the data into such small units. The sort of selected tuples is carried out in the table handler process within the S processor. A further advantage of this approach is that we can sort any column of a table on an as needed basis. We are not restricted to carrying out selections and joins on tables for which there is an index.

Data from the S processors is then directed to one or more of the relational engines. These engines comprise two B processors and an R processor that does the actual operation. The resultant data stream can either be sent directly to the MIS front end, or, in the case of nested operations, re-directed to another relational engine using the B processors and the communications network.

From the foregoing it is apparent that there is a need for control within the database engine. In the next section we look at how the control of the database machine is achieved and the software infrastructure that has been developed.

5 THE DATA DICTIONARY AND SYSTEM CONTROL

One of the early decisions taken in the design of the IDIOMS database machine was to base the dictionary structure upon that contained in the Working Draft Database Language SQL2 (Database Language Draft, 1990). This proposes an Information Schema which describes the structure of the database being managed. It is equivalent to the catalogue of DB2. In the parallel IDIOMS machine it was decided that the dictionary should hold physical placement data and resource availability information so that it can be used by the query optimizer which is contained in the data dictionary. The operational model of the IDIOMS database engine is one of query decomposition into dataflow graphs, with nodes of the graph undertaking project, select, join and other operations. In a parallel environment this can be further extended by undertaking parts of the query concurrently on different processors (Kerridge, 1991b).

Earlier it was stated that the data is range partitioned. This partitioning means that queries that use the partitioning column(s) in their predicate can be optimized to access only those partitions where it is known that data appropriate to the query is stored. As part of the IDIOMS project a data storage description language (DSDL) has been developed (Sheffield Univ. internal report, 1991). This allows the partitioning of data to be specified. The partitioning information is then stored in the dictionary so that it can be used by the query optimizer (Unwalla and Kerridge, 1993).

This decision is further reinforced by the use of the transputer as the processing element. As well as providing memory, processor and communications capability the transputer also contains a process scheduler (Inmos, 1988). In fact the transputer contains a high and low priority scheduler. The former is a non-preemptive scheduler that allows a process to execute until it needs to communicate. This enables implementation of lightweight processes that are the basis of OLTP systems. The low priority scheduler is a pre-emptive scheduler which is ideal for MIS query processing. Thus the traditional process scheduling aspects of an operating system are actually provided by the transputer hardware.

The transputer was designed to support dedicated embedded systems. These normally manifest themselves as real-time control systems. However, a database machine is an embedded system. It accepts commands in the form of OLTP transaction requests or MIS queries and then carries out the transaction or supplies a stream of data corresponding to the query. The processes that actually access the disk data storage have been encoded to deal with the table structures that occur in relational database systems. Thus the file management system normally provided as part of an operating system is not required. The IDIOMS database machine does not use a traditional operating system. It merely accepts queries or transactions and returns the corresponding results.

This has one major benefit in that portable database management systems, usually, build a direct interface to data storage by using the system level calls provided by the operating system. Thus a layer of software has to be traversed which is totally redundant. Secondly, because operating systems provide a general purpose process scheduling strategy, assuming a number of concurrent independent users, most database systems implement their own process scheduling strategy running as a single process within the host operating. Yet again, this is a software layer which can be avoided by the use of the transputer.

6 PERFORMANCE

The performance of the IDIOMS machine has not yet been fully evaluated. We do, however, have some preliminary results which enable comparison with existing TSB hardware, but even this is not a realistic comparison. Thus the following should be treated as very speculative, but indicative of likely performance. The performance of the IDIOMS machine is to be evaluated in the period up to September 1992.

TSB have prepared a banking data set of 50,000 accounts, which comprises one of their test data sets. Each account record is about 5000 bytes long, which should be compared with the 100 bytes of the TPC-B benchmark (Gray, 1991). The peak rate of current TSB equipment for that number of accounts is about two transactions per second. This data has been loaded onto the IDIOMS machine and the OLTP performance measured at around two transactions per second per disk, that is, 18 transactions per second. The rate is quoted in this way because a linear speed up has been observed with the number of disks.

This is not surprising as the only overhead is the routing of a transaction to the correct T processor. In this manner we have shown that the design is scalable.

It has to be stated that the IDIOMS mechanisms contained no means of transaction recovery or rollback, which is included in the current TSB system. However, a completely separate parallel architecture has been developed for recovery which has minimal overhead (Oates and Kerridge, 1991a, b; Oates, 1991) and this is currently being implemented.

A further experiment has been undertaken by mounting the TPC-B dataset for a 1 tps system (Gray, 1991). This has been evaluated in several modes. The raw OLTP performance was about 40 transactions per second, representing a performance of about 4.5 tps per second per disk. The OLTP system was then run with the S processor also accessing the shared data storage. The S processors did not process the data in any way, they just kept issuing random requests for data. This represents a worst case situation for the OLTP system. The performance was now reduced to 0.5 transactions per second per disk. These figures do at least give the range of processing rates that can be expected. A more realistic test has been undertaken that involves processing the data acquired form the S engines. A join of two 300 tuple tables was undertaken, resulting in the production of 300 rows. If the join elements were pre-sorted then the total time was two seconds otherwise it took 19 seconds to undertake a full cartesian product (nested-loop) join. The relational engines are capable of undertaking about 5000 join comparisons per second. During join processing the OLTP dropped to about half that when there was no MIS processing. The above results are preliminary, but give confidence that the system will be able to perform satisfactorily. The system will be evaluated not only on the TSB data but also on a benchmark based upon the TPC-B data set into which has been combined the data for the set query benchmark (Gray, 1991). It is intended to report on these results later this year.

7 CONCLUSIONS

This chapter has discussed the design strategy of a share nothing parallel database machine. It has shown how the use of transputer-based processor technology has enabled a radically different approach to integrated OLTP/MIS operation. This is the environment in which the use of parallel technology will have its most dramatic effect enabling data being used to provide decision support during transaction processing. This could open up many uses for data which is currently infeasible due to the lack of processing power that is provided by current database systems.

REFERENCES

Data Storage Description Language for Database Language SQL, Department of Computer Science, University of Sheffield, Internal Report, CS-91-05.

Database Language SQL2, ISO/IEC JTC 1/SC 21/ N 5215, Committee Draft, December 1990.

Gray, J. (1991) *The Benchmark Handbook*, Morgan Kaufmann Publishers, California.

Inmos Ltd (1987) *Transputer Data Book*.

Inmos Ltd (1988) *The Transputer Implementation of Occam, in Communicating Process Architecture*, Prentice-Hall.

Kerridge, J. (1991a) The Design of the IDIOMS Parallel Database Machine, in: *Aspects of Databases* (M. S. Jackson and A. E. Robinson, Eds.), Butterworth-Heinemann.

Kerridge, J. (1991b) Transputer Topologies for Data Management, in: *Commercial Parallel Processing* (P. Valduriez, Ed.), Unicom Ltd.

Oates, R. and Kerridge, J. (1991a) Adding Fault Tolerance to a Transputer-based Parallel Database Machine, in: *Transputing'91* (P. Welch *et al.*, Eds.), IOS Press, Amsterdam.

Oates, R. and Kerridge, J. (1991b) Improving the Fault Tolerance of the Recovery Ring, in: *Transputer Applications'91* (T. Duranni *et al.*, Eds.), IOS Press, Amsterdam.

Oates, R. (1991) Transaction Recovery Architectures for Parallel Database Machines, PhD Thesis, University of Sheffield.

Su, S. (1988) *Database Computers – priniples, architectures and techniques*, McGraw-Hill.

Thompson, P. J. and Waithe, S. W. (1991) The Design and Implementation of the IDIOMS On-Line Transaction Processing Simulator, in: *Transputer Applications'91* (T. Duranni *et al.*, Eds.), IOS Press, Amsterdam.

Transtech Devices Ltd. (1991) SCSI TRAM Databook, TTM-11.

Unwalla, M. and Kerridge, J. (1993) Control of a Large Massively Parallel Database Machine Using SQL Catalogue Extensions and a Data Storage Description Language in Preference to an Operating System, submitted for publication.

Walter, D. and Kerridge, J. (1991) A Scalable Communications Network for a Parallel Database Machine, in: *Occam and the transputer – current developments* (J. Edwards, Ed.), IOS Press, Amsterdam.

8 Parallel Architectures for Smart Information Systems

S. H. Lavington and C. J. Wang
Department of Computer Science
University of Essex

1 INTRODUCTION

Smart information systems, or knowledge-based systems, are defined as computer applications which incorporate non-trivial data-manipulation features such as the ability to adapt, or to deal with dynamic heterogeneous information, or to carry out inferencing. We use the term 'inferencing' to include related techniques of reasoning and deductive theorem proving. Practical examples of smart information systems include deductive databases, Management Information Systems, Expert Systems, AI planners, Intelligent Information Retrieval, etc. More generally, such applications deal primarily with (large amounts of) symbolic, i.e. non-numeric, data which is usually complex and usually describable in terms of sets, relations, graphs, etc.

Smart information systems tend to suffer from the twin problems of slow and complex software. It is paradoxical that whilst device technology provides ever faster and cheaper processing elements, computer applications get ever more demanding so that slowness and complexity of software remain issues. The challenge addressed by novel computer architectures is how to decrease run-times in a cost-effective manner, without adding to the programmers' burden.

Most high-performance computer architectures have been biased towards numeric applications, which typically assume a target activity of arithmetic operations between (two streams of) regular, linearly-addressed elements. The target activity for smart information systems is radically different. In this chapter we explore the top-down functional requirements of smart information systems, analyse generic activities, and propose an appropriate novel architecture. The philosophy behind this architecture is to exploit the natural parallelism in whole-structure operations, via an 'active' memory unit which both stores and processes structures such as sets, relations and graphs. The whole-structure operations are then made available to the high-level programmer as convenient data-processing primitives. We briefly describe a prototype hardware design for an add-on active memory unit, based on SIMD parallelism, which implements

116 Parallel Information Processing

the whole-structure operations directly. Finally, we give examples which show how the unit's functionality can be made available to a C programmer.

2 FUNCTIONAL REQUIREMENTS OF SMART INFORMATION SYSTEMS

Unlike scientific applications, there appear to be few attempts at analysing the basic requirements of knowledge-based systems. One problem is the difficulty of distinguishing generic tasks from well-used but *ad hoc* techniques. If the aim is to specify requirements for parallel architectures that will be directly usable by knowledge-base software, regardless of particular application or language, then a statement of generic functional tasks is vital.

The necessary software for a smart information system incorporates a knowledge-representation formalism together with knowledge-processing algorithms. Choosing a scheme for information representation is one of the first steps in the problem-solving cycle. There are many representational schemes, not all of which (alas) have a formal basis. Examples include relational, object-oriented, frame-based, production rules, clausal logic, semantic nets, neural nets, non-standard logics (e.g. for belief systems), etc. The algorithms which act upon the knowledge base perform such tasks as pattern-matching/selection/recognition; making inferences of some sort (including deduction, reasoning, theorem proving and constraint satisfaction); handling beliefs and uncertainty; learning/adaptation; and data and object management (including sharing, protection, persistence, versioning, integrity, etc.).

For a given knowledge-manipulation task, there is usually a choice of practical techniques and strategies which depend partly on the knowledge representation adopted and partly on the computational platform (hardware and software) available. For example, marker-propagation algorithms can also be expressed as relational operations such as closure and intersection; also, matching algorithms in production rule systems can either be expressed as tree traversals or n-ary relational operations. Each approach may be suitable for a different platform. For example, the architecture of the Connection Machine (Hillis, 1987) was inspired by address-induced, sector representations which suggest marker-propagation algorithms; the architectures of the DADO and NON-VON machines were inspired by the tree-structures of the RETE and TREAT matching algorithms for production rule systems (e.g. Stalfo and Miranker, 1984).

Given the above variety of techniques and their apparent dependence on existing computational platforms, the analysis and quantification of generic tasks and their functional requirements is not easy. It is, however, helpful to go back to the first stages of problem-definition for any smart information system. Abstracting away from choice of programming language, etc., the important generic activities may be grouped under four (somewhat overlapping) functional headings:

- representation and management of knowledge
- pattern recognition (including selection)
- inference (including reasoning and deduction)
- learning.

Actually, pattern-matching may often be an important component of all four activities, not just the second one – an observation to which we return later. The data structures over which pattern-matching could be required include lists, trees, sets, relations, graphs, etc. AI programmers often seem to use lists to represent sets (because of a language-culture?). At some level of detail, sets and lists are of course inter-definable. However, the set is the more fundamental mathematical notion. Since ordering, and indeed graphs and trees, can be represented in the relational paradigm, it is convenient to take a relational or set-based approach to the generic data structures encountered in smart information systems. This allows us to call upon the accepted notions of **tuple** and **set** as the common building blocks from which all relevant data types may be constructed. It also promotes a focused debate on the desirable repertoire of data-manipulation primitives for smart information systems.

In summary, the functional requirements of smart information systems can be described abstractly in terms of operations on sets. The set primitives may be used to implement a number of generic tasks, namely: the representation and management of knowledge; pattern recognition; inference; and learning. More practically, any novel architecture which aims to support smart information systems has to have three attributes:

- a practical memory scheme for the low-level representation, accessing, and management of (large amounts of) set-based information;
- a strategy for carrying out set manipulations rapidly, e.g. by exploiting inherent parallelism;
- an agreed procedural interface whereby the set operations may be presented to the high-level programmer as convenient data-processing primitives.

In the next two sections we present a more formal description of the important notions of **tuple, tuple-set** and **pattern-directed search**. These establish the framework for appropriate low-level information representation and access schemes. Bearing in mind the importance of pattern-matching activities, which seem to imply *content*-addressability rather than locational (e.g. linear) addressability, a fresh architectural approach to set operations is called for. In sections

5 and 6 we develop a novel approach, which essentially consists of moving operations to the data, rather than moving data into processors.

3 A REPRESENTATIONAL FRAMEWORK

We introduce a semantics-free, set-based formalism for storing information, which is intended to support a wide variety of knowledge-representation schemes. Let the basic elements of our formalism be a universe, D, of atomic objects, Ai. The atomic objects comprise the members of two infinite sets and one singleton set:

C,   the set of constants (i.e. ground atoms);
W,   the set of named wild cards (i.e. an abstraction of the variables of logic programming languages);
∇,   the un-named wild card (i.e. an individual distinct from all the members of the other two sets).

Thus:

$$D = \{C_1, C_2, \ldots\} \cup \{W_1, W_2, \ldots\} \cup \{\nabla\}$$

Within this formalism, the symbol A will be used to denote an atomic object of unspecified kind (see below).

A word should be said about ground atoms. These may represent actual external entities such as a numerical constant or a lexical token. They may also represent some higher-level <type> information, or an abstract entity including a <label>. The notion of a <label> as a short-hand name for a composed object is mentioned again later.

Having established our domain of atomic objects, let information be represented as sets of tuples composed from this domain. That is, we assume the existence of a constructor *make-tuple*. Tuples may be of any length, and may consist of any choice of component atoms. The ith tuple thus has the general format:

$$T_i = <A_{i1}, A_{i2}, A_{i3}, \ldots, A_{im}>$$

where $A_{i1}, A_{i2}, \ldots, A_{im} \in D$. The m atoms are often referred to as the fields of the tuple. The scope of a wild card atom is the tuple and its extensions. If a tuple is required to be referenced within another tuple (or within itself, in self-referential systems), then a ground atom can be used as a <label>. This gives a straightforward method for representing structured information and complex objects. It is up to the higher-level knowledge modeller to ensure <label>

uniqueness, and to enforce a strict (e.g. Gödel-number) or congruence semantics. In other words, we see no theoretical reason for singling out <labels> for special treatment at the lowest level of information representation.

Tuples may be grouped into tuple-sets, via a *make-tuple-set* constructor, according to typing and semantic information. The tuple-set is the basic unit of information from the memory-management viewpoint (i.e. 'paging' and protection). Obviously, logical tuple-sets of varying granularity can be described, down to the single tuple. This suggests a mechanism for memory management, as discussed briefly in section 6.

Practical examples of data structures built using the *make-tuple* and *make-tuple-set* constructors are given in section 9. Facilities must naturally exist for creating, deleting, modifying and retrieving the tuples that constitute a knowledge base. Retrieval is achieved as a result of pattern-directed searching. Indeed, many of the useful operations on bulk data structures involve matching of atoms, i.e. essentially searching. (By 'bulk structures' we mean large collections of complex data such as sets, bags and relations.) Because of its importance, we now consider searching over tuple-sets in some detail.

4 A FORMALIZATION OF SEARCH

Pattern-directed search is conceptually a single function with three arguments: the interrogand, the matching algorithm to be used, and the tuple-set to be searched. Its result is in general another tuple-set (being a sub-set of its third argument). Operationally, the search proceeds as follows. Each member of its third argument is compared with the interrogand, which is itself a <tuple>; if they match, as determined by the matching algorithm, then that tuple appears in the output set.

The matching algorithm may specify:

(a) search mode (see below);
(b) a compare-operator, i.e. logical or arithmetic versions of $=$, $\neq$, $>$, $\geq$, $<$ or $\leq$;
(c) a compare mask, to inhibit a part or the whole of one or more field from taking part in the comparison;
(d) a means, e.g. Hamming distance, of measuring nearness.

Topic (d) is especially relevant to neural network or connectionist paradigms – an area so far omitted from our analysis of approaches to knowledge-base systems. Setting aside the underlying neurological model and the usual implementation in terms of floating-point calculations and threshold logic in individual processing nodes, let us consider the perceived benefits of the neural network approach. At the functional level, these benefits are:

- Learning or adaptation. Using some sort of specialization/generalization mechanism, a network evolves an interior weighted connective structure to produce a mapping between the input and output signal patterns. In general, the learning phase only requires qualitative knowledge of the domain problem. This makes neural networks suitable for solving problems in applications domains where an algorithm does not yet exist or is not known to the programmer.
- Graceful degradation or fault tolerance. Neural networks employ a distributed approach to knowledge representation, since many simple units act collectively to fulfil the overall system functionality. Networks may thus be able to cope with missing input data or to tolerate a certain amount of hardware damage. The system performance will degrade according to the degree of damage, and might recover by re-learning even though any hardware damage is not repaired.

Although the above perceived benefits set neural networks apart from most conventional symbolic programming paradigms, neural network technology has by and large been used principally to achieve pattern matching – a generic task found in various forms throughout smart information systems. Many neural network applications equate to the implementation of nearness pattern matching, according to metrics equivalent to Hamming distance or Euclidean distance. A means of measuring nearness during searching is thus very important. Mechanizing nearness measurement is a current research issue, and is not considered further in this chapter. However, it is possible that a future knowledge-base memory system will be able to support aspects of both the conventional AI (symbolic) and the neural network (sub-symbolic) approaches.

Confining ourselves to an analysis of search modes for symbolic information, un-masked equality is generally the most relevant type of compare operator and mask. Various modes of search are possible, depending upon whether un-named and named wild cards are given their full interpretation or are treated as if they were constants. We call these two cases 'interpreted' and 'uninterpreted'. Furthermore, either of these two possibilities can be applied to atoms in the interrogand or to atoms in the stored tuple. There are thus 16 possible modes of search (not all of which turn out to be useful). Five of the more obvious modes are:

- identity matching: bit-patterns are compared, regardless of the kind of atom (i.e. wild cards in both interrogand and stored tuple are 'uninterpreted'),

- simple matching: un-named wild cards in the interrogand are interpreted, as in conventional content-addressable memory (CAM),
- one-way matching (F): both kinds of wild card in the stored tuple are interpreted; this search mode is similar to the functional programming paradigm,
- one-way matching (D): both kinds of wild card in the interrogand are interpreted (the database paradigm),
- two-way, or unifiability, matching: all wild cards are interpreted.

In section 9 we give an example of a C procedure, which allows a programmer to specify a particular search option.

5   AN ARCHITECTURAL FRAMEWORK

Returning to the theme of candidate architectures, the previous two sections suggest that an appropriate memory scheme for smart information systems consists conceptually of a very large table for holding the variable-length tuples of section 3. Furthermore, this table requires to be accessed associatively (i.e. by content), according to the pattern-directed search modes described in section 4, to yield resultant tuple-sets. We consider the practical consequences of such an idealized memory specification later. First, however, it is necessary to consider how to perform parallel processing on the tuple-sets that emerge from the memory.

Current parallel architectures differ in the way that processor-store communications are organized. There is a range of possibilities. At one extreme there is the shared memory design, in which several processors share access to, and communicate via, a single memory (e.g. Encore Multimax). At the other extreme there is the fully distributed design, in which each processor only has access to its own local memory, and processors communicate directly with each other (e.g. the European Declarative System, EDS). The EDS is one of five prototype 'knowledge-base machines' described in Wong (1991). Besides the EDS, two other machines, namely Bull's Delta-Driven Computer and the Dutch PRISMA machine, have a distributed memory architecture. The big issue for each of these machines is likely to be the strategy for distributing both data and work amongst nodes, in order to achieve an acceptably scalable performance for non-trivial information systems.

One perceived advantage of distributed memory designs is that the overall store bandwidth is increased linearly as more processors are added to the system. However, when handling large data structures, the overhead of inter-processor communication often outweighs the delays caused by contention in a shared memory design. An alternative approach is to reduce the store bandwidth requirement by making the memory more active. The I-Structure store introduced by Arvind *et al.* (1987) is a step in this direction. Instead of holding an array in the dataflow graph itself, Arvind proposed that it be held in a separate store which is capable of performing array update operations in response to commands which are primitive to the source language. Extending the I-Structure notion somewhat, we might envisage a physically-bounded region of memory which contains all shared data and the means ('methods') for performing operations upon that stored data. If used in a multi-processor environment, the shared memory would accept one command at a time.

Using the regular form of representation for symbolic data described in section 3, it is possible to imagine an active form of memory that is capable of performing whole-structure operations such as set intersection *in situ*. This yields several advantages. The store bandwidth requirement is considerably reduced, since only high level commands and printable results cross the processor-memory interface. Given the regular format, an efficient SIMD approach can be taken to exploit the fine grain parallelism available in the majority of required operations (see later). The need for a mapping from backing store formats (e.g. files) to more efficient RAM representations is eliminated. The architecture provides a natural framework for the notion of data persistence.

6 AN ACTIVE MEMORY ADDRESSED BY CONTENT

In the spirit of Arvind's I-Structure store, we propose an add-on active memory unit which will both store and manipulate bulk data types. In addition to the general functional requirements of symbolic applications discussed in section 2, there are some more specific operational features that are desirable. These include persistence, support for garbage collection, concurrent-user access, etc.

Object-based persistent languages, for example PS-ALOGOL (Persistent Programming research Group, 1987), allow data structures created in RAM to survive longer than the programs that created them. From an architectural point of view, the most important attribute of a persistent object store would appear to be the ability to access objects of various sizes without requiring *a priori* knowledge of their physical location or cardinality. In addition, a persistent object store should allow:

- maintenance of structural relationships between objects;
- protection of (logical sets of) objects;
- ability to modify large structures in place.

These requirements imply some form of isolation from physical addressing, so that names used for objects at the applications programming level are carried through to the storage level, regardless of memory technology. This 'universal naming' may be mechanized by some form of one-level associative (i.e. content-addressable) memory. In particular, we might envisage that the tuple-sets of section 3 are all held in one very large, associatively-accessed, table. When retrieving information from this table, the atoms in an interrogand are the same bit-patterns as the named atoms used by an applications programmer.

In an associative, i.e. content-addressable, memory, some of the problems of garbage-collection are reduced because physical slots which become vacant can be re-used without formality (physical location is irrelevant to data retrieval). A more intriguing problem is how to manage data movement (i.e. 'paging') within a hierarchy of associative units. This is related to protection (i.e. locking). In Lavington *et al.* (1987) we present a scheme for memory management known as 'semantic caching' which uses descriptors similar to the tuple interrogands of section 3 to identify logical tuple-sets of varying granularity. Relatively straightforward logical tests on descriptors will determine whether a particular tuple-set is wholly, partly, or not at all contained in the fast cache section of an associative memory hierarchy. More details will be found in Lavington *et al.* (1987).

There are several examples of the application of CAM techniques to symbolic processing. At the disk level, there are database machines such as Teradata (Page, 1990). At the other extreme, there are special-purpose VLSI chips such as PAM (Robinson, 1986). We know of no affordable CAM technology that will offer the flexibility to store large quantities of tuple-sets of a variety of formats, as implied by the general data type representation proposed in section 3. Relying on disk alone tends to push the processing of data structures back into the locus of computational control (i.e. a CPU), which goes against the philosophy of whole-structure processing and the active memory. In the next section we describe prototype SIMD hardware that appears to offer direct support for a useful range of primitive operations on data structures, in the context of an associatively-accessed active memory unit.

7 PROTOTYPE PARALLEL HARDWARE MECHANIZATION OF THE ACTIVE MEMORY

From the top-down requirements presented in sections 3 and 4, it is clear that support for primitive operations on bulk data types greatly benefits from the provision of large volumes of low-cost associative (i.e. content-addressable) memory. Fortunately, a scheme has been developed which uses SIMD techniques and conventional components to provide pseudo associative memory at no more than twice the cost per bit of normal RAM. A knowledge-base server known as the Intelligent File Store (IFS/1) using these techniques has been in operation for some years (Lavington, 1988). The techniques have been extended to support relational algebraic operations (Robinson and Lavington, 1990).

Based on this experience, a prototype active memory unit known as the IFS/2 is now nearing completion (Lavington et al., 1991).

The IFS/2 appears as a shared-memory unit to a host computer. Within the shared memory, and invisible to software, hardware hashing is used to distribute data across the available storage. This storage is also split into modules, each module being equipped with a search engine. In response to a user's query, the area of associative search is thus limited by hashing and the search itself proceeds in SIMD fashion, keeping all available search engines busy. This scheme achieves two things:

(a) the automatic and applications-independent distribution of work and data amongst available equipment;
(b) an associative memory that is modularly extensible, i.e. its search time is independent of actual memory capacity.

Briefly, the IFS/2 is an extensible architecture based on nodes. Each node has an array of SIMD search modules under the control of a transputer, acting as associative cache to an associatively-accessed SCSI disk. The present implementation has nine search engines, 9 Mbytes of cache and 700 Mbytes of disk per node, and three nodes. The 27 Mbytes of semiconductor associative memory are actually used for two purposes: half is used as a cache for the disk (thus implementing a one-level associative memory); the other half acts as three relational algebraic buffers used in set and graph operations within the active memory unit. The transputer node-controllers are linked to other transputers which look after tuple-descriptor housekeeping (see below), the implementation of complex functions on tuple fields, presentational tasks such as the sorting of responders, and communication with a host computer.

The implementation of the IFS/2 active memory unit is described more fully in Lavington et al. (1991). From a programmer's viewpoint, the IFS/2's storage appears as a very large table of tuples of the form described in section 3. Additionally, the IFS/2 precedes each stored tuple by a <class-number> which refers to an entry in a Tuple Descriptor Table (TDT) maintained by firmware. A new TDT entry is created each time a new tuple-set is declared. Each TDT entry gives the format (i.e. number and classification of atoms) for that tuple-set, together with other housekeeping information. The format information is used to control activity during unifiability search, etc. (see section 4). Including a <class-number> with each stored tuple ensures that many independent users can store many structures in the active memory without risk of these being confused during search commands, etc. In the present implementation, 16 bits are used for the <class-number>; each tuple-set format can specify up to 128 fields.

Typical operating times for the prototype are as follows, when the data is all held within the 27 Mbytes of semiconductor associative memory. We assume ternary relations R, S, and T as test data, where: |R|, |S| = 1000 and |T| = 100. Note that the times for all but the **join** operation are relatively independent of relation cardinality.

insert a tuple:	~ 65 microsecs.
member:	~ 35 microsecs.
delete a tuple:	~ 35 microsecs.
search with one wild card:	~ 120 microsecs, plus 20 microsecs per responder.

join:

$$R \bowtie_{(1,2,3) = (1,2,3)} S = R \cap S : \text{up to 108 millisecs.}$$

$$R \bowtie_{3 = 1} T : \text{up to 27 millisecs.}$$

For small volumes of data, e.g. simple sets of cardinality less than 50, the IFS/2 prototype is unlikely to out-perform an assembler program running on a modern general-purpose workstation of comparable clock-rate (25 MHz). However, the cost-effectiveness becomes more attractive for larger data volumes and/or more complex operations. For cardinalities of about 1000, the speed-up can be expected to be between 10 and 100. We have observed IFS/1 speed-ups of up to 1000 times when querying a 100,000-tuple relation holding historical share-transaction information as 5-field tuples (Walther, 1989). The prototype thus demonstrates that the active memory principle has the potential of being implemented efficiently.

8 THE HIGH-LEVEL LANGUAGE VIEW

In the previous sections we have demonstrated the possibility of mechanizing whole-structure operations on persistent information, using the notion of **set** and **tuple**. The underlying architectural principle is that of an active memory unit, which provides add-on functionality to a conventional computer. There is now the question of integrating this low-level functionality into conventional programming systems.

Programming languages based on higher-level set primitives do exist. Perhaps SETL (Dewar *et al.*, 1983) is the best example. SETL has been used with good effect for software prototyping, but runs inefficiently because its higher-level primitives have to be mechanized by inappropriate (i.e. von Neumann) architectural support. Nevertheless, SETL demonstrates that set and relational primitives find acceptance amongst software implementers. SQL may, of course, be regarded as another way of presenting relational operations. We are currently implementing an SQL interface to the IFS/2. Interfaces are also planned for CLIPS, an OPS5-like production-rule development environment, and for Prolog. These higher-level programming systems build on a C procedural interface briefly illustrated in section 9.

It is not the purpose of this chapter to invent yet another programming language. We content ourselves with presenting a repertoire of useful set and relational and graph operations relevant to smart information systems, and discussing (in section 9) their run-time support via C library procedures which make direct call to the IFS/2 parallel hardware. The repertoire of useful set and relational operations is straightforward, and can be described as follows:

(1) **Operations on data of type set:**

   member, intersect, difference, union, duplicate removal, subset.

(2) **Operations on data of type relation (a subtype of set):**

   insert, delete, select, project, join, product, division, composition.

(3) **Aggregate primitives for sets/relations:**

   cardinality, maximum, minimum, average, sum, count, count unique.

The actual format for the corresponding low-level commands and their procedural parameters are discussed in section 9, where sample C program fragments are given.

Operations on graphs, as represented by relations, are more open to debate. A suggested repertoire is as follows:

(4) **Whole-graph operations producing one or more graphs as result. Each resultant graph is a tuple-set of node-arc pairs.**

   Transitive Closure (Relation Closure). Find Component Partitions. Find all maximum cliques

(5) **Graph operations producing either a set of discrete nodes or a set of discrete edge pairs as result.**

   Find the set of vertices reachable from a set of one or more specified vertices. Find the set of edges reachable from a set of one or more specified vertices (i.e. return a subgraph). Find the set of vertices at distance N from a specified vertex. (This is sometimes referred to as the Nth wave.) Find the path(s) between two specified vertices.

(6) **Graph operations producing a boolean result.**

Is the graph connected? Is node i accessible from node j? Is node i connected to node j? Is a graph cyclic or acyclic? Sub-graph matching: is a specified graph a subgraph of another specified graph? Say whether a specified set, N, of vertices in a specified graph, G, is a clique (i.e. every pair of nodes in N is connected by an edge in G).

(7) **Labelled graph aggregate operations, producing an integer result.**

Give the shortest path between nodes a and b. Give the longest path between nodes a and b. For a graph having weighted arcs, given the arc average. For a graph having weighted nodes, give the node average.

Graph traversal is breadth-first, with a set of vertices being produced at each step. These sets of nodes are recycled within the active memory, and they may also be stored – as in the operation to find the set of reachable vertices in a graph. This has applications in deductive databases, for example, where query evaluation can be seen as graph traversal. Further comments on recursive query handling will be found in Robinson and Lavington (1990).

9   LOW-LEVEL COMMANDS

The higher-level primitives of section 8 are supported by a lower-level procedural interface. The IFS/2 active memory commands are embedded as library procedures in C. To give the flavour of the active memory interface, we present fragments of C code to illustrate the way a C systems program running on a host computer can manipulate persistent data held in the active memory.

By way of example, the IFS/2's main pattern-directed search command has the C procedure format:

ifs_search(*matching_algorithm, code, cn, query, &result*),

where:

matching_algorithm specifies one of the search modes of section 4;

code specifies three parameters for each field in the interrogand, namely a bit-mask, a compare-operator (=, >, etc.), and whether this field is to be returned in the responder-set;

cn is the tuple-set identifier (or 'class-number'), specifying the tuple-set to be searched;

query holds information on the interrogand, in the form of a tuple-descriptor giving the characterization of atoms (see section 3) and the actual field values;

&*result* is a pointer to a buffer in the host which contains information on the result of the search. This buffer contains a header giving:

(i) a repeat of the *query* parameter;

(ii) the descriptor of the responder tuple-set (including a new class_number allocated to it by the IFS/2);

(iii) the cardinality of this responder tuple-set. In the software simulator version of the IFS/2, the header is then followed by a buffer containing the first n fields of the responder-set itself; in the actual IFS/2 hardware, the responder-set is held in the unit's associative memory, according to the active memory's default of treating all information (including derived 'working' sets) as persistent.

When manipulating persistent structures, e.g. via the active memory's relational algebraic operations, the present IFS/2 procedural interface builds on the existing C file-handling syntax. This is illustrated by the following fragment of host C program. We assume that three structures called Alf, Bill and Chris are being manipulated, and that each structure is stored as a single base relation. Of these, let us assume that Alf already exists in the IFS/2's persistent associative memory, that Bill is to be created during the execution of the present program, and that Chris is the name we wish to give to the result of **joining** Alf and Bill. In other words:

Chris := **join** (Alf, Bill),

according to specified, compatible, join fields. The following program fragment assumes that the types IFS_ID, IFS_BUFFER, and IFS_TUPLE are defined in the included library file ifs.h; the last two are structures and the first is a 32-bit integer holding a structure's <class-number>. Assume that we already know from a previous program that the <class-number> of Alf = 1. The program loads tuples from a host input device into the new structure Bill, and then performs the required join:

```
#include "ifs.h"
main()
{
```

```
IFS_ID              Bill,
                    Alf = 1,
                    Chris;
IFS_BUFFER          *Bill_buf;
TUPLE               t1;

Bill = ifs_declare(<type>);
if ((Bill_buf = ifs_open_buf(Bill, "w")) != NULL);
{
        while ( <there are more tuples to be written> )
        {
                <set t1 to next tuple>
                ifs_write(Bill_buf, t1);
        }
        ifs_close_buf(Bill_buf);
        /*the join command*/
        Chris = ifs_filter_prod(Alf, Bill, <join parameters>);


}
}
```

ifs_filter_prod is a generalized relational command which has the following C procedural format:

ifs_filter_prod *(cn1, cn2, expr e, expr_list el)*

This forms the cartesian product of tuple-sets cn1 and cn2, then filters the result by (e, el) as follows:

expr and *expr_list* are structures defined in the header file 'ifs.h'. A structure of type *expr* represents an expression constructed from the usual boolean and arithmetic operators. The third argument in **ifs_filter_prod** should represent a boolean expression; the fourth should be a list of integer-valued expressions which define the contents of the output relation. These two arguments together specify a combined **selection** and **projection** operation, which in IFS/2 terminology we call a **filter**. The various relational **join** operations are special kinds of **ifs_filter_prods**.

It is important to note that all **ifs** commands in the above program fragments are sent down a communications-link to an attached active memory unit, where they cause hardware actions that procede independently of the host CPU. The result is a reasonably direct route between a high-level primitive and its corresponding hardware support.

10 CONCLUSIONS

To be useful, architectural support for smart information systems must not only offer raw performance improvement. Perhaps more importantly, it must reduce software complexity because complexity is the main cause of total system cost to the end-user. The approach taken in this chapter has been to identify frequently-used generic tasks, and then to move responsibility for these tasks to hardware. By analogy, this is equivalent to providing add-on hardware support for common tasks such as floating-point arithmetic or graphics primitives.

In the case of smart information systems, the most difficult job is to devise a commonly-agreed formalism for knowledge representation and a consequential repertoire of useful operations on the resulting data structures. The formalism and repertoire must be applications- and language-independent. We propose a representation based on the well-understood notions of tuple and set which, together with a rich choice of actions for pattern-directed search, form a suitable basis for defining whole-structure operations on sets, relations and graphs.

We have described an add-on **active memory** unit, in which SIMD techniques are employed to exploit whole-structure parallelism in a manner that requires no effort on the part of the applications programmer. This unit, known as the IFS/2, also offers a solution to the hardware problem of partitioning data and work amongst resource-nodes in a modular architecture. A prototype hardware implementation at Essex has indicated that speed-ups in the range 10 to 100 times are readily achievable for whole-structure operations. A simple C procedural interface provides a smooth path between higher-level data-processing primitives and low-level hardware support.

11 POSTSCRIPT

Since writing this chapter (January 1992) the IFS/2 hardware unit has been re-engineered and a 'production' version demonstrated at the annual SERC/DTI Information Technology Conference in March 1993. The CLIPS and SQL interfaces described in section 8 have been implemented. The performance has been reported in a paper entitled 'Exploiting parallelism in primitive operations on bulk data types: somersaults', by Lavington *et al.*, *Computers and Artificial Intelligence*, Vol. 12, No. 4, 1993, pages 313 − 336. The IFS/2's procedural interface of section 9 has now been replaced by a more composed, expression-tree interface. The graph operations have been generalized into a family of Least Fixpoint operators.

12 ACKNOWLEDGEMENTS

It is a pleasure to acknowledge the contribution of other members of the IFS team at Essex. Particularly, Jenny Emby and Andy Marsh contributed to the IFS/2 hardware design; Martin Waite, Jiwei Wang and Neil Dewhurst were responsible for the software simulator; Jerome Robinson and Edward Tsang have contributed to the definition of relational and graph operations. The work described in this chapter has been supported by SERC grants GR/F/06319, GR/F/61028 and GR/G/30867.

REFERENCES

Arvind, Nikhil, K. K. and Pingali, R. S.(1987) I-Structures: Data Structures for Parallel Computing, MIT LCS (CSG Memo 269), Cambridge, MA, February.

Dewar, R. B. K., Schonberg, E. and Schwartz, J. T. (1983) *High-Level Programming – An Introduction to the Programming Language SETL*, Courant Institute of Math. Sciences, New York.

Hillis, W. D. (1987) *The Connection Machine*, The MIT Press.

Lavington, S. H. (1988) Technical Overview of the Intelligent File Store, *Knowledge-Based Systems*, 1(3), June, pp. 166–172.

Lavington, S. H., Emby, J. M., Marsh, A. J., James, E. E. and Lear, M. J. (1991) A Modularly Extensible Scheme for Exploiting Data Parallelism, *Third International Conference on Transputer Applications*, Glasgow, 1991. Published in *Applications of Transputers 3*, IOS Press, 1991, pp. 620–625.

Lavington, S. H., Standring, M., Jiang, Y. J., Wang, C. J. and Waite, M. E. (1987) Hardware Memory Management for Large Knowledge Bases, *Proceedings of PARLE, the Conference on Parallel Architectures and Languages Europe*, Eindhoven, June 1987, pp. 226–241 (Published by Springer-Verlag as *Lecture Notes in Computer Science*, Nos. 258 & 259).

Page, J. (1990) High Performance Database for Client/server Systems, *UNICOM Seminar on Commercial Parallel Processing*, London, June, pp. 21–42. Also published in: *Parallel Processing and Data Management* (Valduriez, Ed.), pp. 33-51, Chapman and Hall, 1992.

Persistent Programming Research Group (1987) PS_ALGOL Reference Manual, Fourth Edition, Persistent Programming Research Report No. 12., Department of Computing Science, University of Glasgow and Department of Computational Science, University of St. Andrews.

Robinson, I. (1986) A Prolog Processor Based on a Pattern Matching Memory Device, *Proceedings Third Int. Conf. on Logic Programming*, London, pp. 172–179 (Springer-Verlag, *LNCS* 225).

Robinson, J. and Lavington, S. H. (1990) A Transitive Closure and Magic Functions Machine, *Proceedings of the Second International Symposium on Databases in Parallel and Distributed Systems*, Dublin, July, pp. 44–54 (IEEE Computer Society Press).

Stalfo, S. J. and Miranker, D. P. (1984) DADO: A Parallel Processor for Expert Systems, *Proc. IEEE Conf. on Parallel Processing*, pp. 92–100.

Walther, H. (1989) Performance Measurement of the Associative Memory IFS at the Artificial Intelligence Applications Institute at Edinburgh, 13th November 1989 – 24th November 1989, UBILAB Report 2/89, February 1989, Union Bank of Switzerland, Zurich.

Wong, K. F. (1991) Architectures of knowledge-based machines, *ICL Technical Journal*, 7(4), November, pp. 815–841.

PART 3

Software Tools and Programming Models

9 The PVM Concurrent Computing System

V. S. Sunderam
Department of Mathematics and Computer Science
Emory University, Atlanta

1 INTRODUCTION

High-performance computing, particularly in scientific domains, is increasingly based on parallel processing. One form of parallel or concurrent computing, using portable software systems or environments on general purpose networked computing platforms, has gained tremendous popularity in recent years. Several such software systems that support this model are in widespread use. Two important factors contributing to their success are cost effectiveness (as compared to traditional hardware multiprocessors), and high usability as a result of widely portable implementations, support tools and straightforward interfaces. Examples of such systems are Isis (Birman and Marzullo, 1989), Linda (Arango et al., 1990), Express (Kolawa, 1991) and PVM (Sunderam, 1990). It should be noted that these systems, referred to hereafter as 'environments', are distinct from distributed operating systems, which are native kernel level implementations. Wide-ranging experiences (in terms of quantity and diversity of use) during the past several years has firmly established the viability and effectiveness of concurrent computing tools such as those mentioned above, and it is the general consensus of the high-performance scientific computing community that these systems will continue to play an active role in concurrent computing in the near-term future.

Concurrent computing environments offer several programming interfaces, but with the exception of a few (notably Linda), they are uniformly based on some variant of message passing. While early transitions to this model from traditional vector machines and share-memory multiprocessors met with some resistance, message passing is now widely accepted as the normal programming and computing model for most parallel machines, as well as for many of the software environments that emulate parallel computers. Essentially, the model is based on collections of asynchronously executing processes that interact and cooperate via the exchange of messages. On many multiprocessors, the process-processor binding is one-to-one, but software systems such as PVM remove this restriction for greater flexibility. Typical manifestations of this model, both on hardware multiprocessors and software environments, consist of user-level libraries that are bound into application programs – these libraries provide facilities for process management, communication, synchronization and certain auxiliary functions.

The PVM system is a software infrastructure that permits collections of heterogeneous machines to be used as a general-purpose, message-passing parallel computer. Under PVM, a user defined collection of serial, parallel and vector computers appears as one large distributed-memory computer. Throughout this chapter the term 'virtual machine' will be used to designate this logical distributed-memory machine. The PVM user library contains functions to start up tasks on the virtual machine and allows the tasks to communicate and synchronize with each other. Applications, which can be written in Fortran 77 or C, can be parallelized by using message-passing constructs common to most distributed-memory computers. By sending and receiving messages, multiple tasks of an application can cooperate to solve a problem in parallel.

PVM supports heterogeneity at the application, machine and network level. Users may exploit this feature in several ways; for instance, PVM allows application tasks to exploit the architecture best suited to their solution. PVM handles all data conversion that may be required if different computers in the virtual machine use different data representations, in addition to making transparent other inconsistencies between machines in terms of architecture and operating system facilities, thereby providing for machine heterogeneity. PVM also permits the virtual machine to be interconnected by a variety of different networks.

The PVM project started in the summer of 1989 at Oak Ridge National Laboratory (ORNL) and is now an ongoing collaborative research project at Emory University, ORNL, and the University of Tennessee (UT), It is a basic research effort aimed at advancing science, and is wholly funded by research appropriations from the U.S. Department of Energy, the National Science Foundation and the State of Tennessee. Owing to its experimental nature, the PVM project produces software that is of utility to researchers in the scientific community and to others. This software is and has been distributed freely in the interest of advancement of science, and is being used in computational applications around the world.

In the next section, we discuss the PVM computing model and describe the programming interface as well as an operational overview, noting aspects that have undergone evolutionary changes over the duration of the project. We then discuss our experiences with scientific computing using PVM, and present some performance figures based on its use. While the predominant use of PVM has thus far been in high-performance scientific computing, it is also evolving into a valuable framework for general purpose distributed computing, particularly in commercial applications involving databases and transaction processing. The system is undergoing enhancements to support the requirements of such applications, and we briefly describe our preliminary accomplishments in this respect. The chapter finally presents some concluding remarks and outlines near- and long-term research and implementation plans.

2 THE PVM SYSTEM

PVM (Parallel Virtual Machine) is a software system that permits the utilization of a heterogeneous network of parallel and serial computers as a unified general and flexible concurrent computational resource. The PVM system (Sunderam, 1990) initially supported the message passing, shared memory and hybrid paradigms, thus allowing applications to use the most appropriate computing model for the entire application or for individual sub-algorithms. However, support for emulated shared-memory was omitted as the system evolved, since the message-passing paradigm was the model of choice for most scientific parallel processing applications. Processing elements in PVM may be scalar machines, distributed- and shared-memory multiprocessors, vector super-computers and special purpose graphics engines, thereby permitting the use of the best suited computing resource for each component of an application. This versatility is valuable for several large and complex applications including global environmental modeling (Narang et al., 1990), fluid dynamics simulations (Lozier and Rehm, 1989), and weather prediction applications. However, the full effectiveness of the PVM system can be realized, with significant benefits, on common hardware platforms such as a local network of general purpose workstations.

The PVM system is composed of a suite of user-interface primitives supporting software that together enable concurrent computing on loosely coupled networks of processing elements. Some of the prominent advantages of the system are:

- the ability to execute in existing network environments without the need for specialized hardware or software enhancements or modifications,
- support for multiple parallel computation models, particularly useful in conjunction with support for multiple hardware architectures,
- integral provision of debugging and administrative facilities, using interactive graphical interfaces,
- support for fault-tolerance and partially degraded execution in the presence of machine or network failures,
- auxiliary profiling and visualization tools that permit post-mortem analysis of program behaviour.

136 Parallel Information Processing

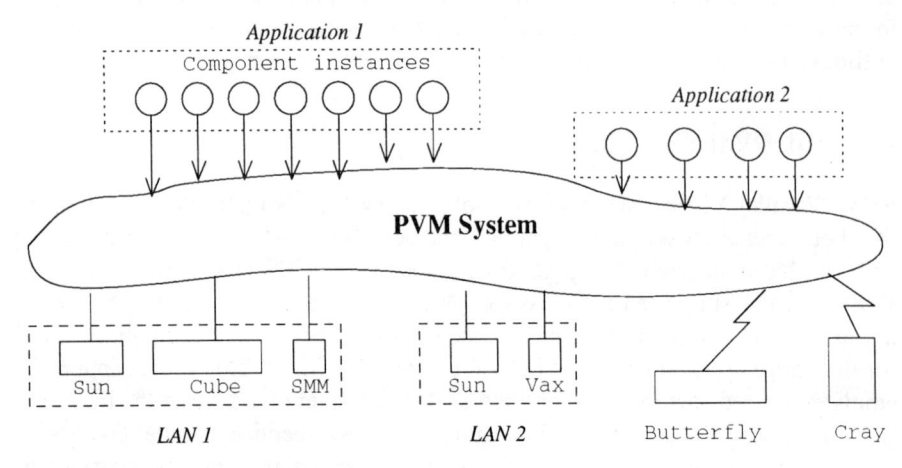

FIGURE 9.1. PVM system overview.

2.1 Architectural description

PVM may be implemented on a hardware base consisting of different machine architectures, including single CPU systems, vector machines and multi-processors. These computing elements may be interconnected by one or more networks, which may themselves be different (e.g. one implementation of PVM operates on Ethernet, the Internet, and a fibre optic network). These computing elements are accessed by applications via a standard interface that supports common concurrent processing paradigms in the form of well-defined primitives that are embedded in procedural host languages.

Application programs are composed of *components* that are subtasks at a moderately large level of granularity. During execution, multiple instances of each component may be initiated. Figure 9.1 depicts a simplified architectural overview of the PVM system.

Application programs view the PVM system as a general and flexible parallel computing resource. This resource may be accessed at three different levels: the *transparent* mode in which component instances are automatically located at the most appropriate sites, the *architecture-dependent* mode in which the user may indicate specific architectures on which particular components are to execute, and the *low-level* mode in which a particular machine may be specified. Such layering permits flexibility while retaining the ability to exploit particular strengths of individual machines on the network. The PVM user interface is strongly typed; support for operating in a heterogeneous environment is provided in the form of special constructs that selectively perform machine-dependent data conversions where necessary. Inter-instance communication constructs include those for the exchange of data structures as well as high-level primitives such as broadcast, barrier synchronization, mutual exclusion and rendezvous.

Application programs under PVM may possess arbitrary control and dependency structures. In other words, at any point in the execution of a concurrent application, the processes in existence may have arbitrary relationships between each other and, further, any process may communicate and/or synchronize with any other. This is the most unstructured form of crowd computation, but in practice a significant number of concurrent applications are more structured. Two typical structures are the tree and the 'regular crowd' structure. We use the latter term to denote crowd computations in which each process is identical; frequently such applications also exhibit regular communication and synchronization patterns. Any specific control and dependency structure may be implemented under the PVM system by appropriate use of PVM constructs and host language control flow statements.

Multiprocessing on loosely coupled networks provides facilities that are normally not available on tightly coupled multiprocessors. Debugging support, fault tolerance in the form of checkpoint-restart, uniprocessor level I/O facilities and profiling and monitoring to identify hot-spots or load imbalances within an application are examples. On the other hand, several obstacles and difficulties are also associated with networked concurrent computing. Among these are generating and maintaining multiple object modules for different architectures, considerations of security and intrusion into personal workstations, and a number of administrative and housekeeping functions. In its present form, PVM supports two auxiliary components that provide some desirable features and overcome several of the obstacles. First, the HeNCE interface is a graphical tool that eases many of the application tasks of specifying components, handling input and output, interacting with PVM during execution, managing multiple objects and providing a debugging interface.

Second, PVM is undergoing extensions to provide a uniform programming interface, in a vein similar to the PICL library (Geist *et al.*, 1990) that supports portable parallel programming and profiling.

2.2 Operational overview

The PVM system is composed of two parts. The first part is a daemon, called *pvmd*, that resides on all the computers comprising the virtual machine. Pvmd is designed so any user with a valid login can install this daemon on a machine. To run a PVM application, the user executes pvmd on one of the machines, specifying a list of other hosts that together form the virtual machine for this particular session. This first pvmd in turn starts up the daemons on each of the others, and the set of daemons cooperate via distributed algorithms to initialize the virtual machine. The PVM application can then be started by executing a program on any of these computers; the usual method is for this manually started program to spawn other application processes, using PVM facilities. Multiple users may configure overlapping virtual machines, and each user can execute several PVM applications simultaneously.

The second part of the system is a library of PVM interface routines (*libpvm.a*). This library contains user callable routines for message passing, spawning processes, coordinating tasks, and modifying the virtual machine. Application programs must be linked with this library to use PVM.

2.3 The HeNCE subsystem

HeNCE is a tool that greatly simplifies the writing of parallel programs (Beguelin *et al.*, 1991a). In HeNCE, the programmer explicitly specifies parallelism between subroutines by drawing a graph where nodes in the graph represent subroutines written in either Fortran or C. The programmer must supply the HeNCE graph and the source code for the subroutine nodes. HeNCE will automatically execute the subroutines in parallel (whenever possible) across a network of heterogeneous machines. The programmer does not need to use any parallel programming primitives and does not need to write any code beyond that supplied for the node subroutines. HeNCE relies on the PVM system (Beguelin *et al.*, 1991b) for process initialization and communication. Programmers wishing to write explicit message passing parallel programs on a network of machines should explore using the PVM system directly.

HeNCE is composed of five integrated graphical tools. The compose tool allows a programmer to specify the parallelism of an application by drawing a graph describing dependencies between user defined procedures. HeNCE uses the graph to automatically write the parallel program. With the configure tool the user specifies a network of heterogeneous computers to be used as a parallel virtual machine and defines a cost matrix between machines and procedures. The build tool uses the configuration and cost matrix to compile and install the procedures written by the first tool on the appropriate machines. The execute tool dynamically maps procedures to machines for execution of the application and collects tracing information. Finally, there is a trace tool that reads the trace information and displays an animation of the execution, either in real time for debugging or later for performance analysis.

2.4 PVM version 3.0

The PVM model, interfaces, implementation and portability have proven sound enough that several hundred sites are actively using the system. Such widespread use has aided system evolution enormously, a substantial part of these changes being attributable to user feedback. As a result, the third major version (3.0) of PVM is imminent; prior versions included 1.0 (not publicly released) and 2.0–2.4 (each with a few minor release versions). The basic computing model remains the same in PVM 3.0; however, the system core has been completely redesigned for improved performance, scalability and fault tolerance while maintaining PVM's high standards of portability and robustness. Important modifications are briefly outlined in this section. Specific syntax and detailed explanations of the 3.0 system are omitted from this chapter since the specification was subject to change prior to system release scheduled for 2Q 1993.

Based on user feedback and internal changes deemed necessary, the user interface has been somewhat modified in 3.0. Most changes are syntactic, although a few semantic changes were also required. One fundamental change involves process identification and addressing; processes in 3.0 are represented by an integer task identifier (called the *tid*), while in previous versions, processes were identified by a component name and instance number pair. The tid is the primary and most efficient method of identifying processes in PVM. Since tids must be unique across the entire virtual machine, they are supplied by the system. PVM 3.0 contains several routines that return tid values so that the user application can identify other processes in the system. Although less efficient, processes can still be identified by a name and instance number by joining a group. A user defines a group name and PVM returns a unique instance number for this process in this group.

A significant new feature in PVM 3.0 is support for certain forms of failure resilience. If a host (i.e. a computer in a virtual machine) fails, PVM will automatically detect this and delete the host from the virtual machine. The status of hosts can be inspected by the application, and if required a replacement host can be added. It is still the responsibility of the application developer to make his application tolerant of host failure. PVM makes no attempt to automatically recover processes that are aborted because of a host failure. Another use of this feature would be to add more hosts as they become available, for example on a weekend, or if the application dynamically determines it could use more computational power.

Version 3.0 also contains provisions for dynamic process groups. In PVM, functions that logically deal with groups of processes such as broadcast and barrier use the user's explicitly defined group names as arguments. Groups may overlap, and a process can belong to multiple groups. Routines are provided for processes to join or to leave a group. Processes can query for information about other group members.

Finally, version 3.0 contains facilities that enable straightforward integration of hardware multiprocessors into a virtual machine. PVM was originally developed for concurrent computation across multiple, interconnected, but independent, machines. As a result, to exploit true multiprocessors such as the Intel iPSC/860, it was necessary to write a PVM program for the 'host' processor that received messages from the external network, and routed them to individual nodes using the native message-passing routines on the machine. Similarly, for messages from a node destined for an external machine, the PVM program on the host converted these messages from native format to PVM format and routed them over the network. With PVM 3.0 the dependence on network specific mechanisms is relaxed, and communication within multiple network types as well as across them is transparently handled. For example, programs written in PVM 3.0 can run on a network of SUN's, on a group of nodes on an Intel Paragon, on multiple Paragons connected by a network, or a heterogeneous combination of multiprocessor computers that are geographically distributed. PVM 3.0 is designed to use vendor specific communication calls within a multiprocessor.

3 SCIENTIFIC COMPUTING EXPERIENCES

The PVM system has been used for the execution of a variety of application codes on different networks, each with its unique mix of processing elements. Example applications that have been executed under PVM include matrix factorization, stochastic simulation of toroid networks and Mandelbrot image computations. In this section we describe in detail two applications that are drawn from the domain of scientific computing, and are large, computationally intensive codes that are well known. The first is an application that models the physical properties of complex substitutionally disordered materials, and the second is a molecular dynamics application.

3.1 Superconductivity studies

The first application models the physical properties of complex substitutionally disordered materials. A few important examples of physical systems and situations in which substitutional disorder plays a critical role in determining material properties include: metallic alloys, high-temperature superconductors, magnetic phase transitions and metal/insulator transitions. The algorithm is an implementation of the Korringa, Kohn and Rostoker coherent potential approximation (KKR-CPA) method for calculating the electronic properties, energetics and other ground state properties of substitutionally disordered alloys (Stocks *et al.*, 1978).

The KKR-CPA parallel algorithm was executed under the PVM system using several combinations of different numbers of IBM RS/6000 Powerstations. For each of these experiments, no source code changes were made; only the

PVM host pool and application input files were modified as appropriate. Owing to the inherent differences in processor speed between the model 320, model 530 and model 550 Powerstations that were used, the number of energies was varied so as to approximately balance the load on each processor. Table 9.1 shows the effective megaflop rate achieved by the PVM system for the KKR-CPA algorithm on different combinations of IBM RS/6000 Powerstations. In the 13-machine experiment, 4 model 320 systems and 7 model 530 systems were physically on a single Ethernet network, while the remaining 530 and 550 systems were geographically distant, and accessed via a 1.5 Mb T1 link. In all other experiments, all RS/6000 systems were interconnected by a single Ethernet network. It can be seen from the table that near linear speedups were attained for this application, owing to the relatively high computation-to-communication ratio. More significant is the extremely high computational rate, particularly considering that speeds in excess of 250 Mflops could be achieved using existing, general purpose RS/6000 Powerstations, interconnected by existing networks that were in simultaneous use for other activities. Of particular note is the relative price-performance ratio of the PVM system on IBM RS/6000 Powerstations as compared to supercomputers and hardware multiprocessors; an abbreviated listing is shown in Table 9.2.

TABLE 9.1. Performance of HiTc on various PVM – IBM RS/6000 Configurations.

Model 320		Model 530	
nproc	Mflops	nproc	Mflops
serial	18.2	serial	24.4
2	31.3	2	45.9
4	63.1	4	92.2
N/A	—	7	161.9
6 (530's) + 4 (320's)			206.5
7 (530's) + 4 (320's)			226.0
1 (550) + 8 (530's) + 4 (320's)			261.0

TABLE 9.2. Price-performance ratios for HiTc applciation.

Machine	List Price	Mflops	Mflops/$M
PVM (4×320+6×530)	$252K	207	822
Cray YMP (8 procs)	$20M	2290	114
iPSC/860 (128 procs)	$3M	2527	842

3.2 Molecular Dynamics Simulations

Another scientific computing application in which very high levels of performance have been achieved using PVM on RS/6000 Powerstations is classical molecular dynamics. Molecular Dynamics (MD) simulations are commonly used to calculate static and dynamic properties of liquid and solid state systems (Plimpton, 1990). This application treats each of the N atoms (or molecules) as a point mass, and Newtons equations are then integrated to move each atom forward in time. Individual force equations are derived for each atom based on the potential energy functional for the system. The algorithms discussed in this section pertain to the general class of MD problems in which (a) only short range forces are of interest; (b) atoms diffuse, i.e. each atom's neighbors change as the simulation progresses; and (c) systems consisting of a few hundred to several thousand atoms (relatively small systems) are considered.

MD algorithms are inherently parallel, as discussed in Nguyen *et al.* (1985). Several parallel algorithms for MD simulations have been developed, and executed on a variety of vector and multiprocessor architectures, ranging from the Cray-XMP vector supercomputer to 1024-node hypercubes. A detailed discussion of the algorithms, speedups and problems in parallelizing this code may be found in the literature. The results reported indicate that MD simulations for small systems (200–2000 atoms) require approximately equal times on the Cray-XMP and on a 1024-node Ncube/2 hypercube. For larger systems (2000–10000 atoms), parallel algorithms on the Ncube/2 can execute at up to twice the speed of the Cray. These findings are consistent with the observation that as the size of the system increases, the communication to computation ratio of the parallel algorithms decreases, thereby reducing the message passing overheads in the parallel implementation.

The MD simulation algorithm was implemented on the PVM system for execution on a network of RS/6000 Powerstations. This algorithm assigns to each processor, a fixed region of space, and updates the positions of all atoms within its box in a given timestep. The PVM implementation of this MD algorithm was adapted from an algorithm originally designed for the hypercube architecture. Given the regular interconnection structure of the hypercube, the control and communication structure is also regular; essentially consisting of iterative phases of PDE solutions, followed by data exchanges along each dimension of the hypercube. The data exchanged between each computational phase consists of atom velocities and force values; typical runs involved the exchange of several hundred messages, each of the order of several hundred KB in size.

The results of the molecular dynamics application for a range of processors and problem sizes are given in Table 9.3. The table compares the execution times of PVM using a network of RS/6000 Powerstations and the iPSC/860 hypercube. For a small number of processors, PVM over a 1.2 MB/sec Ethernet is quite competitive with a hypercube with dedicated 2.8 MB/sec channels. Load imbalances became worse on PVM when eight processors were used because the workstations had different computational rates. With an even more heterogeneous mixture of machines, the load imbalances would be expected to get much worse given this application's method of parallelisation. (These load imbalances are not seen in the KKR-CPA application because its method of parallelization employs a dynamic load balancing scheme.) Nevertheless, it is encouraging to note that the PVM system performs quite well, even for the MD application which inherently has a high communication to computation ratio.

TABLE 9.3. Times in seconds for MD simulations.

	Molecular Dynamics Simulation		
PVM		Problem size	
RS/6000 procs	5×5×5	8×8×8	12×12×12
1	23	146	1030
2	15	91	622
4	12	62	340
8	6	34	184
iPSC/860 procs			
1	42	202	992
2	22	102	500
4	11	52	252
8	6	27	129

4 PVM USAGE AND APPLICATION DOMAINS

As mentioned earlier, several hundred sites are actively using PVM at the time of writing. Along with Express, Linda and Parmacs, PVM appears to be a highly viable toolkit and methodology for concurrent computing on heterogeneous networks of processing elements. In this section, we present feedback regarding PVM usage from a very small cross-section of the user community, to highlight the different application domains and hardware environments in which PVM is being utilized.

- PVM is in use at Los Alamos National Laboratory for numerically intensive computations on clusters of 16-IBM RS6000/560 workstations connected with Ethernet, FDDI and Socc.

- Lawrence Livermore Laboratory mention their use for computer aided tomo- graphy of the soft x-ray emission on the DIII-D tokamak on HP and Sun workstations and Cray supercomputers.
- A scientific computing consultancy uses PVM for large (100,000–500,000 line) scientific applications involving meteorology, photochemistry, particle dispersion and underground transport and aqueous chemistry.
- At the Colorado School of Mines, PVM is used for running seismic migration applications on several workstations. Seismic migration, which gives the subsurface image of the earth from the data recorded at the surface, is computationally intensive, especially in 3-D case. In real 3-D seismic migration, the data set is about 4 Gbytes and the computation required is of the order of several billion floating point operations They conclude that they can run a real problem on 5 IBM/RS6000-520 and 530 in about 15 hours, which is comparable to the performance on CRAY. In this application, PVM is used not only to do the computation in parallel, but also to coordinate the disk I/O in order to make the data I/O in parallel.
- At the University of Utah, researchers are developing a parallel solver for nonsymmetric partial differential equations, which they will eventually integrate into a large-scale combustion model. Currently they use PVM on a network of IBM RS/6000 model 520 workstations, connected by token ring. These processors will soon be upgraded to model 560s, and the token ring network will be replaced by an FDDI network. They also plan to offer PVM as the basis for network parallel computing on an FDDI configuration.
- At a NASA research center, PVM is being used for (1) flow simulations for a variety of problems in hypersonic, rarefied flows using the Direct Simulation Monte Carlo method (a particle method). Some of these simulations have run more or less continuously for several months on multiple SparcStations for a single problem. They are using PVM on a regular production basis on 8 SPARC-2's and have run some benchmarks using up to 32 Sparcs; (2) for a multi-discipline design and optimization code that they are implementing in a multi-computer environment; (3) for a CFD problem as well as a coarse breakdown of an optimization problem within an aircraft design and mission analysis simulation.
- The Jefferson Cancer Institute is part of the Jefferson Medical College, Thomas Jefferson University. The institute conducts basic and applied research in areas which include pharmacology, microbiology, molecular biology, molecular genetics and structural biology. Researchers have endeavored to take maximum advantage of information technologies in all

of these areas. Technologies in widespread use include: relational and object oriented databases, high performance 3D graphics, analytical tools for molecular modelling, emergent computation and genetic algorithms. PVM supports applications in many of these areas which share two common threads: (1) algorithms which lend themselves to emergent approaches; and (2) applications which integrate data and services from multiple machines.

- Several Wall Street firms are investigating the use of PVM for economic forecasting, massively parallel mortgage and interest-rate simulations, and for concurrent computation of yield analyses.
- In the Biophysics Department at the State University of New York in Buffalo, PVM is an integral part of the computing environment. Their main PVM applications concern kinetic analysis of ion channel currents. This problem is solved both by analytical and Monte Carlo simulation methods.
- At Stanford University, PVM is the message passing platform for one of the implementations of Jade, a language for writing serial, imperative programs that run in parallel on a heterogeneous collection of machines. They have implemented a sparse Cholesky factorization algorithm, a program that simulates water, and an implementation of the Barnes-Hut n-body solver.
- Also at Stanford, researchers are developing a method for protein structure prediction, for which they exhaustively search all possible tertiary conform- ations using a simplified representation of a polypeptide chain. They have constructed a parallel interface library that lets them port the code between a distributed-memory Ncube-2 system, a shared-memory Silicon Graphics 4D-240, or a network of workstations running PVM.
- At the (only) supercomputing centre in Taiwan, PVM is used for various scientific applications including Computational Fluid Dynamic equations, and incompressible Navier–Stokes equations.
- Katholieke Universiteit Leuven in Belgium uses PVM for medical image enhancement with a (time consuming) Monte Carlo algorithm.
- At the University of Chicago, researchers are running a code to calculate the primordial abundances of elements from inhomogeneous models of nucleosynthesis.
- At the University of Heidelberg, PVM is being used for molecular biology and biotechnology applications which scan databases of protein sequences for similarities that are significant in terms of protein structures or functions. The application is running on a Parsytec machine under Parix and a port to a CM5 and KSR-1 is planned.
- At Boeing, PVM is being used for a fast-response database query system.

- The Chemical Abstracts Service is using PVM for the storage and retrieval, in a distributed setting, of several thousands of structure diagrams and molecular information.
- Cerfacs in France use PVM for several applications, including a project that will couple a model of the ocean and a model of the atmosphere. PVM is being used to send the boundary information between the two models. The second application is a parallel algorithm for solving the global optimization problem. This algorithm is very coarse grained and extremely well suited for a heterogeneous computation environment. They are using the algorithm to solve optimization problems for planning satellite trajectories for satellites dedicated to collecting altimeter information.
- The Canadian National Research Council EGS (Electron Gamma Shower) developers, with a user base of about 5000, use PVM extensively. EGS is a public-domain Monte Carlo code that does electron gamma transport in the energy range 1 keV–20 TeV. It is ideally suited to a network operating system like PVM since it requires little internode communication.

5 GENERALIZED DISTRIBUTED COMPUTING SUPPORT

The PVM project evolved primarily in a scientific research setting and as such, its facilities were initially oriented towards supporting high-performance, distributed memory parallel programs. The use of PVM, as described in the previous section, has also been predominantly in the realm of scientific computation – thus far. Recently, however, there is evidence of significant interest in the commercial and business computing communities in technologies such as PVM, driven by increasing trends towards both distribution and the need for high-performance computing. Parallel processing in general, and environment-based systems such as PVM in particular, offers a multitude of benefits in computing applications in the commercial sector. Example application areas that could benefit from such technologies include

- groupware applications such as distributed calendar management and teleconferencing,
- group decision support systems,
- parallel processing of complex queries against massive databases,
- high speed on-line transaction processing, and
- distributed transaction processing, for faster response as well as for greater distribution and failure resilience.

As with scientific computing, there are two major motivations for considering environment-based systems such as PVM for the above and similar commercial applications, as opposed to either mainframes or hardware parallel processors. The first is cost-effectiveness – PVM can directly be utilized on *existing* hardware in terms of both computers and networking facilities. Several commercial applications are intrinsically distributed; the PVM software infrastructure provides a robust and straightforward substrate on which to implement such distributed and groupware applications. Furthermore, in typical workstation environments, a large proportion of the computing cycles are frequently idle – PVM is well-suited to utilize those resources for background compute-intensive tasks. Even in situations where hardware acquisition is necessary, clusters of workstations can be far more cost-effective than monolithic multiprocessors, and have the added advantage of being incrementally scalable and upgradable. The second motivating factor is functionality. PVM is a heterogeneous system, and can use the collective and specialized capabilities of different classes and types of computers and networks. The component computers of the virtual machine may themselves be parallel processors, supercomputers, specialized graphics engines, etc., in addition to general purpose scalar machines. This capability is very valuable in applications that inherently contain multiple, different, sub-algorithms. For example, an integrated trading system might comprise a compute-intensive rate simulation running on a hypercube, interfaced to a transaction processing system on clustered, distributed workstations which in turn access a high-speed data-server, and may be augmented with visual interaction and display systems executing on graphics workstations. Such applications are fast becoming prevalent, and heterogeneous software systems such as PVM are ideal in such circumstances, as they are capable of exploiting architectures that are most appropriate for a given subtask.

In recent attempts to utilize PVM for groupware, transaction and database-oriented applications, we discovered that although the primitive facilities were present, the required functionality suggested that a different set of abstractions were needed in order to enable convenient and straightforward implementation of these applications. The design and test implementation of this enhancement to PVM, termed the General Distributed Computing (GDC) layer, has recently been completed and is undergoing analysis and testing for suitability and performance. The GDC facilities consist of infrastructural support for the required operations, and are briefly described below:

- **Parallel IO facilities**: the GDC layer extends PVM functionality by providing support for distributed and parallel input and output to disk files as well as for terminal interaction. The standard Unix file semantics are retained to the extent possible; in addition, facilities for shared but non-conflicting reading and writing, using a variety of different inter-

leaving and consistency semantics are provided. In essence, exclusive, independent interleaved and serialized access are supported by the parallel IO subsystem. In addition, support exists for data compression and encryption, as well as for file shadowing – a valuable feature for reliability.
- **Synchronization and Locking**: the GDC sunsystem provides facilities for mutually exclusive access to resources. The model permits these resources to be application dependent – the provided primitives allow for locking an abstract resource identified by a string valued identifier and an integer. Thus applications may establish a convention according to the nature of their requirements and utilize the GDC facilities without any loss of generality or functionality, but with substantial flexibility. For example, to implement record-level file locking, applications may request a lock on the abstraction identified by the filename and record number. In addition to efficient locks, the GDC subsystem also incorporates certain deadlock detection hueristics and, based on option switches, will either attempt recovery or return control to the user after setting locks to a 'safe' state.
- **Client-Server Support**: the native PVM facilities are geared towards asynchronous, communicating processes, and do not provide sufficiently high-level access to applications using the client-server paradigm. The GDC subsystem alleviates this deficiency by permitting server components of applications to **export** services that are identified by symbolic names, and for client components to **invoke** these services in a location-transparent, hetero- geneous, and efficient manner. These features comprise a significant extension of the standard remore procedure call model in that (1) PVM and GDC automatically locate remote services; (2) support for load balancing, using multiple servers, is provided; (3) invocation semantics may be either procedure-argument based or message based; and (4) a certain level of failure resilience is built into the system.
- **Transaction Processing**: design and initial implementation and testing efforts are in progress for a distributed transaction facility in the GDC layer. This facility provides the normal transaction processing constructs including beginning and ending transactions, aborting transactions, and nested transactions. These features are consistent with the usual atomicity, consistency, isolation and durability semantics of traditional database systems. However, since the GDC layer facilities may be used in conjunction with standard PVM message passing features, certain enigmatic situations arise. For example, if a transaction's scope includes sending and receiving of messages, the correct actions in the case of an abort are unclear, as restoring the system to a previously valid state is complex and possibly intractable. We are exploring several alternatives

and will proceed incorporating these features into the GDC layer as soon as 'correct' semantics are decided upon.

Our preliminary esperiences with the GDC subsystem indicate that enhancing the PVM features to support generalized distributed computing, with specific focus on commercial, business and database applications is very valuable, and is being increasingly accepted and adopted. Our performance measurements have also been very encouraging; during testing, overheads of a few to several tens of milliseconds were observed for most of the facilities outlined above, such as locking, synchronization and parallel input and output with shadowing.

6 CONCLUSIONS AND ONGOING WORK

In this chapter, we have described the PVM system and its evolution, experiences and uses. The PVM system is a valuable environment for the concurrent execution of applications on heterogeneous networked platforms. PVM is attractive from both technical and economic viewpoints; experiences have been very encouraging and have demonstrated PVM's potential for achieving supercomputer level performance at a fraction of the cost, as well as for providing highly effective emulations of parallel machines. The latter point is especially important; literally everyone has access to high performance workstations which, if used collectively can be as effective as true hardware multiprocessors. The PVM software infrastructure is instrumental in enabling a collection of these machines to be seamlessly integrated into a coherent and flexible concurrent computing resource. Its ease of use, coupled with support for multiple concurrent programming paradigms and auxiliary tools for debugging and monitoring support, significantly increases the effectiveness of network-based computing. Ongoing and future work on the PVM system includes support for high speed fibre optic networks, enhancing the program development facilities, support for object-oriented concurrent computing, process-level fault tolerance, and increasing the efficiency of internal algorithms. We believe that the PVM approach is a viable alternative or complement to conventional supercomputing, as well as to traditional distributed computing in the commercial world.

7 ACKNOWLEDGEMENTS

This work was supported by the Applied Mathematical Sciences program, Office of Basic Energy Sciences, U. S. Department of Energy, under Grant No. DE-FG05-91ER25105, and the National Science Foundation under Grant No. CCR-91-18787).

REFERENCES

Arango, M., Berndt, D., Carriero, N., Gelernter, D. and Gilmore, D. (1990) Adventures with Network Linda, *Supercomputing Review*, 3(10), October.

Beguelin, A., Dongarra, J. J., Geist, G. A., Manchek, R. and Sunderam, V. S. (1991a) A Users' Guide to PVM Parallel Virtual Machine, Technical Report ORNL/TM-11826, Oak Ridge National Laboratory, July.

Beguelin, A., Dongarra, J., Geist, G. A., Manchek, R. and Sunderam, V. (1991b) Solving Computational Grand Challenges Using a Network of Supercomputers, in: (Ed. D. Sorensen) *Proceedings of the Fifth SIAM Conference on Parallel Processing*, SIAM, Philadelphia.

Birman, K. and Marzullo, K. (1989) ISIS and the META project, Sun Technology, pp. 90–94, Summer.

Geist, G. A., Heath, M. T., Peyton, B. W. and Worley, P. H. (1990) A machine-independent communication library, in: (Ed. J. Gustafson) *The Proceedings of the Fourth Conference on Hypercubes, Concurrent Computers, and Applications*, pp. 565–568, P. O. Box 428, Los Altos, CA, Golden Gate Enterprises.

Kolawa, A. (1991) The Express Programming Environment, *Workshop on Heterogeneous Network-Based Concurrent Computing*, Tallahassee, October.

Lozier, D. W. and Rehm, R. G. (1989) Some Performance Comparisons for a Fluid Dynamics Code, *Parallel Computing*, 11(2), pp. 305–320.

Narang, H. *et al.* (1990) Design of a simulation interface for a parallel computing environment, in: *Proc. ACM Southeastern Conf.*, April.

Nguyen, H. *et al.* (1985) A Parallel Molecular Dynamics Strategy, *J. Comput. Chem.*, 6, pp. 634.

Plimpton, S. (1990) Molecular Dynamics Simulations of Short-Range Force Systems on 1024-Node Hypercubes, in: *Proc. Fifth Distributed Memory Computing Conference*, (Ed. D. Walker and Q. Stout), IEEE Computer Society Press, pp. 478–483.

Stocks, G. *et al.* (1978) Complete Solution of the Korringa-Kohn-Rostoker Coherent Potential Approximation: Cu-Ni Alloys, *Phys. Rev. Letters*, 41, pp. 339.

Sunderam, V. (1990) PVM: A Framework for Parallel Distributed Computing, *Concurrency: Practice and Experience*, 2(4).

10 Configuration Tools for a Parallel Processing System

M. Ward, J. Hayley, J. Meadows
ICL, Wenlock Way
Manchester

1 INTRODUCTION

Parallel MIMD machines (e.g. nCUBE, Meiko) are now becoming established in the marketplace, handling large volumes of data and delivering computing power at a justifiable cost. ICL's Corporate Systems business is based mainly on commercial applications, with an emphasis on database systems. For many of our customers, these applications are 'mission-critical' and vital to the normal operation of their businesses. This leads to stringent requirements in terms of availability, fault-tolerance and manageability.

The methods adopted for resilience of data will allow non-stop file access by employing a software solution which exploits the natural redundancy available in a parallel architecture. In the event of a disk failure the user applications carry on without loss of performance and without losing their data. If an element (i.e. an individual processor) failure occurs, applications connected to the failing element see a fail and a new 'connect request' can be issued; applications connected to other elements are unaffected.

The key objectives for the file system and its management are:

- The system should provide a method of mirroring user and system data to provide resilience to disk loss and element failure.
- The system administrator should be able to specify that mirrored data can be on a remote element.
- Any resilience features should be transparent to application software.
- A disk naming scheme to enable unique identification of all disks and their physical locations is to be used.
- The system should be able to dynamically re-allocate repaired disks back to their original configuration.
- The management of the system should be no more difficult than the management of a single UNIX system.
- Graphical interfaces for file system management should be employed.
- All designs should be able to support any number of elements and disks.

The Esprit project EPOCH (European Parallel Operating System based on Chorus) is developing tools to simplify the management of a complex commercial parallel system containing up to 64 elements and 732 disks. In this chapter we review the EPOCH architecture and the file system, and then go on to describe the tools for file system management. An extension of this work into the area of planning for the filestore layout is also described.

The EPOCH file system is based on the use of Volumes which are a special form of disk partition produced by VERITAS™ Volume Manager (VxVM). VxVM provides a complex mapping of UNIX file systems and raw disk partitions onto the underlying physical disk resources. By using VxVM, it is possible to protect data against disk or element failure by maintaining multiple copies of the data; this is called a mirrored volume. Individual copies are known as plexes.

The aim of the System Management software is to give a simplified uniform management view of the machine, since trying to control such a complex system would be a nightmare if each element were to be managed independently. We have therefore provided a novel way of abstracting the components of the machine into groups of like objects which are managed as a single entity.

The work described here and previous Esprit work (EDS project, Ward et al., 1990) is being exploited by ICL in the *GOLDRUSH Mega*SERVER™ product. *GOLDRUSH* (Skeat, 1994; Butler Group, 1994) is an open database server which can act as a back-end to either UNIX™ or mainframe systems, and which provides enhanced performance for applications based on relational database technology.

2 EPOCH ARCHITECTURE

The EPOCH system (Borramann et al., 1993) contains up to 59 Processing Elements (PE), 4 Communication Elements (CE) providing external communications and a Management Element (ME). All elements are interconnected by a high-speed message passing network (DeltaNet) (Hotzner and Tomann, 1990).

The filestore is realized by use of 3.5" SCSI disks connected via SCSI-2 interfaces to their owning elements. Each PE has two wide-SCSI interfaces, each capable of supporting up to 14 disks. (In early configurations, each PE can have up to 20 GBytes of storage on 12 disks.) The CE has a single wide-SCSI interface and two independent couplers for external communications (FDDI).

The system exploits buffering and caching within the disk drives. In addition, to meet performance requirements, a substantial part of the PE's main

---

™Veritas, VxVM, VxVA and VxFS are registered trademarks of VERITAS Software Corporation in the USA and other countries.

GOLDRUSH and GOLDRUSH Mega SERVER are trademarks of International Computers Limited in the UK and other countries.

UNIX is a registered trademark in the US and other countries, licenced exclusively thorugh X/Open Company Limited.

memory (of 256 MBytes) is used to provide a suitable combination of file system and application-level caching.

The Management Element (ME) is a standard ICL UNIX Server (running the UNIX SVR4.2 Operating System) incorporating extra hardware to drive the DeltaNet. It is used to host the system management applications (Figure 10.1).

Each element runs an instance of the UNIX operating system based on Chorus™/MiX V.4 (Chorus systèmes, 1991) providing an application interface/ environment no different from that of a standard UNIX SVR4 machine. The file system is based on VERITAS VxFS which enhances the SVR4 baseline to reach 'commercial file system' standards in order to meet the needs of the Relational Database Management System (RDBMS).

Although disks are physically connected to a single element, they are viewed at the system level as being connected to all elements, thereby achieving a single coherent global filestore and thus providing a single image at the RDBMS application level.

The disk resilience scheme is based on the use of the VERITAS Volume Manager (VxVM) ported into the Chorus/MiX environment. Additional features to provide remote disk mirroring have been added by extending Chorus/MiX to make it capable of driving remote disks over the DeltaNet.

During system start-up, each element 'mounts' its own local filestore. This enables local file systems to be progressively added into the standard UNIX hierarchy of directories and files. Each file system resides on a single volume, whose plexes map onto VxVM subdisks. Since these sub-disks may physically reside on any real actual disk, then each disk potentially contains the plexes of many volumes (see Figure 10.2). At this stage each PE/CE is fully operational, with the file system hierarchy on each element being local and independent of other elements.

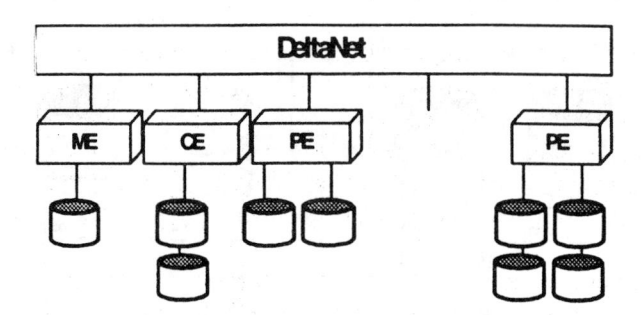

FIGURE 10.1. EPOCH hardware.

™Chorus is a registered trademark of Chorus systèmes.

154 Parallel Information Processing

At the next stage of system establishment, a series of 'remote cross-mount' operations are undertaken to attach the underlying file systems of other elements to the local file hierarchy of this element. This is undertaken in a pre-defined way so that once completed, the global file hierarchy looks the same from all elements. File path names and access to shared files at the RDBMS application level are thus identical, regardless of PE and physical location of the data. (Note that certain partitions, such as the boot file system and those containing local UNIX software, swap files, dump files, etc., are deemed to be 'local only', are replicated on each element and do not form a visible part of the global coherent filestore hierarchy).

Read and write access to the coherent filestore is via standard SVR4 SVID system call interfaces. The standard Virtual File System (VFS) structures allow different file systems to co-exist, and to support both local and remote file access (including Raw I/O). Remote access within the coherent filestore (PE-PE and PE-CE) uses an extension to the standard Chorus distributed file access. Access to the ME filestore is achieved using NFS.

Additional file system functionality at the platform level is provided by the System Management, System Establishment and Recovery components. System Establishment and Recovery includes local and central file system components which handle the establishment and resilience of the coherent filestore, thus presenting and preserving the Platform Interface to the RDBMS software layer.

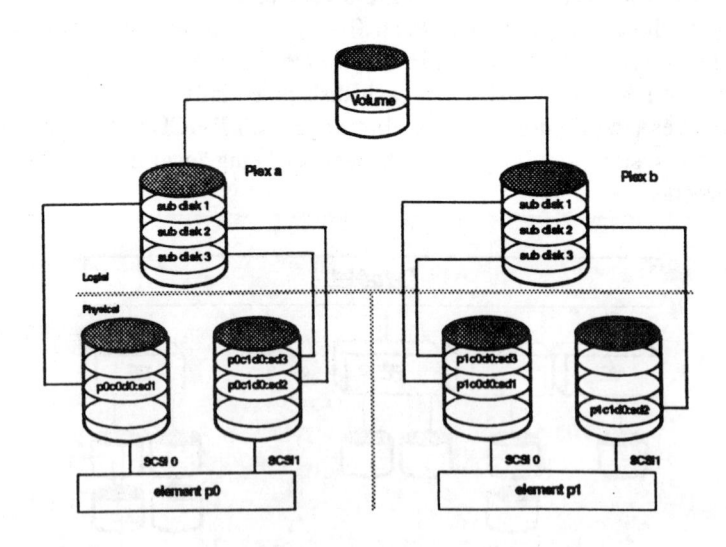

FIGURE 10.2. Disk volumes.

2.1 File system architecture

The file system software component structure within the UNIX Operating System is illustrated in Figure 10.3. This shows the major components together with the access paths for local and remote disk I/O to a mirrored filestore. The diagram shows the case for ordinary file access.

- **File Access.** This is the standard UNIX Virtual File System (VFS) layer which provides the system call interface into the file system software components.
- **Distributed file access.** This acts as the client/server agent for PE-PE remote I/O requests. It transparently routes I/O requests and data across the DeltaNet using inter-processor communications (IPC).
- **File System.** The VxFS file system maps files onto a VxVM Volume (see below). VxFS is now standard on UNIX SVR4.2 systems and provides EPOCH with 'commercial strength' file management. Its benefits include high-speed recovery in the event of an element failure.
- **Volume Manager.** VxVM presents a 'virtual disk' interface to the file system software. Mirroring, volume, plex and sub-disk management are carried out at this layer. This component translates between virtual and physical disk driving and uses the standard UNIX DDI/DKI interface.

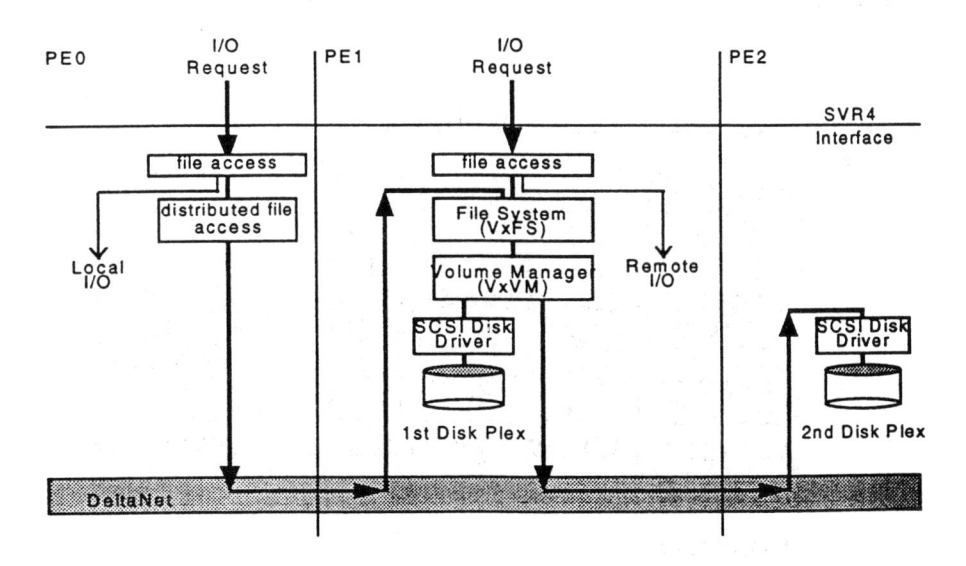

FIGURE 10.3. File system software structure.

156 Parallel Information Processing

- **SCSI Driver.** This provides physical device driving across SCSI appropriate to the selected hardware disk products.

3 CONFIGURATION MANAGEMENT

For a single-node UNIX machine, tools such as VERITAS VxVA (VERITAS) and SUN Net Manager provide excellent graphical interfaces, thereby simplifying the System Administrator's task from one of understanding UNIX commands to that of manipulating coloured graphical objects. These tools provide management of the vertical stripe (see Figure 10.4). However, if we were to treat EPOCH as 64 independent nodes, these tools would be of significant advantage for the management on each element (the vertical stripe), but would pose a real problem for the management of 64 elements due to the repetition and user time required! Therefore, we need to regard the machine as a collection of objects operating in parallel (the horizontal stripe). For this, more sophisticated management tools are required.

Tools from third party vendors were considered: monitoring tools such as Hewlett Packard's OpenView and administration tools such as Tivoli Works were evaluated, however, no-one appears to be considering the management of the filesystem for MPP platforms.

The fundamental concept behind Configuration Management is the use of 'sets' to hide the complexity of managing multiple instances. We have to manage 59 PEs, 4 CEs and a total of 732 disks, with each disk containing sub-

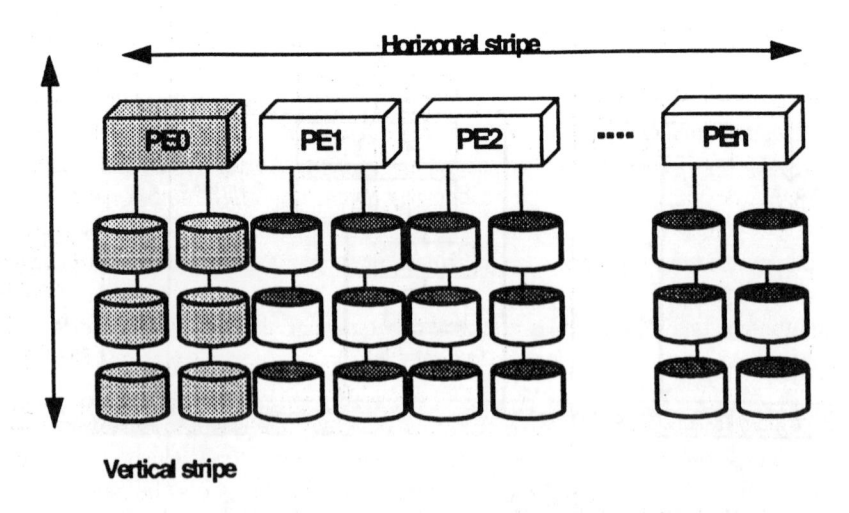

FIGURE 10.4. Management complexity.

disks from many volumes. So, instead of the traditional way of thinking in terms of disks and partitions (a vertical stripe for the management of a single node), the administrator needs to think about volume_sets and disk_group_sets (the combined vertical and horizontal stripe required for management of the parallel machine) thereby exploiting the replication properties of the machine.

Thus we give the System Administrator a 'single image' view of the system in various ways: by providing displays (showing which elements are running a database installation, or how much space is available in a group of disks holding a specific database table), and by allowing actions to manipulate a collection of objects from a single command (such as **create_volume_set**). This example (as you will see later), is very complex since it involves the use of many elements and disks. More general actions (such as **df** – the command that reports on free disk space) can be performed by broadcasting a standard UNIX command to a collection of objects. All of these methods are capable of being scaled to cope with very large numbers of elements, disks, volumes, etc.

A set can be defined to be any chosen subset of elements in the system. This not only allows a collection of objects to be managed as a single entity across many elements, but also simplifies the layout of the elements by reducing variation in the number of different 'vertical stripes'. For example, it is possible to create a database service which has an identical disk and volume layout across all the elements supporting that service.

This symmetry of layout is exploited in the EPOCH. Configuration tools make the system easier to plan, easier to configure and easier to operate. It also enables the performance of each element to be more uniform and more predictable. However, there is a trade-off here between complexity, flexibility, and manageability: in the limit, absolute performance might require a slightly different layout on each and every element, on the other hand, the use of symmetric layouts and a relatively small number of 'vertical stripe' layouts can give near-optimum performance and makes the system considerably easier to manage.

For the fine-tuning of the chosen configuration, separate capacity management tools are provided which allow the System Administrator and Database Administrator to observe the behaviour of sets and their component objects; (details of these tools are outside the scope of this chapter).

A number of requirements for management were noted in the Introduction: these include the provision of graphical user interfaces, and tools that allow the management of EPOCH to be no more difficult than that of a single-node UNIX machine. By providing these tools, we are able to improve productivity of the System Administrator and reduce the likelihood of operator errors.

An additional feature of the tools is that they do not impose any run-time contribution on the costs of running a database workload. Costs are incurred only when the System Administrator interacts with the tools themselves.

158 Parallel Information Processing

All of the tasks so far have been concerned with the day-to-day administration of the system. However, a significant task for the System Administrator and the Database Administrator is laying out the filestore. We have found that a configuration planning tool is essential in order to try out example layouts before committing them to the machine.

3.1 Set definition

As we described earlier, sets provide a mechanism for collectively naming a group of elements. The set may then be used as a single object to carry out functions on all elements within the set. Actions on sets include create_set, extend_set, delete_set and contract_set.

Sets may be created and modified via the graphical user interface and can be dynamically updated by some operational activity, either by an application, or by the System Administrator. A number of set types have been defined (Figure 10.5).

The basic type of set is the element_set which allows us to refer to a collection of elements (e.g. p0, p5, p8, c0, where p0, p5, etc. is the element identifier). A pre-defined set is created called **all_elements**.

Disks are organized by the Volume Manager into disk groups. A disk group is a named collection of disks that are logically owned by a specific element. Volumes are created within a disk group and are restricted to using those disks within that disk group. (When the volumes are mounted, they become part of the local file system.)

A simple way to replicate this structure across many elements is now required. Firstly we define a disk_group_set to replicate the disk group across an element_set. To make this easier to manage, the arrangement of disks in a disk group is identical across all elements of the disk_group_set. Typically, we

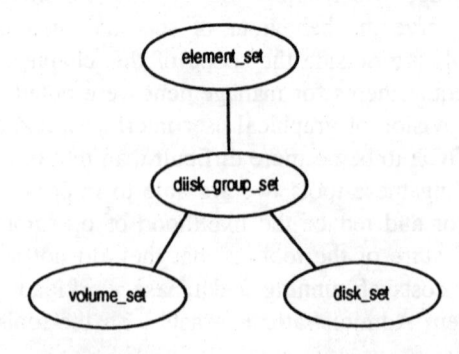

FIGURE 10.5. Set hierarchy.

only create two disk_group_sets, one for the system filestore (locally plexed) and one for the application filestore (remotely plexed).

Next we need to specify the disks within the disk group (i.e. their SCSI names); this information is replicated across the disk_group_set and is called the disk_set. There is one disk_set for each disk in the disk group (the vertical stripe) that underlies the disk_group_set.

Finally, the volume structure is replicated. A volume_set is the replication of the volume structure using a sub-set of the disks in the disk_group_set. An important characteristic is that every volume in the volume set is given identical attributes, since this simplifies the management of volumes. These attributes include size, plex-type (local-mirror, remote-mirror or simplex), file system details and mount point.

Usually, separate volume sets will be created for each separate RDBMS object, e.g. log, journal, table, etc. If desired, a volume_set can have fewer elements than the parent disk_group_set, i.e. the horizontal stripe is narrower than the width of the whole machine.

3.2 Configuration management tools

A UNIX daemon process which runs on the ME holds the EPOCH configuration database. A function call interface is provided to enable trusted application programs to create, modify and query the database. This process makes library calls to generate VxVM objects such as disk groups, volumes and plexes, and it provides interfaces to create file systems and to mount/unmount them across the named element_set.

An X-Windows/Motif-based graphical user interface program has been implemented to display two views of the configuration: the upper part of the window shows the hierarchy of sets (the set window) and the lower part of the window is used to display the configuration of an individual element (the element window) (Figure 10.6). Each set type is colour coded. The set data may be queried (double click) and can be created using the 'edit' function. A command line interface program is also provided which takes scripted commands from a file. The set database may be written to a file for archiving.

3.3 Configuration planning tools

So far we have discussed the use of platform-level tools as a means of simplifying file system layout. GOLDRUSH is aimed at the RDBMS users who like to plan their layout before committing to the machine; for these users, a planning tool is provided. This tool has an added advantage since it simplifies the laying out of filestore for the application-level objects.

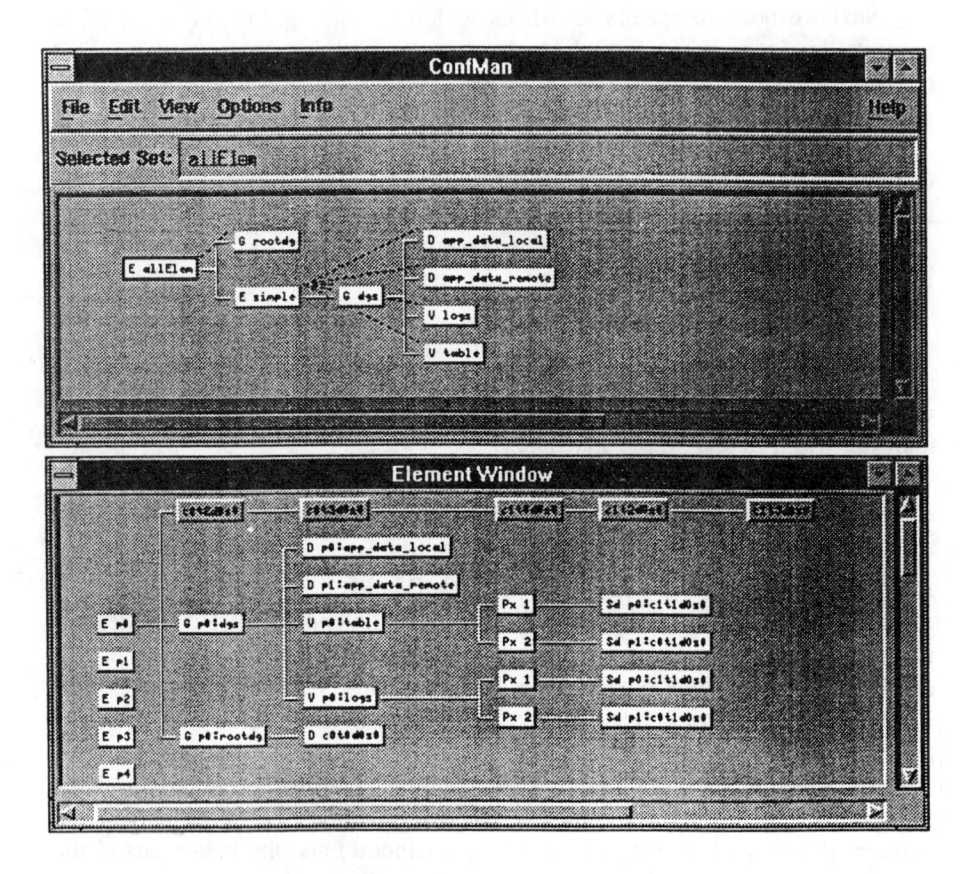

FIGURE 10.6. Configuration management user interface.

The tool is a Windows application which runs on a PC. It uses graphics and mouse control and adopts a easy-to-use point-and-click methods of specification, and pictorial summary displays. For example, to create an element set, the elements are presented as a matrix, and the System Administrator then selects the elements in the set by clicking the mouse over a particular element (highlighting it). After completing this task, the Administrator names the set.

Firstly the hardware is defined, i.e. element types and quantity, disk sizes and SCSI attachment. Next the element_sets, disk_group_sets and disk_sets are defined in much the same way as previously. To install an RDBMS on the element_set, the Database Administrator (DBA) needs maximum flexibility within the rules normally applied (e.g. keep logs and data on separate disks). The DBA is then presented with the layout in pictorial fashion, just as if it had been produced in the traditional way – using the white-board!

3.4 Example: creating a database table

The system is to be set up to use three elements (p0, p1 and p2), each of which has a locally mirrored system filestore and a remotely mirrored filestore for application data. In this example, INGRES logs and journals will be added to the filestore layout (Figure 10.7).

1 Create an element_set
To use a limited part of the EPOCH machine an element_set 'simple' containing just 3 elements p0, p1 and p2 is defined:

   create_element_set(list=p0,p1,p2, name="simple")

2 Create disk_group_sets
A disk_group_set requires the name of the set and the elements in the set. When a disk_group_set is created, disk groups for each element are created by prefixing the set name by the element name. For the system filestore a disk_group_set 'rootdg' is created:

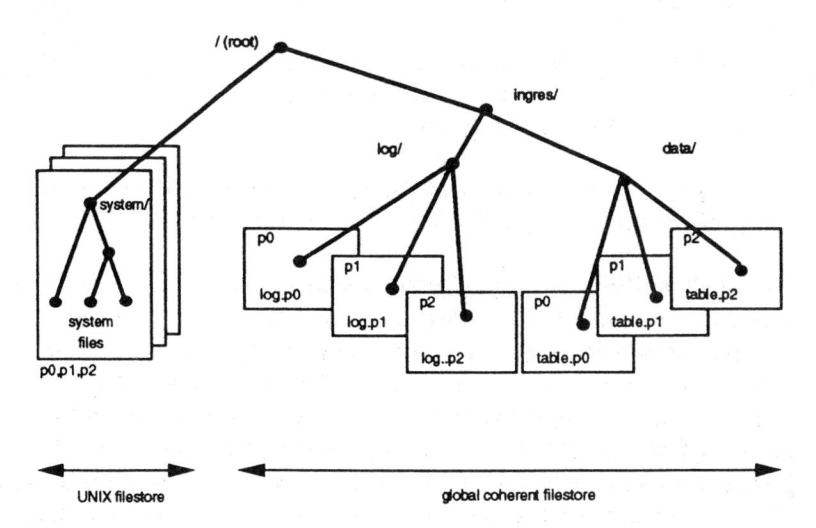

FIGURE 10.7. Example filestore layout.

create_disk_group_set(based-on="simple", name="rootdg")

- disk group 'p0:rootdg' on element p0
- disk group 'p1:rootdg' on element p1
- disk group 'p2:rootdg' on element p2

For the application a separate disk_group_set 'dgs' is created:

create_disk_group_set(based-on="simple", name="dgs")

- disk group 'p0:dgs' on element p0
- disk group 'p1:dgs' on element p1
- disk group 'p2:dgs' on element p2

At the end of this step the disk groups have been created, but each disk group is empty.

3 Create disk_sets

For the system filestore, a local mirrored arrangement is chosen and disks c0t0d0 and c1t0d0 are added to the disk_group_set 'rootdg'. Note that the category is set to local (indicating that these disks are to be used for locally mirrored file store):

create_disk_set(based-on="simple",parent="rootdg",disk_name=c0t0d0, category=local)

- disk 'p0:c0t0d0' to disk group 'p0:rootdg'
- disk 'p1:c0t0d0' to disk group 'p1:rootdg'
- disk 'p2:c0t0d0' to disk group 'p2:rootdg'

create_disk_set(based-on="simple",parent="rootdg",disk_name=c1t0d0, category=local)

- disk 'p0:c1t0d0' to disk group 'p0:rootdg'
- disk 'p1:c1t0d0' to disk group 'p1:rootdg'
- disk 'p2:c1t0d0' to disk group 'p2:rootdg'

Now disk filestore space for the application data is created using disk c1t1d1 locally and c0t1d1 remotely. The disks are mirrored in a cyclic fashion using p2 as the remote plex for p1, p3 as the remote plex for p2 and p0 as the remote plex for p3. The local plex is created first:

Configuration Tools for a Parallel Processing System 163

create_disk_set(based-on="simple",parent="dgs",disk_name=c1t1d0, category=local)

- disk 'p0:c1t1d0' to disk group 'p0:dgs'
- disk 'p1:c1t1d0' to disk group 'p1:dgs'
- disk 'p2:c1t1d0' to disk group 'p2:dgs'

The remote plex is mirrored on a different element to ensure resilience of the global filestore to element failure. Note that the category is set to remote.

create_disk_set(based-on="simple",parent="dgs",disk_name=c0t1d0, category=remote)

- disk 'p1:c0t1d0' to disk group 'p0:dgs',
- disk 'p2:c0t1d0' to disk group 'p1:dgs',
- disk 'p0:c0t1d0' to disk group 'p2:dgs'.

4 Create volume_sets

Having organized the filestore space into disk groups, the next stage is to use volume sets to create file systems and/or raw volumes corresponding to sets of filestore objects needed by the RDBMS software. A simple INGRES database service is set up with some parallel log files called logs and a parallel database table called **table**.

The first step is to create the log files in a volume set:

create_volume_set(based-on="simple",parent="dgs",name="logs", plex-type=remote-mirror,lmount=vxfs, ... , mountp="/ingres/log/log.#")

The volume set has been created in the disk_group_set 'dgs'. Each volume is remotely mirrored across PEs, and each one forms a VxFS file system. Other parameters define attributes such as size, location of plexes, etc. When a volume set is specified, a mount point must be specified for each element in the set. This determines (for each of the newly created files and volumes) their full path names within the global filestore hierarchy. To avoid the user having to type up to 64 separate mount point names, a wild-card facility is available in the Configuration Management Tool that replaces any '#' characters in the mount point string with the element identifier. Thus, the string */ingres/log/log.#* in the example above creates the following volumes:

- volume 'p0:logs' within disk group 'p0:dgs', mounted on '/ingres/log/log.p0'

- volume 'p1:logs' within disk group 'p1:dgs', mounted on '/ingres/log/log.p1'
- volume 'p2:logs' within disk group 'p2:dgs', mounted on '/ingres/log/log.p2'

The volume set for the database table would be created in a similar way:

create_volume_set(based-on="simple",parent="dgs",name="table", plex-type=remote-mirror,lmount=vxfs,........, mountp="/ingres/data/table.#")

After completing these steps the following files and directories will appear in the EPOCH global file hierarchy, and hence will be visible and accessible from the RDBMS software running in every processing element:

/ingres
/ingres/log
/ingres/log/log.p0
/ingres/log/log.p1
/ingres/log/log.p2
/ingres/data
/ingres/data/table.p0
/ingres/data/table.p1
/ingres/data/table.p2

4   CONCLUSIONS

We have shown that in order to simplify the filestore management of a parallel system, it requires either an investment in a team of System Administrators, or some new ways of making the task no more complex than managing a standard UNIX machine. Novel methods have been adopted to take advantage of the regularity of the parallel system and the 'set' concept for each machine object has been defined. A Configuration Management Tool has been produced to manage the on-line system and a Configuration Planning Tool developed for assisting with the planning aspects of the filestore layout.

5   ACKNOWLEDGEMENTS

This work was done within the framework of the ESPRIT III project EP6059 EPOCH (European Parallel Operating System based on Chorus). We would like to thank our colleagues at Siemens and IAO for their contribution to the project.

REFERENCES

Borrmann, L., Gelenbe, E., Hofstetter, I., Istavrinos, P., Klaus, K. and Ward, M. (1993) EPOCH – European Parallel Operating System based on Chorus, Parle93 Poster Session.

Butler Group (1994) Technology Audit GOLDRUSH MegaSERVER, Open Systems Series No. 2.

Chorus systèmes (1991) An Overview of CHORUS MiX V.4, CS/TR-91-12.

Hotzner, R. and Tomann, S. (1990) Design and Simulation of a multistage Interconnection Network, *CONPAR 90*, Lecture Notes in Computer Science, Springer-Verlag 457, pp. 385–396.

Skeat, F. (1994) Goldrush – Parallel Technology, submitted for publication.

VERITAS, VxVA. VERITAS Visual Administrator, VERITAS Software Corporation.

Ward, M., Townsend, P. and Watzlawik, G. (1990) EDS Hardware Architecture, CONPAR 90, Lecture Notes in Computer Science, Springer-Verlag 457, pp. 816–827.

11 Customizable Resource Management for Parallel Database Systems

K. R. Mayes, J. Bridgland and S. Quick
Centre for Novel Computing
University of Manchester

1 INTRODUCTION

The purpose of this chapter is to examine the ways in which database management systems (DBMS) can be supported by operating systems. The requirements of any language, with respect to the demands made on operating system abstractions, vary with the richness of that language (Weiser et al., 1989). Thus it is difficult for a single set of abstractions to support all languages. In general, it may be said that a run-time system specializes the operating system abstract machine for use by a particular language. Commercial databases are no exception to this, in that like any high-level language system, databases have complex run-time systems. So how are database management systems supported? There have been three routes to implementing commercial databases on operating systems: using unmodified general purpose operating systems; using modified general purpose operating systems; and using specially-designed operating systems.

Where database systems have been implemented on top of an unmodified general-purpose operating system (e.g. Stonebreaker, 1981), persistent store and scheduling provision have been found to be generally inadequate for database performance requirements. Seltzer and Olson (1992) pointed out that the modifications to UNIX, which have taken place since the early work of Stonebreaker, mean that buffering and file system write semantics can be supported, at user-level, using the system call interface. In conformance to this approach, database management systems implemented on general purpose operating systems use raw disk I/O and maintain their own buffer cache (for efficiency, portability and reliability) (Yoo and Rogers, 1993). Moreover, just as many existing parallel language implementations multiplex their own process structure, at user-level, onto a smaller set of operating system-provided processes (Pierson, 1989), so parallel databases often provide their own threads libraries.

The second approach for database run-time system support is to rewrite parts of the kernel of the general-purpose operating system. For example, parts of the UNIX kernel have been rewritten to support on-line transaction processing (Yoo and Rogers, 1993). The great advantage of specializing parts of a conventional operating system kernel is that much code supporting multiple users, virtual memory and low-level I/O can be reused. To support ORACLE on the Meiko Computing Surface, using the Solaris operating system, a distributed lock manager and parallel file system have been added to the system software (Holman, 1992). The ICL Goldrush Megaserver similarly has a general-purpose operating system interface – specifically, it has an SVR4 interface emulated on a microkernel (Guillemont et al., 1991). However, for database support, modifications have been made to support distributed lock management and lightweight communications. File management is provided by the new VxFS file system standard on SVR4.2 systems (ICL, 1993).

The third approach is to run databases on operating systems which have been specifically designed to support a particular database computational model. In general these are the specialist backend database servers. For example, the NCR/Teradata machine has its own TOS operating system, with the general-purpose operating system residing on the front-end host (Page, 1992). The EDS system, as described by Watson and Townsend (1990)[1], had an operating system which was specialized, at the design stage, to support an Extended SQL computational model. The Chorus-based EDS microkernel is interesting in that it was designed to support Lisp and logic programming as well as a database (Wong and Paci, 1992). Such specialized systems do not tend to run general software; this may be restricted to the host machine. Although the EDS machine kernel did support a UNIX interface in addition to language-specific interfaces, it could be hosted by proprietary or UNIX systems (Watson and Townsend, 1990).

There is a fourth alternative for the provision of operating system-level resource management, namely customizable operating systems. The remainder of this chapter will view database requirements in relation to customizable systems. Section 2 provides a background to customizable systems and suggests that they may be appropriate for the support of database management systems. Section 3 describes the resource management requirements of parallel databases. Section 4 briefly describes support for parallel database systems in a customizable system currently being developed.

---

[1] The EDS system was the prototype of the ICL Goldrush Megaserver. It is a distributed-store multicomputer with an internal network.

2 APPLICATION-ORIENTED RESOURCE MANAGEMENT AND DATABASE SYSTEMS

Application-oriented systems are well known in the areas of general computing environments and in real-time control systems. Similarities between general/numeric computations and decision support systems on the one hand, and between on-line transaction processing and real-time control systems on the other, indicate that similar, general solutions to performance problems may be appropriate. Such customizable systems have been produced to support real-time control systems (e.g. Gheith and Schwan, 1993; Marsh et al., 1992), customizable threads packages (e.g. Bershad et al., 1988), communications protocols (Hutchinson and Peterson, 1988), more general kernels (Campbell and Islam, 1993; Mukherjee and Schwan, 1993) and languages (e.g. Philbin, 1992). These approaches allow great flexibility in terms of resource management policy, even to the extent of dynamic, run-time policy change (e.g. Mukherjee and Schwan, 1993).

As mentioned in the introduction, it may be that the resource management requirements of an application and its run-time system differ from the resource management provided by a general purpose operating system. In general, it is the function of the run-time system to specialize the operating system interface[2]. The customization approach allows the alternative of providing precisely the required operating system interface. This is a more application-oriented approach to management of resources. The essence is to separate *policy* from *mechanism*, thereby 'unbundling' the interface primitives to allow higher levels of software to 'rebundle' them as required. This approach dates back to the Hydra system (Wulf et al., 1974) which separated resource management policy from the mechanism of its provision. Microkernels such as Mach (Black et al., 1992) and Chorus (Gien, 1991) allow user-level provision of services by means of server processes. Nanokernel systems such as Psyche (Scott et al., 1989) support user-level library provision of resource management.

There is thus a question of whether or not customizable systems could be of use in database support. A major concern in implementing a commercial product like a database management system is to achieve a balance between (amongst other things) performance and portability. One way of implementing a fast database is to invest much time and effort in designing and implementing a specific operating system from scratch. Unfortunately, such a specialized system will tend only to provide support for non-portable, proprietary, database management systems. On the other hand, a portable database management system will use system call primitives commonly found in general-purpose operating systems such as UNIX. Such databases will be portable between different platforms and, conversely, a single platform can support different data-

---

[2]That is, the *semantics* of the operating system interface; interface syntax is (relatively) unimportant and can readily be emulated.

bases. Here, the user-level run-time system, mapping the database semantics onto that of the operating system primitives, is likely to be large and possibly inefficient. Altering the operating system internals, whilst keeping the same interface, to more closely match the database requirements will increase performance. However, similar performance will only be achieved on similarly-modified operating systems, so again portability suffers.

It may be that customizable systems offer a compromise between specialized and general purpose approaches, in that a customizable system will, by definition, be capable of supporting both types of system. Customized resource management required by the run-time system is provided beneath either a specialized, or general purpose, customized interface. There is thus the prospect of running proprietary databases on non-proprietary architectures and, similarly, of running general-purpose databases in specialized resource management environments. Such potential advantages indicate that investigating customizable systems support for databases is worthwhile.

Putting resource management at user-level also facilitates interaction between the application and the system software. The DBMS is often able to determine which data is likely to be re-referenced (and should therefore be cached) and how to cache this data (i.e. which block replacement policy to use). Stonebraker (1981) concluded that 'In order for an operating system to provide buffer management, some means must be found to allow it to accept *advice* from an application... .'

3   RESOURCE MANAGEMENT REQUIREMENTS FOR PARALLEL DATABASE SYSTEMS

Given that a case can be made for investigating customization of resources for database support, it remains to determine which management issues are of importance in database management systems. There are perhaps three aspects of resource management where interactions with the operating system level are critical to the performance and characteristics of the parallel database management systems. These are persistent storage implementation, transaction scheduling policy, particularly with respect to the interaction with locking, and fast, lightweight communications on distributed store multicomputer systems. A general-purpose operating system such as Unix has facilities such as file system, process management and IPC designed to serve time-sharing users. Databases have specific requirements which strongly influence performance. As noted in the introduction, databases which run on general purpose operating systems usually provide their own user-level threads packages and use raw disk I/O.

3.1 Transaction scheduling and synchronization

Process scheduling mechanisms also influence performance due to the overheads associated with context switching and synchronization associated with locks and message passing. Stonebraker (1981) suggested that an ultimate solution might be to provide a 'special scheduling class' for database management systems. A typical lock-related problem is caused by the operating system descheduling a process holding a short-term lock which will be required by other processes. There can also be problems arising from interactions between scheduling policies and message passing. For example, the Mach scheduler was modified to provide handoff scheduling specifically intended to optimize message passing. Mach's message passing subsystem uses handoff scheduling inside the kernel, immediately suspending a sender and scheduling a blocked receiver. This avoids the run queue entirely and 'aids performance' (Black, 1990). However, kernel handoff scheduling caused problems for Duchamp (1991) implementing a transaction manager, causing the creation of 25 to 35 threads when 1 thread only was needed. In addition to the specificity of requirements for data handling systems, parallel database performance is also influenced by *dynamic* scheduling policy. Franaszek and Robinson (1985) noted that scheduling policies which take into account the state of transactions – for example, whether the transactions are executing or waiting on a lock – could increase the level of concurrency. User-level thread packages are able to take into account the state of applications; they are flexible and avoid a kernel overhead by being multiplexed on top of kernel-level threads-of-control. However, problems remain with blocking, for example I/O, system calls and with lack of coordination between kernel- and user-level scheduling (Marsh *et al.*, 1991). Solutions are available in systems such such as Psyche (Scott *et al.*, 1989) and Scheduler Activations (Anderson *et al.*, 1992), which overcome these problems by decoupling kernel- and user-level threads.

Thus databases require fast, flexible thread schedulers which can take into account the state of transactions, which do not interfere with locking, which interact sensibly with communication primitives, and which, if implemented at user-level, do not suffer from the problems associated with some threads packages.

3.2 Persistent storage

There are two basic aspects of persistent storage systems which can affect performance of database management systems: disk block manipulation and data caching. Disk block allocation, mode of access (sequential/random), use of indirect blocks for locating files and block size can all influence performance. For example, building INGRES on top of the existing UNIX file system caused problems due to mismatches between INGRES file access mode and UNIX disk block allocation (Stonebraker *et al.*, 1983). In addition to disk management factors, the performance of data management and persistent object stores are influenced by the need for sophisticated use of caching (Sechrest and Park, 1991). The caching activities and physical memory management of the operating system may be too inflexible to support these. Most portable database systems implement their own storage access mechanisms by directly using low-level operating system interface routines (Unwalla and Kerridge, 1992).

A further aspect of database management exists which is perhaps the equivalent of the so-called 'dusty deck' Fortran codes. It may be that data accumulated over several years may need to be accessed in ways not predicted at the time the data began to be collected. Such systems, which are not readily adapted to changing business requirements, have been termed 'legacy systems' (Brodie, 1992). This means an adaptable means of storing and retrieval is needed.

Thus, to provide efficient persistent store management, the system must allow the DBMS full control over caching. This includes allowing the DBMS (or application) to specify which data should be cached and which data should be *flushed* from the cache when the cache becomes full. It must be possible to specify when *dirty* data should be written from the cache to the disk – the *write policy*. Prefetching may also improve performance by fetching data into the cache before it is needed. The system must provide an interface which allows the DBMS to control prefetching. A DBMS may also need to guarantee that a block has been written to the disk. This is important for committing transactions and where the order in which blocks are written is critical. The system must provide an interface which allows detailed control over the flushing of blocks from the cache to the disk. To increase efficiency, the operating system must be carefully designed to reduce intermediate copying of data and to reduce the number of traps-to-supervisor. Finally, a storage representation which allows the database to adapt to changing needs is highly desirable.

3.3 Communications

In a scalable distributed-store multicomputer communications between distributed database components has a critical effect on performance. In tightly-coupled multicomputers with internal networks, lightweight message passing protocols are both possible and desirable. Lightweight protocols reduce the overhead associated with protocol processing, and allow efficient use of communication bandwidth. Parallel implementations of databases typically require maintenance of coherency of shared data. This in turn requires efficient implementations of a distributed lock manager. Distributed lock managers, as found in the ICL Goldrush machine (ICL, 1993), are dependent on the lightweight communications protocol to minimize overheads. Parallel processing of database transactions needs to be matched with high bandwidth file access. A parallel, global, file system needs coherency to be maintained, and must be supported by fast internal network traffic to access remote files (Holman, 1992; ICL, 1993).

The EDS parallel relational database architecture, a more specialized system designed to run ESQL, had hardware support for fast message passing. The ESQL computational model was relatively communications intensive, and so high performance message passing was critical in high system performance. Network interface hardware was able to send and receive messages without intermediate copying. In this architecture, each node of the EDS multicomputer had a Sparc processor dedicated to processing network interrupts, causing waiting threads to become schedulable on the other Sparc of the node (Watson and Townsend, 1990).

Thus the ability to access network devices efficiently and to define lightweight protocols is an important requirement for parallel database management systems.

4 LIBRARY-BASED RUN-TIME RESOURCE MANAGEMENT IN ARENA

Arena is a customizable system currently under development (Mayes et al., 1994). Although customization of resource management could be implemented at any level in the system, Arena places it at user-level. There are two ways in which user-level policy can be implemented: by providing a user-level *server process* or by providing a *library* of routines which, after linking, are accessed in the application address space. By using the library approach, the bulk of the conventional operating system functionality can become effectively part of the run-time system. Young et al. (1991) noted that the implementation of a distributed transaction processing system as a library resulted in reductions in costs associated with other types of system: that is, costs associated with system calls or with remote procedure calls to other system components.

The design of the run-time executive and resource management components of the Arena system is based on the general approach taken by the Flagship system software (Leunig, 1987; Mayes and Keane, 1993). In the Flagship project, the low-level interface of a graph reduction machine was implemented on conventional hardware as a 'hardware ADT', and resource management was represented as interacting manager ADTs. The Arena run-time executive, or 'hardware object', presents an abstraction of conventional hardware features such as register contexts; virtual addressing contexts; physical store. The basic approach to defining the generic interfaces of the hardware object and of the user-level resource managers is to provide a minimal set of primitives which can be combined to support a variety of application paradigms. Like Flagship ADT instances, Arena objects are passive; their interface operations are invoked by the normal procedure call mechanism.

The point is that a small hardware-dependent executive should provide mechanism routines only, allowing all policy into the run-time systems. Restricting such hardware-dependency to a small executive should facilitate portability: a particular hardware object will be an instantiation of the hardware abstract class for specific hardware. A set of resource manager objects will use the facilities provided by the hardware object. A particular resource manager object will be an instantiation of a particular manager abstract class for specific resource management policies.

The system is application-oriented, and so the unit of work supported by the hardware object is a single application. A single application may, for example, be multi-threaded, use multiple address spaces, and be distributed over several nodes of a distributed machine. The Arena system emphasizes the performance of individual applications, but will also provide support for secure multi-user and general-purpose environments. That is, a number of computations will be able to exist in the system concurrently, with the hardware object allocating processor resources to each. The hardware object must provide protection in terms of access to physical resources. Protection between computations must be afforded by the hardware object. Protection within a computation must be the responsibility of the managers of the computation.

4.1 Arena scheduling

Scheduling in Arena is the responsibility of the Process Manager (PM), which will reside at user-level. This is supported by the facilities of the hardware object which gives access to the processor state. Two-way interaction between the PM and the hardware object allow user-level handling of events.

4.1.1 Process manager level
The interface of the PM consists of primitives which result from the 'unbundling' of the conventional UNIX-like process-plus-address space entity. An address space can be created independently of a thread of control. This decoupling has potential advantages in terms of allowing flexible implementation of process models. The address space is potentially a unit of thread scheduling, though little about thread scheduling is imposed, and other thread schedulers can be defined.

Thread switching is implemented by a pair of calls to hardware object interface routines *getRegisterContext( )/setRegisterContext( )*. In Arena, all thread state is maintained at user-level; there is no thread state at supervisor-level. Unlike many other systems which provide user-level scheduling, there are no kernel-level threads to provide 'virtual processors'. The degree of supervisor-level involvement in thread switching is determined only by the facilities provided on a particular processor for accessing thread registers and stack. That is, if thread state can be saved and restored by user-level operations, then the switch is done entirely at user-level.

A PM can implement any scheduling scheme. Locks are customizable, as is their interaction with the scheduler policy. The central PM routine is the thread switching routine. Interrupts and exceptions can be handled at user-level by means of user-definable and schedulable threads. Thus hardware timer events can be handled at user-level to implement preemptive scheduling.

4.1.2 Hardware object level
The hardware object does no scheduling of threads or address spaces. It simply saves and loads register contexts, including address translation context, accessing designated thread context block. All thread context blocks reside at user-level. There is some state shared between the executive and the user-level PM; consisting of a few flags, counters and the state of the event handling threads. These latter are, however, only scheduled according to user-level policy. The executive handles low-level events and, where designated, makes 'upcalls' into user-level by setting flags in the state shared with the PM and loading the thread switching routine of the PM.

4.2 Arena persistent store

Section 3.2 showed the requirement of a DBMS on the backing store for efficient operation. The following sections show how each of these requirements is met by the design of Arena. The Arena backing store allows the user full control over caching, prefetching, allocation policy and write policy.

As with scheduling, there are two main levels in the design of the Arena backing store. At the lowest level is the hardware object which implements security. Above this level are the Backing Store Manager (BSM) and Name Manager (NM). The policy decisions are implemented in these mangers, which reside at user-level.

4.2.1 Backing store manager level
The BSM controls high-level policy with respect to backing store. It implements caching, cache block replacement, prefetching, write policy, naming and an object system.

Caching policies
As discussed in section 3.2, a DBMS may require a number of different caching policies. To allow for this, each BSM may implement any number of caching

policies. The BSM may choose to make decisions on which policy would be most appropriate based on past access methods. It may also accept a hint from an application advising it on how a block should be cached. A hint may be ignored or a different caching policy may be used if the requested method is not available.

Prefetching
Stonebraker (1981) stated that INGRES could nearly always determine which disk block it would access next. If this block could be brought into the cache before it was needed, the application would not have to wait for a disk operation.

Prefetching is implemented in the BSM by two methods:

- the BSM allows an application to explicitly request that a block is prefetched via the BSM interface, and
- as with caching, a BSM may be coded to observe disk access patterns and from this information, attempt to prefetch data which may be used in the near future.

Allocation – The Object Model
The BSM provides two access models: physical and logical. With physical access, addresses are physical disk addresses and no interpretation is performed. With logical access, *disk objects* provide a structured view of the disk. The disk object model presents a mechanism for controlling the allocation and representation of data on the disk. In general purpose operating systems, the file system generally provides a single mechanism for allocating files. If this mechanism is inappropriate, the performance of the application may suffer. Disk objects allow any number of different allocation policies to co-exist. The basic structure is that of a hierarchy formed from a tree of objects. Each object controls the allocation, including the expansion and reduction, of each of its children. For example, one object may organize its children contiguously (at the cost of having to re-organize its children when space becomes fragmented) while another may disperse the blocks of its children over the disk (at the cost of increased access time). Applications create objects with parents which provide the necessary properties. Disk objects can also be used to group child objects together. For example, if it is known that three objects will often be accessed at the same time, they may be grouped under the same parent which guarantees to keep them close together on the disk. Disk objects may also implement their own data representation. For example, a special disk object may be designed which stores sparse matrices or certain tables efficiently.

Each disk object is of one type, or class, which defines the actual access function to be used. An abstract class is defined from which all disk object classes are derived. This class defines a standard interface providing various operations such as read, write and create_a_child. Not all operations are implemented by all classes. For example, a 'data' disk object would not implement the create_a_child method. New disk object classes can be added to the system at any time. This allows for extensibility.

The disk object hierarchy provides a physical hierarchy on the disk. The Name Manager allows each user to create their own logical hierarchy by the use of textual names. A computation provides an environment which enables users to access their own directory object. Within this directory object are the names and *access keys* to other objects on the disk. The mapping of textual names to disk object identifiers occurs at the BSM level.

Write policy

The BSM also implements a *write-policy* which determines when new data should be written to the disk from the cache. A DBMS may require more control so that the order in which blocks are written to the disk can be controlled, or so that changes are known to be committed. The BSM allows this by providing an interface giving full control over the flushing of data from the cache.

4.2.2 Hardware object level

The hardware object deals solely in terms of disk blocks. It provides access to the disk at the block level. Each block on the disk is either free or has already been associated with a disk object identifier. Any number of disk blocks may belong to the same identifier. However, to access a disk block, the correct key must also be provided. Three keys are used – read, write and allocation. The purpose of the allocation key is to enable blocks to be moved from association with one identifier to another.

Allocation of blocks

The allocation interface enables blocks to be allocated in a number of different modes from *soft* to *hard*. The actual blocks comprising a disk object would be allocated in *hard* mode. Some additional blocks may be 'reserved' by allocating them in *soft* mode in anticipation of the object growing. Its purpose is to enable applications to register an 'interest' in a block whilst allowing the block to be reclaimed if resources become exhausted[3].

A read-only map of the usage of the disk is visible at user-level so that applications can locate a suitable area of the disk for a new object. An application may, for example, use this map to position data, which will be accessed concurrently, close together on the disk to reduce any seek latency. There is a balance between the increased flexibility afforded by a user-level implementation of policy and the decrease in performance associated with frequent

---

[3] An example of where this might be used is in the creation of a log file. The application may expect the log to grow without knowing its final size. It can allocate extra blocks after the end of the actual log data in soft mode so if the log grows, it can do so contiguously.

crossing of the trap interface. To reduce the number of traps-to-supervisor, the hardware object provides an interface allowing multiple operations to be specified in one system call. For example, a number of reads and writes on several different disk objects can be specified in one system call.

4.3 Communications

The Arena system is intended to run on both multiprocessor and multicomputer architectures. As will be described in the next section, the initial target machine for Arena is a prototype EDS machine which is a distributed store multicomputer with an internal network. The design for communications has three components. A Communications Manager (CM) provides a high-level set of communications primitives. A Network Manager (NWM) provides a lower-level message-passing interface, mapping the CM abstractions on to the hardware object interface which presents an abstraction of the network device.

Each multicomputer node has its own local hardware object and instances of resource managers. Where an Arena computation is distributed, a set of the resource manager objects for that computation occurs on each node on which the computation is running. Communication between nodal components of the computation resource management occurs via the NWM object instances, mediated via the hardware objects and network drivers.

4.3.1 Communication manager level

The CM provides the usual IPC primitives based on the 'port' abstraction found in many communication-oriented kernels. Further unbundling of the port abstraction into operations creating and manipulating message queues and thread queues, say, is possible. However, it was probable that this might impose an implementation bias into the interface. A port is itself a reasonably unitary notion equivalent to, for example, an address space or a thread of control. A CM instance entirely defines the structure of a port. The CM provides the interface for application-level communication between, possibly distributed, threads of control. It interacts with the PM to implement whatever policy are required by the application with respect to blocking. A major determinant of the behaviour of a message-passing system is whether the communication primitives are blocking. That is, whether the thread of control which invokes a communication primitive should block while awaiting delivery, or reception, of a message. The Arena CM interface will enforce no policy with respect to blocking of sender or receiver threads. For example, it may be that enforced blocking of the thread is too restrictive. It is possible that an application may benefit from being able to test a port for the presence of a message. A CM object interacts with its PM object to request suspension and resumption of threads. Since both objects are implemented at user-level, the run-time system programmer has complete control over the policies applied.

4.3.2 Network manager level
The NWM provides an interface for lower-level access to the hardware object send and receive primitives. The NWM object is responsible for user-level buffering policies and provides manager-level interfaces for use by the Store Manager and Backing Store Manager[4] in addition to the CM. Protocols residing in a particular NWM will interpret message headers and route incoming messages to the appropriate manager. The multiple NWM instances of a distributed application apply identical protocols.

4.3.3 Hardware object level
The interface provides access to the network device driver. The driver code resides at this level for reasons of security and efficiency. However, the NWM will provide a network event handling routine which will run as a user-level thread. The hardware object interrupt handler will make this runnable so that the user-level network protocol code can be executed. The hardware object level will simply deal with the network hardware headers of the messages.

4.4 Current status of Arena

The initial target hardware is a thirteen-node EDS machine[5]. This is a distributed store multicomputer, where each node has two Sparc (MMU-cache-coherent) processors sharing nodal store. This machine thus presents a model for scalable hybrid multicomputer/multiprocessor architectures. The system is in the early stages of implementation. The major components of the hardware object, that is those dealing with execution contexts, have been implemented on the Sparc processor. The current size of the hardware object is approximately 50 Kb of text. The nature of customizable systems is such that an incremental approach to implementation is facilitated. A series of Process Manager instances of increasing complexity are being coded. The version currently being linked with the hardware object is intended to test and obtain measurements of the event handling mechanism.

The customizable backing store management described in section 4.2 is also being designed and coded. The EDS machine does not have local disks and so work on the BSM will rely on incore disks to emulate physical disk access. Other work has shown that physical disks can be accurately modelled (e.g. Ruemmler and Wilkes, 1993).

---

[4]The Network Manager object may provide support for virtual shared memory and distributed backing store.

[5]The EDS machine architecture (Ward and Townsend, 1990) is scalable to 256 nodes.

5 SUMMARY

This chapter has been mainly concerned with describing the motivation behind a design for a system supporting customizable user-level resource management, and with showing that such a customizable system could provide an alternative for the implementation of parallel database management systems. The resource management requirements of a parallel database have been examined and it has been shown how a customizable system can satisfy these requirements.

6 ACKNOWLEDGEMENTS

The authors would like to thank Andy Nisbet, John Gurd, Brian Warboys and all the members of the Centre for Novel Computing. Thanks also to John Keane of UMIST, and to Paul Watson of ICL. This work is supported by EPSRC grants GR/J 84045, 93315512 and 91309499.

REFERENCES

Anderson, T. E., Bershad, B. N., Lazowska, E. D. and Levy, H. M. (1992) Scheduler activations: Effective kernel support for the user-level management of parallelism, *ACM Transactions on Computer Systems*, 10(1), pp. 53–79.

Bershad, B. N., Lazowska, E. D. and Levy, H. M. (1988) Presto: A system for object-oriented parallel programming, *Software – Practice and Experience*, 18(8), pp. 713–732.

Black, D. (1990) Scheduling support for concurrency and parallelism in the Mach operating system, *IEEE Computer*, 23(5), pp. 35–43.

Black, D., Golub, B. D., Julin, D. P., Rashid, R. F., Draves, R. P., Dean, R. W., Forin, A., Barrera, J., Tokuda, H., Malan, G. and Bohman, D. (1992) Microkernel operating system architecture and Mach, *Proc. USENIX Workshop on Microkernels and Other Kernel Architectures* (April), pp. 11–30.

Brodie, M. L. (1992) The promise of distributed computing and the challenges of legacy systems, *Proc. 10th British National Conference on Databases*, LNCS 618, pp. 1–28.

Campbell, R. H. and Islam, N. (1993) CHOICES: A parallel object-oriented operating system, in: *Research Directions in Concurrent Object-Oriented Programming* (Eds. G. Agha, P. Wegner and A. Yonezawa), MIT Press, pp. 393–451.

Duchamp, D. (1991) Experience with threads and RPC, in: *Mach. Proc. USENIX Symp. on Experiences with Distributed and Multiprocessor Systems* (Summer), pp. 87–104.

Franaszek, P. and Robinson, J. T. (1985) Limitations of concurrency in transaction processing, *ACM Transactions on Database Systems*, 10(1), pp. 1–28.

Gheith, A and Schwan, K. (1993) CHAOSarc: kernel support of multiweight objects, invocations and atomicity in real-time multiprocessor applications, *ACM Transactions on Computer Systems*, 11(1), pp. 33–72.

Gien, M. (1991) Next generation operating systems architecture, *Operating Systems of the 90s and Beyond*, LNCS 563, pp. 227–232.

Guillemont, M., Lipkis, J., Orr, D. and Rozzier, M. (1991) A second-generation micro-kernel based UNIX; lessons in performance and compatibility, *Proc. USENIX Conference* (Winter), pp. 13–21.

Holman, A. (1992) The Meiko Computing Surface: A parallel and scalable open systems platform for Oracle, *Proc. 10th British National Conference on Databases*, LNCS 618, pp. 96–113.

Hutchinson, N. C. and Peterson, L. L. (1988) Design of the x-kernel, *Proc. of the SIGCOMM 1988 Symp.* (August), pp. 65–75.

ICL (1993) GOLDRUSH Megaserver Technical Overview, ICL Corporate Systems, UK.

Lazowska, E. D. (1992) System Support for high performance multiprocessing, *Proc. USENIX Symp. on Experiences with Distributed and Multiprocessor Systems* (March), pp. 1–11.

Leunig, S. R. (1987) Abstract Data Types in the Flagship System Software, Flagship Document FLAG/DD/303, ICL, UK.

Marsh, B. D., Scott, M. L., LeBlanc, T. J. and Markatos, E. P. (1991) First-class user-level threads, *ACM Operating System Review*, 25(5) (*Proc. 13th ACM Symp. on Operating System Principles* (October, 1991)), pp. 110–121.

Marsh, B., Brown, C., LeBlanc, T. J., Scott, M., Becker, T., Quiroz, C., Das, P. and Karlsson, J. (1992) The Rochester checkers player, *IEEE Computer*, February, pp. 12–19.

Mayes, K. R. and Keane, J. A. (1993) Levels of atomic action in the Flagship parallel system, *Concurrency: Practice and Experience*, 5(3), pp. 193–212.

Mayes, K. R., Quick, S., Bridgland, J. and Nisbet, A. (1994) Language- and application-oriented resource management for parallel architectures, *Proc. 6th ACM-SIGOPS European Workshop*, pp. 172–177.

Mukherjee, B. and Schwan, K. (1993) Experimentation with a reconfigurable microkernel, *Proc. USENIX Symp on Microkernels and other Kernel Architectures* (September), pp. 45–60.

Page, J. (1992) A study of a parallel database machine and its performance. The NCR/Teradata DBC/1012, *Proc. 10th British National Conference on Databases*, LNCS 618, pp. 115–137.

Philbin, J. (1992) Customizable policy management in the Sting operating system, *Proc. US/Japan Workshop on Parallel Symbolic Computing: Languages, Systems and Applications*, LNCS 748, pp. 380–401.

Pierson, D. L. (1989) Integrating parallel Lisp with modern UNIX-based operating systems, *Proc. US/Japan Workshop on Parallel Lisp*, LNCS 441, pp. 312–315.

Ruemmler, C. and Wilkes, J. (1993) Modelling disks, HP Laboratories Technical Report HPL-93-68.

Scott, M. L., LeBlanc, T. J. and Marsh, B. D. (1989) Design Rationale for Psyche, a general-purpose multiprocessor operating system, University of Rochester Computer Science and Engineering Research Review 1988-1989, pp. 5–13.

Sechrest S. and Park, Y. (1991) User-level physical memory management for Mach, *Proc. USENIX Mach Symp.*, November, pp. 189–199.

Seltzer, M. and Olson, M. (1992) LIBTP: Portable, Modular Transactions for UNIX, *Proc. USENIX Conference* (Winter), pp. 9–25.

Stonebraker, M. (1981) Operating system support for database management, *Comms. ACM*, 24(7), pp. 412–418.

Stonebraker, M., Woodfill, J., Ranstrom, J., Murphy, M., Meyer, M. and Allman, E. (1983) Performance enhancements to a relational database system, *ACM Transactions on Database Systems*, 8(2), pp. 167–185.

Unwalla, M. and Kerridge, J. (1992) Control of a large massively parallel database machine using SQL catalogue extensions, and a DSDL in preference to an operating system, *Proc. 10th British National Conference on Databases*, LNCS 618, pp. 138–155.

Ward, M. and Townsend, P. (1990) EDS hardware architecture, *CONPAR 90-VAPP IV*, LNCS 457, pp. 816–827.

Watson, P. and Townsend, P. (1990) The EDS parallel relational database system, *Proc. PRISMA Workshop* (September), LNCS 503, pp. 149–166.

Weiser, M., Demers, A. and Hauser, C. (1989) The Portable Common Runtime Approach to Interoperability, *Proc. 12th ACM Symp. on Operating System Principles*, pp. 114–122.

Wong, K-F. and Paci, M. (1992) Performance evaluation of an OLTP application on the EDS database server using a behavioural simulation model, *Parallel Processing and Data Management* (Ed. P. Valduriez), Chapman and Hall, pp. 317–350.

Wulf, W., Cohen, E., Corwin, W., Jones, A., Levin, R., Pierson, C. and Pollack, F. (1974) HYDRA: The kernel of a multiprocessor operating system, *Comms. ACM*, 17(6), pp. 337–345.

Yoo, H. and Rogers, T. (1993) UNIX kernel support of OLTP performance, *Proc. USENIX Conference* (Winter), pp. 241–247.

Young, M. W., Thompson, D. S. and Jaffe, E. (1991) A modular architecture for distributed transaction processing, *Proc. USENIX Conference* (Winter), pp. 357–363.

12 Performance Evaluation of Large Parallel Database Machines: Techniques and Tools

I. Jelly*, J. Kerridge[+], C. Bates[++]

* *Computing Research Centre*
 Sheffield Hallam University
[+] *Department of Computer Science, Sheffield University*
[++] *National Transputer Support Centre, Sheffield*
 I.E.Jelly@shu.ac.uk, J.Kerridge@dcs.shef.ac.uk

1 INTRODUCTION

The ability to store and manipulate large volumes of information is a crucial requirement for the operation of most large commercial organizations. These rely upon their database systems to provide the effective implementation of tasks such as order processing, invoicing and ledger maintenance. Most current databases systems are able to support this role without providing detailed management information which could be extracted from the data if there was sufficient spare processing capacity. Future systems will need to support both the transaction processing capability and the management information needs of an organization at the same time on the same data. Increasingly parallel hardware will be needed to meet the demands for this enhanced functionality and to provide better performance for large data volumes. We have already seen the emergence of parallel implementations of Oracle on a number of different parallel platforms such as N-cube, Meiko and Parsys, and new parallel systems such as the recently announced database machine Goldrush from ICL. In order to evaluate the performance of this new generation of database machines, appropriate benchmarks and general performance evaluation techniques are required. These must reflect the different modes of operation of the systems and indicate how well they scale to a range of problem sizes.

The increasing application of database technology to commercial and administrative systems is leading to greater demands for high performance database machines. It is expected that commercial and administrative use of high performance computing will out number scientific and engineering use by a factor of three to one in the near future (Forster, 1993). The requirements for database systems differ from scientific applications in a number of respects. The data that is stored is symbolic rather than numeric and thus imposes a totally different workload upon the processing system. Such systems also require high performance disk systems that are closely integrated with the processing system. A feature of large database applications is that the supporting hardware only undertakes database processing, i.e. they are not general purpose machines. The need for improved processing performance has been heightened by organizations' need for more extensive use of the data they maintain. This manifests itself in the need to extract information from the data, rather than just supporting the mission critical procedures of the organization. This information is used to provide decision support systems. Increasingly, data mining techniques are being used which analyse the data in order to extract patterns and trends which are hidden within the data. This analysis requires much more processing power than is needed to support a transaction processing system, especially if the data mining activity is to be undertaken on the same data that is used by the transaction processing system. There is a need for database machines to be able to support varying styles of interaction with many of these being carried out at the same time. This also raises the need for higher performance database machines.

The user is then confronted with the problem of evaluating the performance of different database machines in the context of their own application requirements. Possible performance evaluation techniques involve benchmarking, simulation or reimplementation of all or part of the user's existing application. Each of these approaches has major drawbacks and may not produce the required quality of information. In order to remedy this, there is a need for suitable application mimics which provide a realistic model of the user's application but can be generated and tested easily.

This chapter describes work on the specification of a synthetic database, based on a financial model, which forms the basis for benchmarking and performance tuning of large SQL database machines. In order to generate the large quantities of data and transactions involved in its employment, a set of software tools have been developed.

The chapter is structured as follows: section 2 of the chapter briefly reviews the development of database machines and places the current development of parallel database machines into context. Current issues concerning the evaluation of database performance are then discussed in section 3 and existing benchmarks reviewed. The role of applications mimics and their use as a design aid for large database systems is considered in section 4. Section 5 describes in detail how a mimic of a banking system can be constructed emphasizing the need for realistic symbolic data which contains relationships between the data items that occur in real life. Section 6 discusses the support tools that are required in order to carry out a performance evaluation. The way in which the performance evaluation should be undertaken is described in section 7. Finally, some conclusions are drawn in section 8.

2 PARALLEL DATABASE MACHINES

Initial developments in the use of parallel database machines centred around the use of shared memory multi-processors. This approach was adopted because it was a relatively easy task to port the software from the single processor/memory implementation that had previously existed. It soon became apparent, however, that such shared memory architectures would not yield the scalable solution required because the shared memory became a bottleneck.

A concurrent development occurred with the use of distributed systems supporting a large organization. In such systems a network of processors was set up, each maintaining an integral part of the company's database. That is, each part would operate mainly independently of the others, but it was possible for more than one part to collaborate to solve larger, more wide-ranging queries. The performance of such database installations was limited by the interconnecting network. Such systems did however scale, provided there was sufficient network bandwidth to deal with the extra interactions. One operational aspect was highlighted by the design of such distributed systems – namely, the separation of user or client application code from the database or server system code.

The client–server model highlights the difference between the types of code that are used in a database environment and the need for a well defined interface between them. The interface is easily specified by the use of ISO Database Language SQL (ISO, 1987). Thus the client process has to be able to generate SQL queries which are then passed to the database server. The server evaluates the query and returns the resulting rows to the client where they are processed. The advantage of the client–server approach is that the client can vary in capability from a mainframe through workstation and PC to dumb terminals operating through a front-end processor. From the organization's point of view this approach protects their investment in user application code. The actual implementation of the database server is removed from consideration when the user part of the system is modified, provided an SQL interface is used.

The advent of the scalable distributed memory multi-processor has resulted in their increased use for database applications. Current implementations have tended to port existing database systems as a multi-instance facility accessing a shared file system, rather than designing a software architecture appropriate to such machines. This has meant that internal software structures, fundamental to database operation, for example, concurrency management, have not been designed to take advantage of the parallel machine architecture. This also limits the level to which the database systems can be scaled. Projects such as IDIOMS

(Kerridge, 1991, 1994) have shown the feasibility of building SQL based database servers which are able to fully exploit the scalable attributes of distributed memory multi-processors. This has been achieved by re-designing the underlying algorithms and removing the need for a traditional filing system, shared or otherwise, by directly accessing the disk storage. The concepts demonstrated in IDIOMS are to be fully developed in the EUREKA project HPPC/SEA-IRISS.

Future generations of high performance database servers will rely heavily upon parallel processing technology, based upon distributed memory multi-processor architectures if scalability, at low cost, is to be achieved. It is therefore vital to ensure that some mechanism not only for benchmarking but also for evaluating the performance of a design is available. Performance evaluation depends upon software support for a realistic mimic of the sort of applications which many organizations operate. Our investigations suggest that a small number of application mimics is likely to provide a good basis of evaluation of a wide range of current commercial systems.

3 DATABASE PERFORMANCE EVALUATION

The emergence of new parallel database platforms requires the development of appropriate performance evaluation techniques. To date the majority of work into performance evaluation of parallel systems has focused on scientific and engineering applications. However, high performance databases exhibit a number of different characteristics that necessitate special consideration where performance issues are concerned. The two most important differences between database machines and those developed for general scientific applications are: first, database machines are dedicated, special purpose architectures designed to run only one application, i.e. the database management system. Secondly, overall performance is highly dependent on the I/O system. The complex interaction between hardware, operating system, database management system and application software gives rise to different performance evaluation perspectives: the hardware designer may wish to know about inter-processor connect utilization, the DBMS implementor cache usage and the application user transaction throughput. Because of these factors, performance evaluation techniques such as benchmarking with low level kernels are unsuitable for database systems.

Traditionally users have used benchmarks for performance evaluation prior to purchase. However this only allows a user to limit the number of machines that are being considered for an application procurement. There then needs to be a means whereby the user can further evaluate possible machines in a well structured manner. For many organizations it is not feasible to just *dump* out parts of their existing data for use as a benchmark because the data is structured in a manner appropriate to current processing techniques which are typically not based upon true database technology, rather large filing systems. It would also take too long to dump out the required data. There is thus a need for an application mimic which is sufficiently close to reality to be a satisfactory representation of an organization's workload but which can be tailored so that it can be used to construct reasonable representations of the expected workload.

An important aspect of current developments is that parallel database machine hardware offers the opportunity to scale the system more easily than current technology once it has been installed. Prospective purchasers will therefore wish to evaluate how easily the machine can be scaled and what effect this will have on the way the data is organized. Thus any performance evaluation system has to be able to construct scaled data sets which can be related one to the other. In addition the volumes have to be realistic, thus it will be necessary to build evaluation systems which have many millions of records in them.

Performance evaluation issues for large database machines thus include the following:

- appropriate measures of performance
- techniques of measuring performance
- valid comparisons between different systems
- exploration of scalability issues
- designing for performance
- impact of different application modes on performance
- impact of different machine architectures on performance.

3.1 Existing benchmarks

The importance of the availability of appropriate, recognized benchmarks is two fold: first it allows potential purchasers to obtain valid comparative information on the performance of different systems, and secondly they provide a valuable standard for system designers. In order to support users and designers, benchmark tests must model the functionality of real applications. Currently, although there are a number of recognized database benchmarks, none adequately meets this requirement for large high performance parallel systems.

It has been seen that high performance database systems are increasingly required to support both OLTP and MIS functionality. However this is not reflected in the existing benchmarks where normally only one operational aspect is considered. The most widely used database benchmarks are those defined by the Transaction Processing Performance Council (TPCA, TPCB and, more recently, TPC-C) (Gray, 1991; Dietrich *et al.*, 1992; Serlin, 1991). These offer the user a measure of OLTP performance, results being expressed in transactions per second and transactions per US$. Because of the simplistic nature of the database model used, a highly optimistic view of the actual capabilities of the system under test is usually given (England et al., 1992). MIS query operation are tested in the Wisconsin and Set Query benchmarks (Dewitt, 1991; O'Neil, 1991) but only the AS^{3}AP set attempts to measure both OLTP and MIS functionality (Turbifill et al., 1991). Unfortunately AS^{3}AP suffers from a number of drawbacks which undermine its usefulness as a performance evaluation tool. These limitations can be summarized as: unrealistically small row lengths in the table definitions, a typical mix of queries and transactions with no attempt to model realistic database functionality, and finally the use of integer data in the key and other frequently accessed fields. This use of integer data represents a failure to understand the typical characteristics of real databases where information such as 'account-number' is always specified in the form of character strings. It can lead to considerable error in the timing of database functions as the duration of fundamental CPU operations on integer and character data differs widely.

4 APPLICATION MIMICS FOR BENCHMARKING AND DESIGN SUPPORT

A collaborative project involving the University of Sheffield, Sheffield Hallam University and the National Transputer Support Centre has researched the development of a new benchmark for large high performance databases machines (Kerridge et al., 1994; Jelly et al., 1994). The intention is to provide a new standard for evaluation of SQL databases (running on either conventional or parallel platforms) which meets the requirements of the current users of large database systems. The Sheffield benchmark models the functionality of modern commercial systems and includes both on-line transaction processing (OLTP), management information systems (MIS) and batch processing. The benchmark consists of a model or 'mimic' database with sets of associated OLTP and MIS queries, and the software tools required to generate the large volumes of data and transactions required to run the system. In order to support investigation of the scalability of database systems, the generated database and queries can be appropriately sized.

The development of a realistic application mimic serves not only as the vehicle for benchmarking of database systems but provides support for the design of new systems. It has been developed in manner which provides considerable flexibility in its usage. By the definition of default values, a standard database model can be generated to form the benchmarking systems; alternatively, the use of different parameters allows system developers to emulate different database design features and compare the high level 'user's view' of performance with detailed investigations into system dependent aspects such as indexing strategies, load balancing and communication overheads.

4.1 Requirements for an application mimic

One of the key features of a well respected benchmark is that it mimics current practice in an application environment. As shown in the previous section there are a number of limitations in current database benchmarks. This section identifies the important features that must be incorporated if a realistic synthetic system is to be achieved. In order to provide a good model as a basis for testing the system must mimic a typical 'real' database in the following features:

- database structure
- data volumes
- mix of and realistic volumes of OLTP operations
- mix of MIS queries
- maintenance of audit information.

In addition, the design must take account of aspects such as the manner of data representation. It has already been seen in section 3.1 that most current benchmark systems do not manipulate symbolic data and it is necessary to rectify this.

The mimic database structure is based on the system used in the IDIOMS project which was built for the TSB Bank plc. The database design developed for that project is representative of a large class of commercial systems, ranging from banking, insurance, mail order and public/private monopoly utilities. As these systems comprise some of the largest databases currently in operation, the decision to base the application mimic system on a banking model appears to be sensible. The synthetic database has been designed to include information on customers, their accounts and standing orders.

A major problem for the development of a realistic application mimic is the difficulty in generating the required data volumes. For a realistic model the typical data scaling requirements run from 100,000 to 10 million rows per table. In order to support the production of this amount of synthetic data, a software tool has been developed to generate these for the mimic system. However it is not sufficient merely to generate data in volume: it must also model real data if the system is to be a marked improvement on current benchmarks. The manner in which synthetic data can be made to appear as close to real world data is discussed in section 5.

Previous analysis of the TSB database operation had already provided an analysis of the most commonly used banking transactions and the profile of their distribution by transaction type. By incorporating this information into the synthetic OLTP set, the mimic system provides a realistic test of normal database usage. One important aspect of the mimic is the inclusion of the creation/ deletion operations as part of the normal OLTP functionality: this means that

192   Parallel Information Processing

the ability of the system under test to manipulate indexes will be tested because invariably the creation of a new account or customer will cause index modification.

In order to achieve an equivalent set of realistic MIS queries, an analysis has been carried out of the exiting MIS type benchmarks and the current (and projected) requirements of commercial users. This has resulted in a categorization of MIS queries from which a typical mix of individual queries can be generated. Categories include such management requirements as statistical reporting, and security checking.

A further aspect of real database systems is that they generally include some aspect of auditing and security and it is thus necessary to ensure that any application mimic contains a realistic representation of these features. By including the requirement to maintain audit information during transaction processing and query response, the database system not only mimics accepted commercial practice but provides information at completion of testing that can be used to validate that the tests have been correctly conducted.

5   A FINANCIAL SYSTEMS APPLICATION MIMIC

The synthetic database mimic is based upon the operation of the banking system used by TSB plc. The mimic bank maintains account, customer, standing order, movements and a history of the preceding set of movements. Every time a transaction occurs on the account which involves a change to the balance of the account a record is made in the movements table. Once 25 movements have occurred the movements are transferred to the history table which overwrites the previous contents for that account. Current banking systems do not permit the retention of history information on-line. Banks would like to be able to do so but the costs are currently prohibitive. The availability of history information allows the extraction of much more accurate management and decision support information.

5.1   Data creation

The main problem in creating reasonable synthetic data for a real application is that the real data contains relationships between data items which are not explicitly stated. For example, in a customer record there is an informal relationship between town name, postcode and telephone area code. Thus queries can be formulated which access the data using each of these fields separately. The responses should in some way be consistent. It is therefore critical that fields which contain symbolic data maintain some degree of correlation. Similarly, the initial balance of an account is dependent upon the type of account, business or personal. Subsequently, the way in which the accounts are manipulated will vary. For example, a business account will have a much larger number of credits than a personal account which will tend to have a single monthly credit followed by a number of much smaller debits.

An important feature of the database generation mechanism is that the data is generated in a completely computed manner, rather than using a random number generator. We introduce the concept of *semantic computability*, to represent the ability to structure the data so that from certain key data attributes the values of many other data items can be calculated. This concept is used subsequently when transactions are generated because it is known precisely what the parameters of an account or customer are directly from the database definition file. There is no need, when creating a transaction, to determine whether or not a particular customer or account exists.

The mimic bank is considered to have 100 areas, each of which may have 100 branches and is thus based upon the usual sort code used by banking systems. For the purposes of the mimic, the areas are associated with administrative areas of the country and the branches are associated with the towns in that administrative area. During database definition a number of parameters can be set which are specific to a particular branch. These include the frequency of business, personal and jointly managed accounts, together with the total number of accounts to be generated for that branch. The accounts are given account numbers in sequence to which is prepended the area and branch codes, together with the business/personal and joint/single indicators. It is possible to generate a total of 10^{10} accounts.

An account number has the following structure:

aabbpjnnnnnn

where *aa* is area number,
      bb is branch number,
      p set to 1 indicates a personal account and 0 indicates a business account
      j set to 1 indicates a jointly, and 0 a singly, managed account,
      nnnnnn is a unique identification within *aabb*.

Part of the account generation process is to identify the customer(s) which manage that account. Customer numbers are generated in sequence based upon the area and branch numbers for the account. Thus a customer number has the structure:

aattrrrshhoo

where *aa* is area number,

tt is town number and the same as *bb*,

rrrs is a road number within *tt*,

hh is a house number within *rrr*,

oo is a unique house occupier number within *hh*.

A town comprises a number of roads, each containing a number of houses, each of which may contain one or more customers or occupiers. The number of roads and houses can be defined or left at a default value. The frequency of multiple occupancy houses can also be set. From the area and branch (or town) numbers the post code and telephone number can be derived. However both of these need to be specialized in different ways. The telephone number is specialized in the following manner:

0 aa bb – rrrshh

where *0aabb* represents the area code and

rrrshh represents the local telephone number.

The post code is generated directly from the area, town and road numbers as *aa tt rrrs*.

Town and road names are generated from a file of root names to which is added a suffix. For example the root *Chestnut* can become Chestnut *Road*, Chestnut *Drive* and Chestnut *Lane* by adding the appropriate suffix. Thus the *rrr* component identifies the root name and the final *s* the suffix. The root names and their suffices can be varied for different countries, not just those based upon English. The house number *hh* is added to a road name to generate part of the address. The *tt* part of a customer number is used to obtain a town name from the file. Finally, the administrative area name is also obtained from a file of such names by using the aa part of the customer number.

The aim in the generation process is to ensure that the same set of data is returned, by a query, regardless of whether access is made by town name, post code, telephone number or road name. Unfortunately, the real world is never as regular as this, at least not in Britain! Hence we have included mechanisms whereby customers can live in one town but have their bank information maintained in a different town. These towns may also be in different administrative areas. The data definition mechanism permits the frequency of such occurrences to be set so that the generated data reflects normal operation. It can be seen that the data is completely computable and is in no way random. This has important benefits when we consider the generation of transactions.

5.2 Transaction creation

Transactions are generated using a random number generator to ensure that the order in which transactions are generated is not biased towards a particular area and branch. The basic format of a transaction is:

class code account source teller {arguments}

Transactions are separated into classes which reflect the way in which they manipulate the database. Thus there are classes which only read, those which update, those which delete information and those which write new data to the database. Within each of these classes there are different transaction codes, thus *debit* and *credit* are both of the class *update* but have different codes. During a definition phase the frequency of each class and code can be defined. In addition any bias towards a particular area, or branch within an area, can be specified to provide a means of generating skewed access to the database being evaluated. The random number is used to provide, by division an area, branch and account number. This can be done accurately because the database definition file retains the number of areas and branches within areas and accounts within branches. From the account number we can determine the type of account and how it is managed, and can thus determine the type of transaction that is likely to occur. The source and teller fields are generated directly, because the source is based upon the area and branch where the transaction comes from, which may not be the same as the area and branch where the account is located. The teller simply identifies whether the transaction is from a counter clerk or from a machine (ATM). These parameters can also be defined before the transaction generation system starts to create transactions. The arguments depend upon the particular transaction, thus a debit would contain an amount and a new customer transaction would contain full details of the customer.

The distribution and frequency of transactions can be varied but default values are already known from an analysis of the workload of TSB Bank. In particular, this identified the fact that about 10 transaction types generated 90% of the workload. The bank has more than 100 transaction definitions in total. Thus the mimic benchmark only implements the most commonly used transactions.

6 SUPPORT TOOLS

The support environment will be provided by four main tools; Data Generation, Transaction Generation, Information about the generated system and Analysis of Results. It is vital that these tools are as portable as possible to different environments so that they can be implemented as easily as possible. To this end all the tools (Cook, 1993) have been implemented in ANSI C.

6.1 Database generation

For the purposes of benchmarking, a database with a large number of default parameters is created. However, when a database system is being designed or evaluated it may be necessary to skew the data. This can be achieved by modifying the default parameters to achieve the desired effect. The size of the database can be set. The database definition file contains a specification of how each customer, account and standing order record is to be constructed (Figure 1). A *set database characteristics* function provides a machine independent means of creating a database definition file.

A *generate database* process takes as input the database definition and a number of other files which allow the parameterization of the generated database. A person names file contains a set of typical first and last names for customers of the country for which the database is being created. Similarly, a town names file contains typical road and town names for the country for which the database is being created. Finally, an account parameters file contains values which represent initial starting values for accounts of different types. The generate database process can be configured so that it generates the database load files account, customer, customer-account and standing order in the format required by the bulk data load facility of the database system being evaluated.

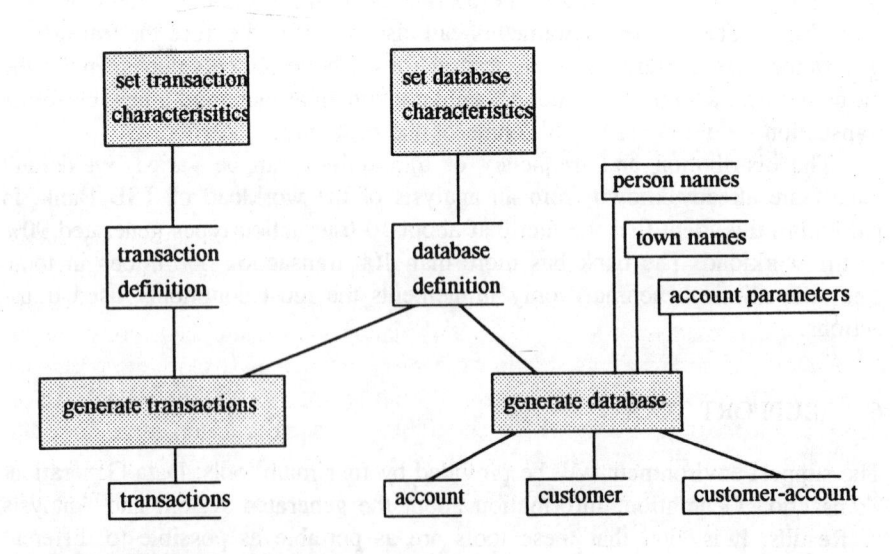

FIGURE 12.1. Generation tools.

6.2 Transaction generation

A machine independent process *set transaction characteristics* provides a means of tailoring the transaction profile. This includes aspects such as the number of different types of transaction and the values contained in the transactions. This information is saved in a transaction definition file. A further process *generate transactions* then takes as input both the transaction and database definition files. Transactions are generated using a random number generator and use the database definition file to ensure that the transactions generated refer to valid accounts and customers, or in the case of new accounts and customers that they did not previously exist. The transaction generator also creates transactions which are not valid to check the operation of the database when information is incorrectly input to the system.

In order to permit validation of the correct operation of the testing run, the transaction generator creates further tables. These include values which relate to the total number of transactions of each type processed and the total value of credits and debits. In addition the generator will randomly select a number of accounts and then monitor the operations that are undertaken on that account. At the end of processing these accounts are checked to ensure that the database contains the correct values. The transactions can be generated so that they can comply with the input format requirements of the database system under test. The generation system also permits the creation of a number of different streams of transactions. This allows the database system under test to be driven by any number of transaction streams.

MIS queries do not need to be generated in the same way because the aim is to run a set of queries which capture typical queries in such an environment. The same queries when executed against different size databases will naturally reflect the scaling factor which has been applied to the database generation.

6.3 Information system

The information system is intended to provide a means of determining the likely effect of a particular query. It takes as input the transaction and database definition files and because the system has been constructed in a computable manner will allow extraction of statistics about the generated data. For example the number of rows which should be returned for a particular query can be determined precisely from the database definition file, so that the output can be checked. Further, the rows which should be returned as a result of an MIS query, can be determined without having to access the database. The information system is provided as an environment independent package which simply has to input the database definition file.

6.4 Results analysis

In order to evaluate the performance of a high performance parallel database machine it will be necessary to obtain monitoring information from the database machine itself. This will include aspects such as processor, memory and disk usage, as well as timing information concerning the processing and residency times of transactions and MIS queries. This analysis is machine specific, due to the monitoring information that is required. Of particular interest will be the ability to analyse what happens to performance when either the data is skewed or access to the database is skewed compared to the way in which data has been partitioned. A further use of such a performance evaluation mechanism will be to provide much more detailed information about the way in which the machine has to be scaled depending upon the change of use which naturally occurs during the life of a database.

7 RUNNING THE APPLICATION MIMIC

The primary role for the application mimic system is to provide a standard benchmark for large SQL database systems, and for this, it is necessary to specify precisely the manner in which the benchmarking process is to be carried out. When used as a design tool the system designer clearly has the freedom to employ the mimic as appropriate for his or her performance evaluation tests.

For benchmarking purposes it is necessary to lay down the specifications for:

- programme of test runs
- the size of each test database
- number of transactions for each size of database
- timing points
- validation of benchmark output
- reporting of results.

The proposed protocol for the benchmarking process is discussed in Jelly et al. (1994). The testing programme and the approach used for performance measurement are outlined here.

7.1 Testing programme

Figure 12.2 shows the testing programme to be run when the application mimic acts in its benchmarking role. A series of differently sized databases and transactions are generated, and two test runs performed on each. After loading the database, the OLTP and MIS operations are tested (consecutively on the first run, concurrently on the second) and then the End of Day processing is performed. The 'End of Day' processing follows the procedure normally adopted in most large commercial systems. It comprises two stages: the handling of standing order payments and statement production, and the production of audit information from the audit trail maintained throughout the interactive phase. This processing stage not only mimics real database operation but provides the information for the validation of the benchmark process by allowing the final state of the database to be checked against the operations recorded in the audit trail. Thus the benchmark covers the three standard database modes of operation: online transaction processing, decision support and batch processing.

First Run
Load database
    OLTP operations
    MIS queries
    'End of Day' processing

Second Run
Load database
    OLTP operations||MIS queries
    'End of Day' processing

FIGURE 12.2. Testing strategy.

7.2 Performance measurement

Previous benchmarks have incorporated two approaches to timing: measurements based on throughput either at a micro or macro level, e.g. transactions/second (Serlin, 1991), equivalent database ratio (O'Neil, 1991), or length of time for a specified number and mix of operations (Dewitt, 1991). This reflects the different interests of those concerned with performance evaluation: the system user is likely to be concerned with such aspects as query response time, transaction residency time; the database manager may focus on throughput over a longer period of time and the platform manufacturer may wish to emphasise such figures as transaction execution time. This divergence of interests is a problem for all performance evaluation, and leads to the general conclusion that the production of a benchmark as a single figure value is inappropriate and may be misleading. Work is currently being undertaken to specify the set of measurements that will appropriately represent the performance of the database system and provide a valid basis for comparison for users and manufacturers.

Timing of the different operational stages is mandatory for the benchmark tests: provisionally it is proposed that each stage in the test runs, i.e. the database load, the OLTP operations, the MIS responses and End of Day processing are all separately timed and these results are reported for the sets of differently sized databases. When the application mimic system is used for design support it is likely that developers will require a finer granularity of timing points: the actual execution time of transactions and queries will be related to system dependent performance aspects such as CPU usage, I/O bandwidths and scheduling policies, as indicated earlier.

8 CONCLUSIONS

This chapter has shown how performance evaluation tools can be constructed which are applicable to any SQL database server and operational environment and has discussed the role of application mimics as the basis for benchmarking and designing database systems within a unified and coherent structure. In particular, it has described ways of generating large volumes of realistic data which is based upon symbolic rather than numeric data. It has also shown how large numbers of transaction can be generated for the mimic application. It has highlighted the need for a means of determining the likely effect of an MIS query without having to access the actual database so that output result can be checked, and has shown how this can be supported by the inclusion of semantic computability within the data. The system can be used to explore the effect of MIS queries which are not part of those supplied with the performance evaluation system but which better reflect the application environment.

REFERENCES

Cook, R. J. (1993) Performance Testing of the IDIOMS Parallel Database Machine, MSc Thesis, University of Sheffield.

DeWitt, D. (1991) The Wisconsin Benchmark: Past, Present and Future, in: *The Benchmark Handbook* (Ed. J. Gray), pp. 119–166.

Dietrich, S., Brown, M., Cortes-Rello, E. and Wunderlin, S. (1992) A Practitioners Introduction to Database Performance Measurement, *Computer Journal*, 35(4), August.

England, R. *et al.* (1992) The Performance of the IDIOMS Parallel Database Machine, in: (Eds. M. Valero, M.R. Jane and E Onate) *Parallel Computing and Transputer Applications'92 (PACTA'92)*, IOS Press Amsterdam.

Forster, H. (1993) The HPCN Programme, in: *Performance Evaluation of Parallel Systems Workshop* (invited talk), University of Warwick, November.

Gray, J. (Ed.) (1991) *The Benchmark Handbook*, Morgan Kaufmann.

International Standards Organization (1987) Database Language SQL, ISO 9075:1987(E).

Jelly, I., Kerridge, J. and Bates, C. (1994) Benchmarking Parallel SQL Database Machines, in: *Proc. British National Conference on Databases*, July 1994, Guildford, UK. LNCS, Springer-Verlag.

Kerridge, J. M. (1991) The Design of the IDIOMS Parallel Database Machine, *Proc. British National Conf. on Databases 9* (Wolverhampton, 1991), in: *Aspects of Databases* (Eds. M.S. Jackson and A.E. Robinson), Oxford, Butterworth–Heinemann.

Kerridge, J. M. (1994) The IDIOMS Parallel Database Machine: Design, Performance and Future Directions, in: *Proceedings of 6th Transputer/occam International Conference*, Tokyo, June.

Kerridge, J., Jelly, I. and Bates, C. (1994) Evaluation of High Performance Parallel Database Machines, in: *Proceedings of European Conference on High Performance Computing and Networks*, Munich, Germany, April 1994, LNCS, Springer-Verlag, Vol 1, pp. 424–429.

O'Neil, P. E. (1991) The Set Query Benchmark, in: *The Benchmark Handbook* (Ed. J. Gray), pp. 209–246.

Serlin, O. (1991) The History of Debit Credit and TPC, TPC-A and TPC-B, in: *The Benchmark Handbook* (Ed. J. Gray), pp. 19–38.

Thompson, P. J. and Waithe, S. W. (1993) The Design and Implementation of the IDIOMS On-line Transaction Processing Simulator, in: (Eds. T. Duranni et al.) *Transputer Applications'91*, IOS Press, Amsterdam.

Turbifill, C., Orji, C. and Bitton, D. (1991) AS^{3}AP: An ANSI SQL Standard Scalable and Portable Benchmark for Relational Database Systems, in: *The Benchmark Handbook* (Ed. J. Gray), pp. 167–208.

PART 4
Applications

13 Real Commercial Applications on Parallel Database Systems

C. Upstill, P. Allen, I. Cramb and N. Winterbottom
Parallel Applications Centre
University of Southampton

1 INTRODUCTION

The University of Southampton Parallel Applications Centre (PAC) is one of Europe's leading independent organizations applying parallel high-performance computing (HPC) technology to problems in industry and commerce.

Based at the University's Science Park at Chilworth, the PAC is a new kind of venture for a UK University. The PAC is run much like a high-technology company rather than a traditional university research group, with a strong emphasis on high-quality work and well-managed projects, deploying a highly professional staff who work to modern software engineering and quality practices within an effective software security regime.

The PAC was established with multi-million pound funding under the joint UK Department of Trade and Industry and Science & Engineering Research Council Parallel Applications Programme. PAC projects cover a wide range of HPC applications from engineering and scientific supercomputing to high-performance databases. Using only fully-supported commercially available parallel systems, the PAC works closely with industrial and commercial end-users and with leading third-party software developers, acting as a porting centre for existing software, and developing new software to commercial standards.

High-performance database systems significantly improve the potential for information management and utilization, bringing substantial commercial benefits. Until recently, the full exploitation of relational databases has been limited by the cost and performance of available computing platforms. High-performance, scalable open parallel systems are poised to transform commercial data processing and take databases into new areas where the cost of conventional solutions is prohibitive.

The PAC's database team is experienced in porting large mainframe databases and applications to the Centre's parallel Meiko/Oracle and Teradata systems. A comprehensive suite of software tools has been developed to assist in the modelling, monitoring and management of parallel database applications.

In this chapter, tools developed at the PAC for parallel database system evaluation, tuning and management are described. Tools under development for analysis, performance prediction and design are discussed.

These tools have proved invaluable for porting real commercial databases and applications to parallel systems. We summarize the PAC's experience in porting large operational database systems from conventional to parallel database technology in collaborations with British Gas, Rover and Ordnance Survey.

2　SOFTWARE TOOLS FOR PARALLEL RELATIONAL DATABASE SYSTEMS

High-performance database systems enable improved information management and improved information utilization, offering substantial commercial benefits. But as the power and complexity of relational database systems increase, the necessity for system analysis and management tools also increases. With parallel systems, new issues affect database design, capacity planning and system configuration. System behaviour and performance become more and more dependent on the ability of database administrators and system managers to identify and remove bottlenecks as and when they occur.

Our experience at the PAC in porting real commercial databases and applications to parallel systems has led to the development of generic software tools for the design, evaluation, tuning and management of parallel high-performance database systems. Taken together, these tools provide a software environment in which we can:

- drive a system to its limits in a controlled and monitored environment;
- generate and display information about system resources and activity in real-time; and
- predict system performance as a function of hardware and software parameters.

We have developed working prototypes in all three categories. These prototypes have proved invaluable in porting commercial operational databases and applications software to parallel systems, in collaboration with blue-chip UK companies including British Gas and Rover Group, and with the Ordnance Survey, among others. The description and figures below indicate how these tools are used.

In the first category, so-called Driver software has been developed to simulate the loads placed on systems by multiple users and applications. The package simulates concurrent users and allows exhaustive database testing, using varying numbers of processors and processes, running transactions which may involve many tens of thousands of lines of code. All key parameters can be changed at run-time. Further development is under way to support mixed-load transaction processing.

In the second category, tools have been developed to gather, process and display system parameters (e.g. physical I/O rate, contention for data, parallel lock manager activity). This Monitor software displays detailed information about system performance in histogram form at run-time, aggregating large amounts of information from many parallel processes.

This package can be used to facilitate detection and removal of bottlenecks within a system – one of the most important aspects of parallel processing. Further development is required to automate the identification and removal of bottlenecks, leading to automated parallel database system tuning.

Most of the software developed so far runs on both our Meiko Relational DataCache (a parallel ORACLE system) and our Teradata DBC, with identical interfaces and substantial use of identical code. All our activities have been oriented towards the construction of generic software, capable of running with any merchant relational database management system without significant change.

In the third category, we are developing modelling tools to predict database throughput and response time, given machine characteristics, database structure and workload profile. The package (labelled Model in the figures) assumes a relational model.

The machine model is currently generic in that it does not attempt to describe design details which are manufacturer specific. A machine is specified in terms of basic resources such as numbers of processors and their speed, numbers of disks and their performance parameters and available memory cache space. It is assumed that the design of the machine and software is such as to make best use of these primary resources.

The objective is to devise the simplest characterization of the system, database and workload which is consistent with predictions of useful accuracy. In principle, we can model any platform, any RDBMS, any database and any transactions. The prototype modelling software runs on a 486 PC. It is being developed against controlled testing of real database systems, using the Driver software to exercise the system and the Monitor software to analyse system behaviour. This is shown schematically in Figure 13.1.

In a typical project life-cycle, our software environment is used for database physical design, implementation and refinement, concentrating on performance issues such as indexing strategies, distribution of data across disks and distribution of work among CPUs.

The fully-developed Model is used for database design, capacity planning, system configuration and performance prediction, as shown in Figure 13.2.

206   *Parallel Information Processing*

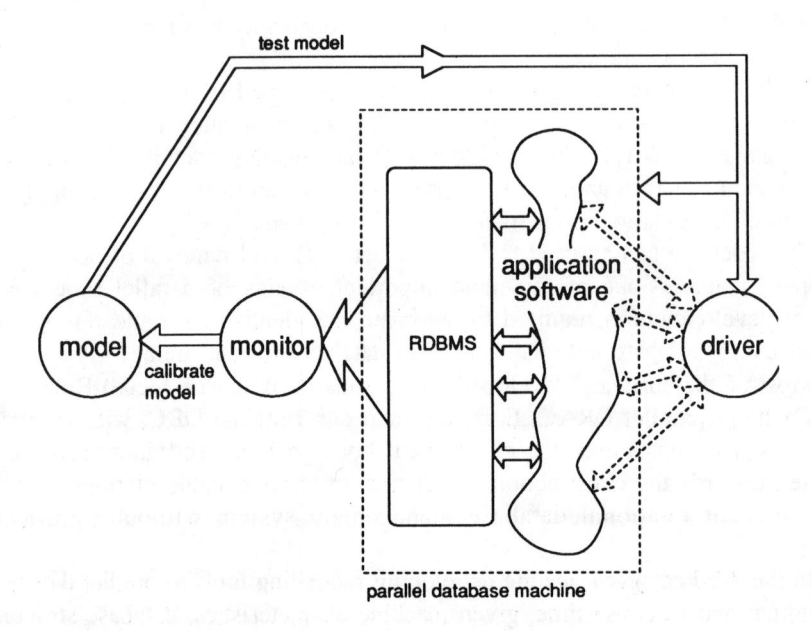

FIGURE 13.1. Development of a Model.

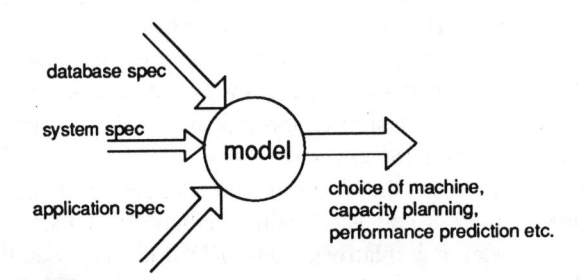

FIGURE 13.2. The modelling process.

Once a prototype system is implemented, the Driver software is used to exercise the system and the Monitor software to analyse system behaviour. The results are used to refine the design and implementation of the database and the application software, as shown in Figure 13.3.

Finally, with a production system exercised by a user population, the Monitor software will be used to analyse system behaviour and the results used to tune the operational database, as shown in Figure 13.4.

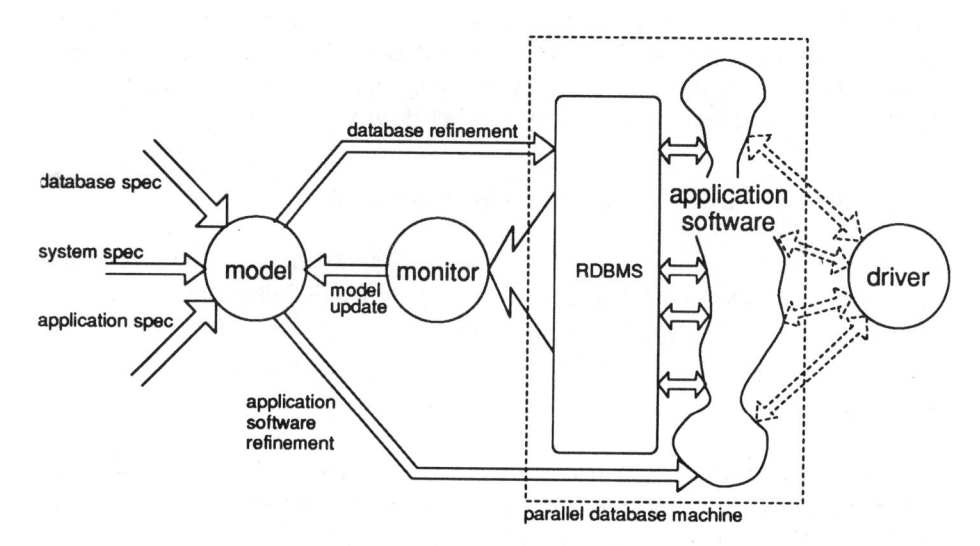

FIGURE 13.3. Refinement.

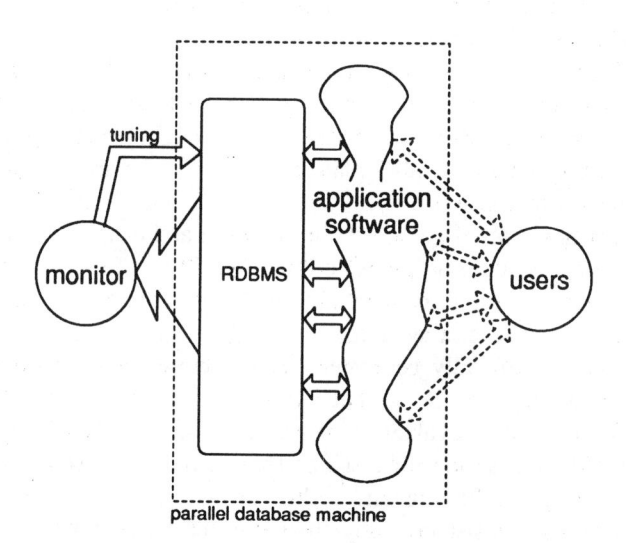

FIGURE 13.4. Monitoring in an operational environment.

In summary, we have produced a suite of prototype tools which has proved invaluable in the porting of large commercial relational database applications from conventional to parallel systems, and in trialing and evaluating the results. These tools are being continually developed to extend their functionality and genericity over a range of platforms. This work is proceeding in the context of porting commercially important databases and applications, to ensure that the requirements of end-users are met in providing for the design, implementation, optimization and management of any parallel database system.

3 COMMERCIAL DATABASES ON PARALLEL SYSTEMS

In this section we give an overview of the PAC's experience in porting large operational database systems from conventional to parallel database technology in collaboration with British Gas, Rover Group and Ordnance Survey.

3.1 British Gas

British Gas plc are the principal supplier of natural gas to the UK energy market, and a rapidly expanding force in energy markets worldwide. Large relational database applications play a critical role in the day-to-day business activities of British Gas. These applications fall into two broad classes, those requiring a rapid throughput of transactions and those where data is accessed via complex queries in MIS and decision support.

The PAC and its collaborators at British Gas are trialing a range of commercial database applications on parallel systems. The aims of this work are to investigate the principal issues associated with managing commercial relational database applications on a parallel platform. Key factors are cost/performance, scalability, reliability and usability.

The project has centred around the installation and evaluation of three databases (data and applications software) on the PAC Meiko Relational DataCache. These provide a broad range of database and transaction types, enabling wide-ranging evaluation of such a system.

The first is an artificially generated data structure, similar to that specified for the TPC-B benchmark. It has been created as a vehicle for our software development, and to allow evaluation of parallel system configurations for high-throughput simple transaction processing. The second is a complex commercial database supporting the buying and selling of gas from North Sea suppliers. Typical transactions consist of many thousands of lines of C with embedded SQL The third is a complex MIS and OLTP application which runs on several DEC VAX machines.

Importing Oracle databases and applications from both VM and VMS environments has proved relatively straightforward. The software tools described above have proved invaluable for porting these databases and applications, and for tuning the system. We are not able to disclose detailed results, but we can state that Meiko/Oracle system has price/performance in line with the manufacturer's claims, and has shown the degree of reliability essential for commercial operation.

3.2 Rover group

Traditionally, large complex businesses have relied on physically separate systems for such tasks as stock control, order processing and management information provision. Parallel technology provides the performance to simultaneously support a wide range of databases and applications in a single system.

Rover Group is Britain's largest motor manufacturer, producing approximately half a million vehicles per year. Rover is moving from build-to-stock to build-to-order, with the objective of building and delivering a vehicle to a customer's requirements in two weeks. Information Technology is critical, and must provide timely access to all corporate information and data from wherever it is needed within the company. Rover intend to use a *corporate repository* – a single authoritative source of data, based on a single data design and logical model. This requires an architecture with the capability to simultaneously support time-critical on-line transaction processing and MIS/DSS applications.

The implementation of such a system on a scale sufficient to meet the information needs of a business as large and complex as Rover is a significant technological challenge. Larger databases exist, and applications exist with greater OLTP demands, but a single repository with support for mixed loads of different types of data processing and applications on this scale means that parallelism is essential to provide the data processing power required.

Rover and the Centre are collaborating in several aspects of applying Teradata's parallel database technology to meet this challenge. The modelling tools described above are proving invaluable in this work.

3.3 Ordnance Survey

As well as commercial databases and applications, we are involved in the use of relational databases to manage and manipulate spatial data. The Ordnance Survey is currently investigating moving from the file-based storage of large-scale data to a relational model. We have ported the Ordnance Survey's prototype Administrative Area Polygon database, and associated applications software, involving many and very complex transactions, from a DEC Station 5000 running ORACLE under ULTRIX to the 21 processor Meiko Relational DataCache at the PAC. We obtained linear or close-to-linear speed-up, clearly demonstrating that this type of application is well-suited to implementation on a parallel platform.

4 CONCLUSIONS

We have developed sophisticated tools developed for the design, evaluation, tuning and management of parallel high-performance database systems. This software environment has proved invaluable for the successful trialing of parallel database systems.

Historically, scientific and engineering applications have been the first to take advantage of new computing technology. This trend has been borne out in the case of parallel computing. However, cost-effective parallel technology is poised to transform commercial data processing, and carry database technology into new areas where the cost of conventional solutions is prohibitive. The PAC and its collaborators will be at the forefront of these developments.

5 ACKNOWLEDGEMENTS

The authors are grateful to their colleague Ming Guo for his contribution to the software tools described in this chapter.

The PAC gratefully acknowledges support for this work from the UK DTI/SERC Parallel Applications Programme, and from British Gas, Meiko, NCR/Teradata, Oracle, Ordnance Survey, Rover Group and Sun Microsystems.

14 Recursive Query Processing on a Connection Machine

Th. Zurek[+], E. M. Minty[*] and P. Thanisch[+]

[*] *Edinburgh Parallel Computing Centre
Edinburgh University*

[+] *Department of Computer Science
Edinburgh University*

1 INTRODUCTION

1.1 Parallel databases

Megapundits in high-performance database technology have been amazingly wrong in their predictions. Ten years ago, the paper *Database Machines: An Idea Whose Time Has Passed* (Boral and DeWitt, 1983) wrote the obituary for parallel database systems. Today, of course, huge profits are made by companies producing database machines and these machines are used to good effect in many branches of industry, commerce and government. If we look back just four years, the megapundits made another prediction, namely that the only hardware architecture suitable for database machines is *shared-nothing* architecture, i.e. an architecture in which each processor has its own memory and secondary storage access and in which the processors communicate via message passing. There is also a presumption that the processors execute asynchronously. We shall refer to a parallel computer that conforms to this architectural description as a *multicomputer*. In this chapter, we would like to dispute the more recent position taken by the megapundits.

Let us focus our attention on the relational data model which allows us to think of the data as if it were organized in tables and which provides a set of simple operations to be performed on these tables. The most computationally expensive of these operations is the *join*, which combines information from two tables to create a new table, which may, in turn, be joined with other another table.

DeWitt and Gray (1990) view the problem as being the efficient, parallel implementation of the join operator. For them, the key computational problem is to implement the join operator so that it executes efficiently once.

We are interested in a rather different class of queries, namely the *linear recursive* queries, which implies that we need to *repeat* an operation, such as a join, some *data-dependent* number of times. For this class of queries, a richer repertoire of operators, such as transitive closure, are potentially useful. We represent parallel query processing strategies at a level of abstraction from the hardware and software implementation that facilitates efficient implementation on a variety of parallel platforms, not just shared-nothing architectures.

To prove our point, we use a target architecture that is radically different from that envisaged by DeWitt and Gray, namely Thinking Machines Corporation's Connection Machine CM-200. In the CM-200, operations are carried out on all the data items synchronously. This results in a single control flow on highly parallelized data. This approach fits well with the concepts of data parallelism, in particular because most of the relational algebra operators allow the data to be split into a large number of portions which can be operated on independently.

The communication effort to be made by the programmer is to describe (mostly regular) patterns of communication to distribute the data amongst the large number of processors. This allows communication calls to be optimized by the compiler and/or performed by highly optimized communication functions provided through software libraries, the hardware itself or the operating system. This, combined with the ability of the CM-200 to perform array operations on large amounts of data at high speed, makes it a platform that is worth considering for problems of database processing.

We concentrate on a particular problem in query processing, namely finding a technique that can produce answers efficiently for the class of *linear recursive* queries. This class of queries is not as general as the class of recursive queries studied by the deductive database community, but it is more general than the class of queries covered by the traditional query languages as SQL, QBE or Quel.

Relational databases only became a practical proposition when researchers developed sophisticated query optimization techniques. These analyse a user's query, expressed in a high-level declarative query language such as SQL, and, using statistical knowledge about the data in the database, choose a sequence of operations that can produce an answer to the query 'efficiently', i.e. using a reasonable amount of processor time and disk operations.

With the added computational difficulty of recursive queries, the need for good query optimization techniques is even greater. In this chapter, we describe the work that must be done to build an optimizer that can exploit the techniques that we have developed for query processing.

1.2 Overview

In section 1.3 we will give a short introduction to the Connection Machine architecture and the underlying paradigm of data parallelism.

In section 2 a query processing model is presented. It is based on the notion of tuple generations as produced by an ordinary bottom-up evaluation of a linear recursive query. These generations will be organized in a matrix. This matrix model provides a kind of gameboard for query processing: several 'moves' (i.e. database operations) are allowed to move over the board (i.e. to process the query) and we can think of several sequential and parallel strategies of combining the moves to 'run' over the board.

Section 3 discusses the optimizing aspects of these strategies and identifies several data and query characteristics that influence the performance of query processing. One result of this analysis is that performance heavily depends on the performance of the join and transitive closure operations that are applied for processing the query. Therefore section 4 presents a parallel join and a parallel transitive closure algorithm and discusses the respective performance issues.

Section 5 gives some performance results for processing linear recursive queries on DAG- and tree-structured database relations. The results are summarized in section 6.

1.3 Introduction to the CM-200

The CM we used is an SIMD computer with 16384 processors connected by a 10-dimensional hypercube network. Each processor has a local memory of 256 kBits so the CM has 512 MBytes total memory. In one step each active processor executes the same instruction but on different data (i.e. SIMD) whereas inactive processors do not participate. The successful use of the CM requires an algorithm that can exploit this data parallelism data parallelism. The large number of processors, the underlying communication network and the parallel mass storage system – the Data Vault – make it suitable for processing large amounts of data.

The Data Vault has 10 GBytes of memory and a possible data transferring rate of 25 MBytes per second. It employs an array of 42 disk drives. Of these 42 drives, 32 hold data. Reading from and writing to these 32 drives means reading and writing on 32 drives in parallel. Having a fast secondary storage system is really important as the sizes of databases are growing with increasingly ambitious database modelling.

Data parallel computing associates one processor with each data element. Therefore parallel data structures are spread across the processors, with a single element stored in each processor's memory. When parallel data structures contain more elements than the system has processors, the system operates in virtual processor mode, presenting the user with a large number of processors with a correspondingly smaller memory and performance. Each physical processor is made to simulate the appropriate number of virtual processors (Thinking Machine Corp., 1991).

2 QUERY PROCESSING

We will now describe a model for processing linear recursive queries. This model is based on the notion of tuple *generations* as they are produced by a naive bottom-up evaluation of a linear recursive query. This is described in section 2.1. Section 2.2 introduces the *generation matrix model* – a query processing model based on tuple generations. In the general query optimizer architecture given by Ioannidis and Wong (1991)[1] this model can be related to the ordering stage, although it also covers also aspects of the planning stage.

2.1 Tuple generations

In this chapter we will deal with linear recursive queries that have the following form[2]:

$$P(X_1, X_2, Z) = E(X_1, X_2, Z)$$
$$P(X_1, X_2, Z) = P(X_1, X_2, Y) \qquad (1)$$

(1) is called the *exit-rule* or *exit-equation* (2) and the *linear recursive rule/ equation* of the query. The term *linear* refers to the fact that the predicate symbol P of the left side of the equation appears only once on the right side. Jagadish *et al.* (1987) and Zurek *et al.* (1993) show that every linear recursive query containing only one linear recursive rule can be transformed to an equivalent query of the form shown above so we can assume this general form.

---

[1] This architecture consists mainly of three stages: *rewriting* (the query) – *ordering* (the operations to evaluate the query) – *planning* (the execution from a structural and physical point of view).

[2] These are *Datalog equations* (Ullman, 1988). Throughout this chapter we rather prefer describing the queries by using relational algebra operators to make the reader aware of the operations that are involved in query processing although the resulting expressions are in 'Datalog style', i.e. we use Datalog-like notations like $P(X,Y,Z)$ and refer to attributes in the relation P by variables X,Y,Z. This also simplifies the notation of a join as the join conditions can be easily derived by matching the variables. Therefore we just notate a join by   without giving the conditions explicitly. This notation is a hybrid of relational algebra and logic programming notation.

Using relational algebra expressions suggests that the techniques proposed in this chapter can be applied to a wide range of query languages and not only to Datalog

The naive way of evaluating a linear recursive query is bottom-up, i.e. starting with the initial relation given by the exit equation further tuples are added by applying the linear recursive equation until no more new tuples are added. We will demonstrate this by an example.

Example

Let us consider a query with (1) as the exit and (2) as the linear recursive rule.

For the purpose of a bottom-up evaluation the rules (1) and (2) are used in the following way:

1. The initial tuples are given by the exit rule (1)
   These tuples are said to be of *generation P_0* so

   $$P_0(X_1, X_2, Z) = E(X_1, X_2, Z).$$

2. Further tuples are added by sequential applications of equation (2) to produce the generations $P_1, P_2, \ldots$:

   $$P_{i+1}(X_1, X_2, Z) = \begin{array}{l} P_i(X_1, X_2, Y) \\ Q(X_1, Y, Z) \end{array}$$

Therefore a bottom-up evaluation produces the generations P_i of tuples in a sequential order starting with the initial relation E as P_0 and joining Q in each step.

Finally the resulting relation P of the query is obtained by

$$P = \bigcup_{i \geq 0} P_i = \bigcup_{i=0}^{M} P_i$$

such that

$$P_j \subseteq \bigcup_{i=0}^{M} P_i \quad \text{for all } j > M \qquad (3)$$

which means that all P_j with $j > M$ do not contribute any new tuple to P. The existence of such an M is guaranteed (Ullman, 1988, 1989).

$$P_3(X_1, X_2, Z) = P_2(X_1, X_2, Z) \bowtie Q(X_1, Y, Z)$$

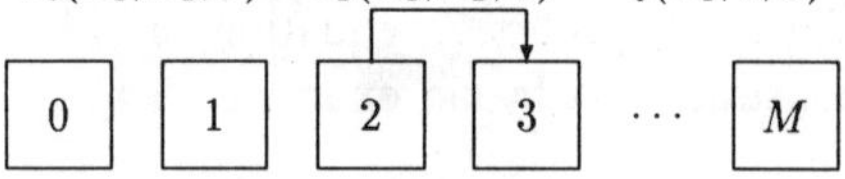

| 0 | 1 | 2 | 3 | $\cdots$ | M |

FIGURE 14.1. Graphical representation of a bottom-up evaluation producing a chain of tuple-generations.

Normally we choose M to be the smallest number such that (3) holds.

The notion of representing the resulting relation as a set of generations of tuples is quite useful. Note that a generation is a set of tuples that were generated in the same way and generations do not have to be disjoint as some tuples might be derived in several ways. The union of all generations represents the result of the query. In figures in this chapter, the set of tuples in a generation shall be represented graphically as a square.

A bottom-up evaluation can then be considered as producing a chain of generations, up to generation M, as in Figure 14.1, where we get generation P_{i+1} by applying the linear recursive rule (or equation) to generation P_i.

We note that a bottom-up evaluation requires M join operations, where M depends on the characteristics of the underlying data (relations).

2.2 Generation matrix

Jagadish *et al.* (1987) presented an alternative technique to process linear recursive queries consisting of an exit rule like (1) and a linear recursive rule (2). This technique computes the transitive closure of relation Q or a relation derived from Q. An important numerical parameter, d, for this technique is obtained from a graph theoretic analysis of the query. We do not want to go into the details of this technique. The reader might refer to Jagadish *et al.* (1987) or Zurek *et al.* (1993).

The important thing about this technique is that it provides a possibility of computing tuple generations other than applying the linear recursive rule (2) to generation P_i to compute generation P_{i+1}. For comparing the bottom-up and the transitive-closure technique we will reorganize the generations in form of a *generation matrix*.

In the last section we introduced tuple generations as subsets of the final result. In Figure 14.1 they are represented as a square in the order in which they are produced by a naive bottom-up evaluation. For our purposes they are reordered and organized in a matrix with generation P_0 as the top left element. This matrix has d columns and M/d rows where

- d is a data-independent parameter given by the query, and
- M is the number defined in (3); M depends on the characteristics of the actual database relation involved in the query and is therefore a data-dependent parameter.

Figure 14.2 shows the generations P_i that form the result P of a linear recursive query. Basically, computing the result of a linear recursive query means computing the generations of its underlying generation matrix. We will now show graphically in which way these generations can be computed: we start in the top left corner as the generation P_0 (square 0) is given by the exit rule (1). Our goal is to proceed to every square (i.e. to compute every generation) in the matrix. Various operations are allowed that correspond to moves from one square to another:

(R)   moving to the next generation to the right (i.e. computing P_{i+1} from P_i) means applying the linear recursive rule r to P_i (see Figure 14.3),

(R2)   moving two generations to the right (i.e. computing P_{i+2} from P_i) means applying the linear recursive rule r twice or applying the 2-step rule[3], r^2, once to P_i (see Figure 14.4),

(Rd)   moving to the generation below (i.e. computing P_{i+d} from P_i) means applying the linear recursive d-step rule to P_i (see Figure 14.5),

(TC)   covering, or moving to, all generations of a column means applying the transitive closure technique using the d-step rule r^d. This move can only be executed if we have already reached or passed P_g where g is – like d – another characteristic of the linear recursive rule (see Figure 14.6).

Finally we can apply (R), (R2) and (Rd) simultaneously to a group of generations (squares) to reach their respective neighbours (see Figure 14.7), i.e. applying a join to several generations, e.g.

$$P_{k+1} \cup P_{l+1} = (P_k \cup P_l) \quad Q$$

---

[3] An x-step rule, r^x, is a rule that has the same effect as applying a linear recursive rule, r, x times. The 2-step and the d-step rules of (2) are shown in Table 14.1.

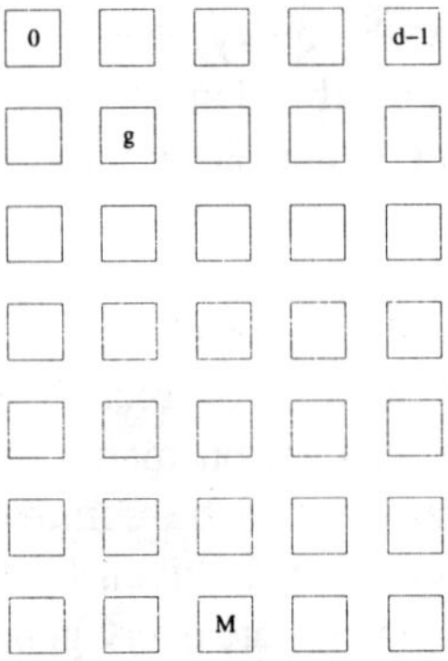

FIGURE 14.2. Generating matrix.

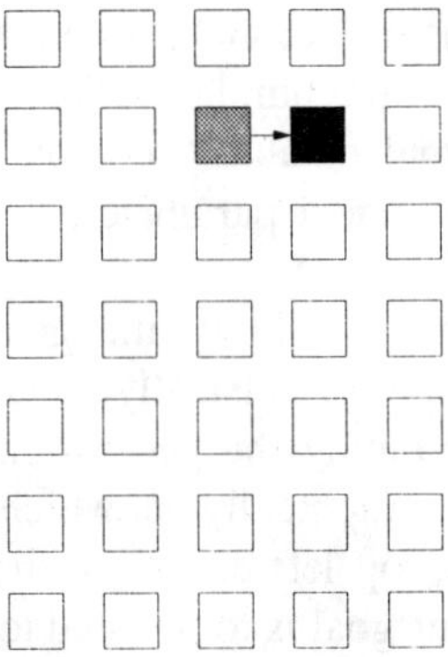

FIGURE 14.3. Moving one square to the right by applying the linear recursive rule r.

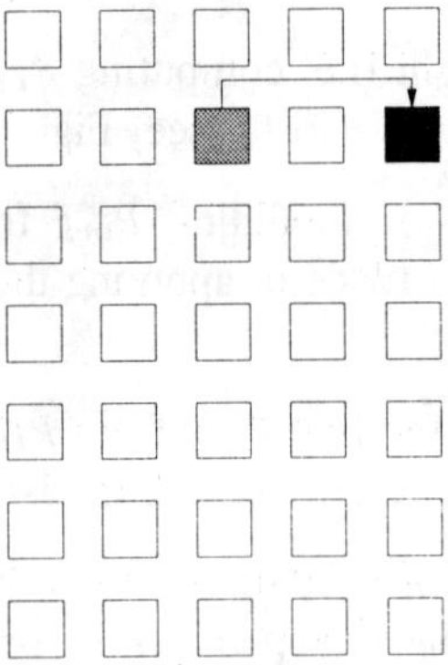

FIGURE 14.4. Moving two squares to the right by applying the 2-step rule r^2.

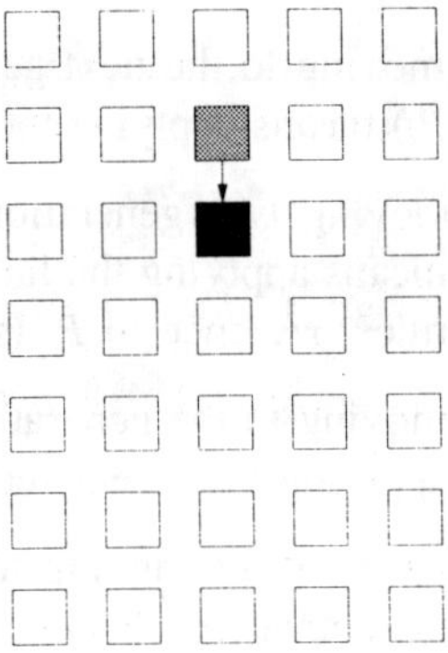

FIGURE 14.5. Moving one square down by applying the d-step rule r^d.

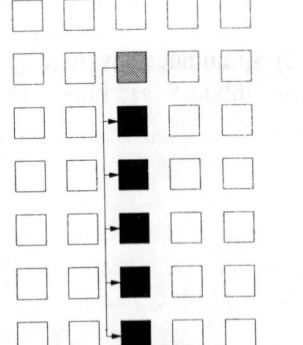

FIGURE 14.6. Covering the rest of a column by applying the transitive closure technique.

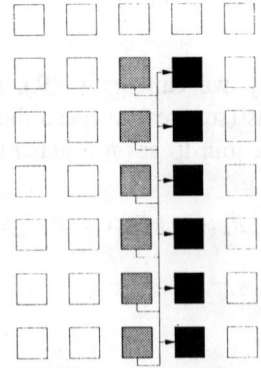

FIGURE 14.7. Simultaneous right move.

A summary of the moves is given in Table 14.1; the costs of the moves are shown in Table 14.2.

TABLE 14.1. Correspondence to operations.

move	corresponding operation
(R)	$P_{i+1} = P_i \bowtie Q$
(R2)	$P_{i+2} = P_i \bowtie Q \bowtie Q$
(Rd)	$P_{i+d} = P_i \bowtie \underbrace{Q \bowtie \cdots \bowtie Q}_{Q^d}$
(TC)	$Q_{a_j}^+$ for $j = 1, \ldots, T$

$Q_{a_j} = \sigma_{X = a_j}(Q(X,Y,Z))$ and $\{a_1, \ldots, a_T\}$ is the set of values of the X-attribute in $Q(X,Y,Z)$.

TABLE 14.2. Costs of the moves.

move	costs
(R)	1 join for each move
(R2)	1 join for each move; 1 join for building $Q \bowtie Q$ (once)
(Rd)	1 join for each move; $(d-1)$ joins for building Q^d (once)
(TC)	T selection operations to build the Q_{a_j}'s; T transitive closures

Obviously we could also generate moves (R3) or (R4) to move three or four generations to the right by deriving the 3-step rule and the 4-step rule. These (Rx) moves do not appear to be of any practical use as they 'jump' over one or more squares that have to be visited anyway. But we should note the general possibility of creating and applying such moves. We will mainly apply the (R) and the (TC) move.

The generation matrix model is one amongst various formalisms for representing parallel computations. The formalism adopted depends, in part, on the way in which the parallel algorithm was designed. For example a parallel algorithm could be represented by a directed acyclic graph (DAG) in which the nodes correspond to sequential tasks and the arcs correspond to a precedence relation. This approach is mainly used for task-farming parallelism. Alternatively, the computation could be represented by a dataflow diagram.

For our present purposes, we use a special-purpose graphical representation where the 'nodes' correspond to intermediate results that are all sub-relations of the result relation. There is a partial order between the nodes in the sense that

- one subrelation may only be generated using our repertoire of simple operations once certain other subrelations have been generated, and
- if two subrelations are incomparable under the partial order, then they may be generated by concurrent, independent operations.

Several strategies/routes of 'running through the matrix' can be considered. The strategy described by Jagadish *et al.* (1987) is the following (see also Figure 14.8):

- Starting at square 0 perform right-moves (R) until you reach square g.
- Move down the column of square g – this corresponds to a (TC) move.
- Perform $(d-1)$ concurrent right moves (R) from all squares of the column in which square g is located to get to the remaining squares – this corresponds to a simultaneous right-move as shown in Figure 14.7.

Alternatively, the naive bottom-up strategy is shown in Figure 14.9.

Table 14.2 shows that the costs of a move are not constant and depend on query-dependent parameters like d and also on data-dependent parameters like T^4 or on the size of the relations involved in a join operation. Therefore predicting the costs of a strategy is not straightforward, although it would be nice if the costs of a strategy could be predicted so that an optimizer could choose the most effective strategy for each individual query.

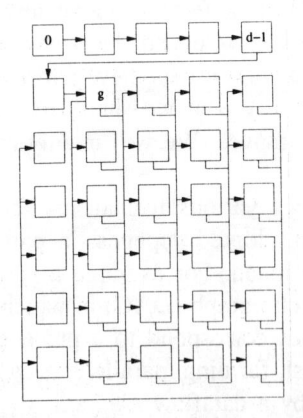

FIGURE 14.8. Transitive closure strategy of moving through the generation matrix.

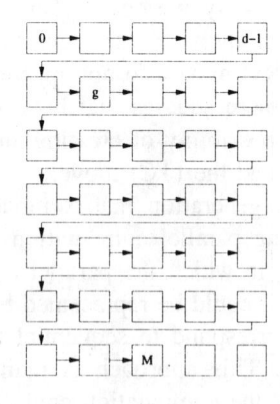

FIGURE 14.9. Bottom-up evaluation of a query.

The performance of a strategy to move through the matrix depends on several issues:

- on the value of d, i.e. the number of columns of the matrix,
- on the value of g as we are forced to perform only right-moves (R) up to square g,
- on the efficiency of a right-move (R), i.e. essentially the efficiency of the underlying join operations as one right-move is in fact executing one join operation,
- on the efficiency of the (TC) move that is dictated by

  - the number T of transitive closures for computing the generations of the column in which square g is located,
  - the efficiency of the underlying transitive closure operation.

Basically the strategy of Figure 14.8 implies

- $d-1$ joins to compute Q^d for the d-step rule r^d,
- g joins to move to generation g,
- T transitive closures to move down the column of g, and
- $d-1$ joins move simultaneously to the remaining generations.

The $g+2(d-1)$ joins and T transitive closures have to be compared with the M joins that are necessary to perform a bottom-up evaluation (see section 2.1). Comparison must also be made on the size of the relations that are involved in the joins and the transitive closures. Apart from that, the efficiency of the transitive closure technique depends also on the length L of the longest path of the underlying relation. One can expect that the transitive closure technique cannot improve the performance to a large extent, or may be even slower if L is small, which suggests that M might be also small, so the number of joins to do a bottom-up evaluation would be also small.

2.3 Parallel aspects

The generation matrix model of section 2.2 provides a framework for analysing several strategies to process a linear recursive query. The moves (R) and (TC) may be combined in several ways for query evaluation. Considerations of sequential strategies dwell upon whether to apply the (TC) move or to go rather for an ordinary bottom-up evaluation, i.e. applying (R) moves. This is a crucial

---

[4] T is the number of values in the X_1 attribute of relation Q of the linear recursive rule (2).

point and we can open the ground for a wide range of new processing strategies by involving parallelism. Parallel issues in the evaluation process are:

- **Data parallel moves**: Figure 14.7 gives already an example in which an (R) move can be applied to several portions of data (e.g. several generations) in parallel. This is called data parallelism as the same instructions are executed on different items of data. In this case data parallelism is possible because there are no constraints in between the portions of data, e.g. generations do not have to be disjoint and can be built independently from one another. This means that (R) moves – and the same applies to (TC) moves – can be performed simultaneously on several generations, e.g. as shown by Figure 14.7.
- **Different moves in parallel**: The (R) and (TC) moves do not interfere with each other so (R) and (TC) moves can be executed in parallel even on the same portion of data, i.e. (R) or (TC) can be applied whenever possible and regardless of whether there is already another activity going on.
- **Parallelizing the (R) move**: Clearly the (R) move can be parallelized internally. As we have already seen, it consists mainly of a join operation[5]. Therefore efforts should be mainly concentrated on implementing one or more appropriate[6] parallel join algorithms.
- **Parallelizing the (TC) move**: The same ideas that have applied to the (R) move can be used for the (TC) move. The dominant operation in this case is clearly the transitive closure. There are several well investigated parallel transitive closure algorithms based on boolean matrix multiplications (Akl, 1989), the Warshall constraints (Agrawal *et al.*, 1990) or hash-join techniques (Zhou *et al.*, 1993).

3   QUERY OPTIMIZER ASPECTS

Usually a database management system (DBMS) incorporates a query optimizing module that decides on the best way to process the query. Given the generation matrix model and the moves and the parallel issues of sections 2.2 and 2.3, a variety of strategies to move through the generation matrix, i.e. of processing a query, can be considered. Naturally it would be nice to find out a way to determine the optimal, i.e. the fastest or cheapest, strategy.

We will now analyse the costs $c(S)$ of a strategy S. Therefore the following notations will be used:

---

[5]Projection and selection operations may also be involved but can be neglected regarding the performance issues that are dominated by the join operation.

[6]For example, regarding the underlying machine's architecture.

- A strategy S is a list of stages s_i

$$S = [s_1, s_2, \ldots, s_n]$$

- A stage s_i is either
    - sequential, i.e. only one single move is executed in the stage, or
    - parallel, i.e. several moves are executed in parallel.

We will denote a stage as a sequence of moves

$$s_i = (m_1, m_2, \ldots, m_{k_i})$$

where $k_i = 1$ for a sequential s_i. For $k_i > 1$ all the m_j may be executed simultaneously, i.e. in parallel.

We will refer to a move m_j of a stage s_i by

$$s_i \cdot m_j$$

- We can consider the m_j to be elements of a set of move types e.g.

$$m_j \in \{(R), (R2), (Rd), (TC)\}$$

although this does not link the moves with the data on which the move is executed and which is also an important performance issue. But this keeps the notation as simple as possible for the moment.

We can now describe the costs $c(S)$ by

$$c(s) = \sum_{i=1}^{n} c(s_i) = \sum_{i=1}^{n} c(s_i \cdot m_1) \tag{4}$$

if S is sequential, i.e. all s_i in S are sequential and

$$c(s) = \sum_{i=1}^{n} c(s_i) = \sum_{i=1}^{n} \max_{j=1}^{k} (c(s_i \cdot m_j)) \tag{5}$$

if S is parallel, i.e. there is a parallel s_i in S. We note that the sequential case (4) is also covered by the (more general) parallel case (5).

Formula (5) gives two factors by which the costs of a strategy are influenced

- the number n of stages in the strategy, and
- the costs $c(s_i \cdot m_j)$ of the moves involved.

We will now track down what basic characteristics and parameters of the data relations; the query and the strategy influence these two factors.

The number n of stages that are necessary to move over the generation matrix is dominated by the size or dimensions of the matrix and the grade of parallelism achieved by the strategy. The dimensions of the matrix are determined by

- the number d of columns where d is given by the query, and
- the number of rows, which depends on the length of the longest path in the directed graph that is defined by the underlying database relation.

The size of the matrix is the same for each of the strategies we want to compare, so this will not cause any difference and can be considered as a given fact to all strategies. Evidently the number of stages can be reduced by packing as many moves into a stage as possible, i.e. executing as many moves in parallel as possible.

The costs $c(s_i \cdot m_j)$ of a single move are not constant and are difficult to calculate, as can be seen in Table 14.2: they are mainly dominated by the performance of the join and the transitive closure algorithms that are used and the parameters d (given by the query) and T (given by the data) so $c(s_i \cdot m_j)$ can be tracked down by calculating the costs of the operations involved in the move and the number of times these operations have to be executed.

The costs of a join operation are determined by

- the size of the databases relations involved in the join, and
- the data skew, i.e. whether the data values are distributed uniformly or not[7]

whereas the costs of the transitive closure operation is dominated by

- the size of the underlying graph, and
- the depth of the transitive closure.

In summary, there is a variety of parameters that influences the performance of the processing strategies. The parameters can be divided into two groups:

- *query-dependent* parameters like d and g, and

---

[7]There is a variety of papers covering the problems data skew causes on parallel joins, e.g. Walton *et al.* (1991), Wolf *et al.* (1993) and Kitsuregawa and Ogawa (1990).

- *data-dependent* parameters like the sizes of the relations involved in the query, T (the number of values for a particular attribute of a relation), the length of the longest path of the underlying graph of a relation, some data skew statistics about the distribution of attribute values and other relevant characteristics.

The first group of parameters can be derived just before the query is processed whereas the data-dependent parameters are usually accessible from the database catalogue that holds several meta-information about the data to provide it to the optimizer. So we can assume that all or most of the parameters mentioned so far are available before the query is processed.

The following sections will discuss the performance issues of an actual implementation of a join and a transitive closure algorithm and the bottom-up and transitive closure strategies of Figures 14.8 and 14.9 on a Connection Machine CM-200. Several parameters regarding implementation, operating system and hardware characteristics are also in the group of data and query parameters that influence the performance of query processing. This leads to a wide range of optimizing decisions that have to be taken to identify the best way of how to process a particular query. Discussing all these aspects exceeds the purpose of this chapter so we will concentrate on giving some ideas and some examples in sections 4 and 5.

4 PARALLEL HASH JOIN AND TC ALGORITHMS

Considerations of sections 2 and 3 worked out that the join and the transitive closure are the two crucial operations in query evaluation according to the generation matrix model. In this section we will give a short description of the two algorithms that were implemented in the experimental database system we used for performance testing. We will concentrate on the issues regarding the performance behaviour of the algorithms. The reader might refer to the bibliography to get some more details about the algorithms themselves.

4.1 Parallel hash-join

The parallel hash-join algorithm was proposed in Kitsuregawa and Matsumoto (1991). We incorporated the actual implemetation described in Minty (1993).

The notion of a parallel hash-join is quite simple. Consider joining two relations R and S on a common attribute X as in

$$R(..., X, ...) \qquad S(..., X, ...). \tag{6}$$

The tuples of R and S holding the same value on the X attribute are sent to two separate cluster spaces on the same processor. A hash function having the possible values of X as its argument gives the actual address of the processor to which the tuples are to be sent. So each processor holds the tuples that have to be joined in its two cluster spaces. Having distributed the data in this way each processor computes the cartesian product of the tuples in its cluster spaces. Finally, the local results have to be put into one relation to form the global result of the join. So the essential steps of the parallel hash-join algorithm are:

1. A parallel clustering phase in which the tuples are spread over the processors depending on their value in the join attribute.
2. A local join phase in which each processor performs a join operation on its local data.
3. A joined relation generation phase in which the global result is built out of the results of the local join.

As we have already mentioned step 2 computes the local cartesian product of the tuples held on one processor. This is done by performing two nested loops over the number r_i and s_i of items in the two cluster spaces of processor i.

In the case of a one-attribute-pair-join (6), a local cartesian product is computed. In (7) there is a two-attribute-pairs-join

$$R(..., X, Y, ...) \qquad S(..., X, Y, ...). \tag{7}$$

In this case step 1 remains the same: tuples are sent to the processors according to their values on the X attribute (alternatively on the Y attribute). Step 2 works out to be a real equi-join as not every pair of tuples is joined (as in the case of a cartesian product) and the values of Y attribute (the X attribute respectively) of the tuples are matched before joining them. So a local join operation is performed on each processor.

The performance of the algorithm is mainly dictated by step 2 which has a time complexity of $O(\max_{i=1}^{n}(r_i * s_i))$ if r_i and s_i are the numbers of tuples of relations R and S on processor i using a total of n processors.

An ideal, uniform distribution of the work load amongst the processors is obtained if the the data is uniformly distributed over the cluster spaces, as shown by Figure 14.10. The function $\max(r_i * s_i)$ and therefore the performance of the algorithm is sensitive to three types of data skew which we will characterize by using the terms given by Walton et al. (1991):

---

[8] Actually, only the addresses of the tuples are sent to reduce the costs of communication.

- **Tuple Placement Skew**: Some values of the join attribute occur in a large number of tuples whereas other values occur only in few tuples (i.e. some r_i and s_i are large whereas the others are small). This implies that some processors will hold a large number of tuples whereas some hold only a small number (see Figure 14.11).
- **Redistribution Skew**: The join attribute has only a small number of different values which means that a lot of processors will hold no tuples ($r_i = 0$ or $s_i = 0$) whereas a small group of processors has to cope with a large number of tuples, i.e. there is a mismatch between the distribution of the join key values in the relations and the redistribution to the n processors (see Figure 14.12).
- **Join Product Skew**: Although there might be a uniform distribution as shown in Figure 14.10 there can be a difference in the size of the local join results due to selectivity[9]: some processors have to build a large result whereas others produce only a small one (see Figure 14.13).

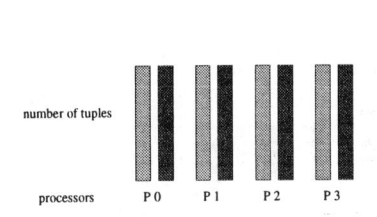

FIGURE 14.10. A uniform distribution of the data amongst the processors.

FIGURE 14.11. Effect of tuple placement skew.

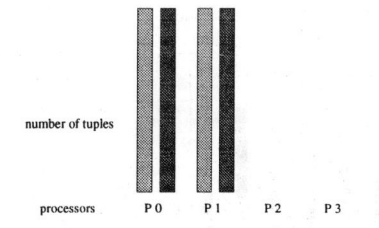

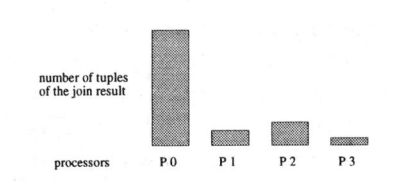

FIGURE 14.12. Effect of redistribution skew.

FIGURE 14.13. Effect of join product skew.

---

[9]In the case of a singe attribute pair join the algorithm we used computes a local cartesian product so no selectivity effects can arise when a uniform distribution is given. Nevertheless, the case of two attribute pairs for the join is sensitive to join product skew.

228 *Parallel Information Processing*

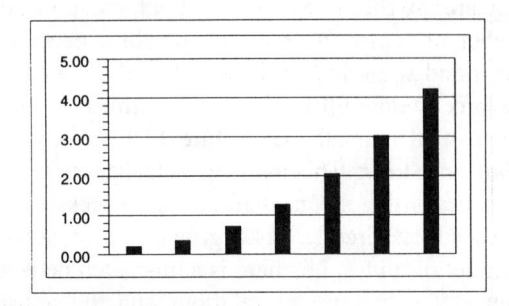

FIGURE 14.14. Tuple placement skew effect on the performance behaviour of the parallel hash-join on a CM-200 using 16384 processors. Results are shown for *tps* = 5, 10, 15, 20, 25, 30. Times are CM busy times in seconds.

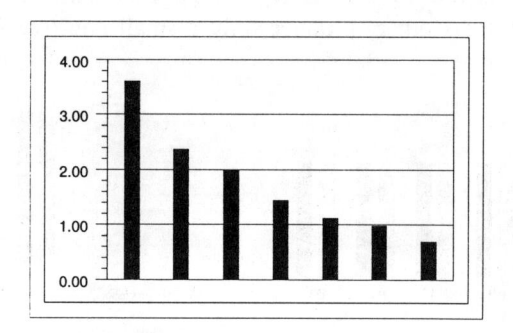

FIGURE 14.15. Redistribution skew effect on the performance behaviour of the parallel hash-join on a CM-200 using 16384 processors. Results are shown for *rs* = 40, 50, 60, 70, 80, 90, 100. Times are CM busy times in seconds.

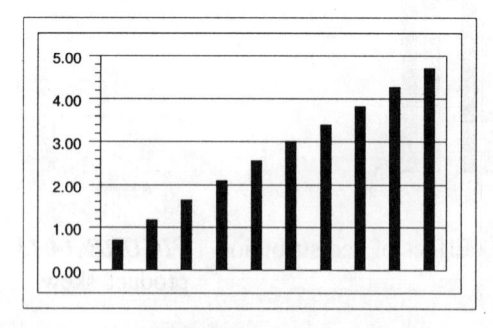

FIGURE 14.16. Join product skew effect on the performance behaviour of the parallel hash-join on a CM-200 using 16384 processors. Results are shown for *jps* = 100, 200, 300, 400, 500, 600, 700, 800, 900, 1000. Times are CM busy times in seconds.

In fact all types of data skew cause a load imbalance amongst the processors. Nevertheless, it is important to differentiate between these three types because they are caused by different facts.

The data skew of a relation can be described by a function $f(v)$ where v is a value an attribute – in our case we concentrate on the attribute that is used for the join. $f(v)$ gives the number of tuples in the relation that hold value v in the respective attribute. If the set or range of values of v is denoted by $range(v)$ and $|range(v)|$ refers to the cardinality the range, then[10]

- tuple placement skew is characterized by large values of

$$tps = \max(f(v)) - \min(f(v))$$

- redistribution skew is characterized by low values of

$$rs = |range(v)|$$

- join product skew is characterized by large values of

$$jps = \max(\text{sizes of local join results})$$

Figures 14.14, 14.15 and 14.16 show the performance behaviour of the parallel hash-join algorithm implemented on a Connection Machine CM-200. In each case the join

$$R(X, Y) \qquad S(Y, Z)$$

was computed where R and S held 100-tuples each in the experiments of Figure 14.14 and 1000-tuples each in all the other cases. In the experiments of Figure 14.16

$$jps = \max(r_i * s_i)$$

because a single attribute pair join was computed. So Figure 14.16 confirms the time complexity of $O(\max(r_i * s_i))$ of the parallel hash-join.

4.2 Boolean matrix multiplication transitive closure

This algorithm (Akl, 1989) uses the *adjacency* matrix A of a graph and computes the powers $A^2, A^4, A^8, \ldots$ up to some A^{2k} such that

---

[10] Please note that the following definitions of *tps*, *rs* and *jps* were made for the purposes of this chapter. In general skew is described slightly different.

$$A^k = A^{2k} \tag{8}$$

which is guaranteed for $k \geq n$ where n is the number of nodes in the graph. A is an $n \times n$ boolean matrix. The powers of A are computed by performing several boolean matrix multiplications.

The matrices have the following properties

- A holds a 1 in position (i, j) iff there is an edge from node i to node j or $i = j$ and holds a 0 in any other cases, and
- A^k holds a 1 in position (i, j) iff there is a path of length k or less from node i to node j and holds a 0 otherwise.

Actually A^k with property (8) is called the *connectivity* matrix and holds the reflexive and transitive closure of the graph represented by a boolean matrix.

The algorithm needs [$\log_2 L$] matrix multiplications if L is the length of the longest path in the graph. The worst case is $L = n$, i.e. the longest path is involving every node of the graph. So in the worst case [$\log_2 n$] matrix multiplications are performed.

There are parallel matrix multiplication algorithms of time complexity O(log n) but from a practical point of view it is unreasonable to use one of these as they require n^3 processors (Akl, 1989). It is reasonable to expect graphs with 1000 or more nodes which would require 1,000,000,000 processors or more. This results in an incredible overload of virtual processors per physical processors which reduces or cancels the benefit of achieving a time complexity of O(log n) for matrix multiplication.

Therefore a matrix multiplication algorithm of time complexity O(n) for n^2 processors is used which results in a total time complexity of O($n$log n) requiring n^2 processors for computing the transitive closure. The actual algorithm that was implemented on the CM-200 was proposed by Cannon (1969). Its suitability for hypercube architectures was established by Johnsson (1987, 1989).

The implementation of the boolean matrix multiplication transitive closure algorithm proved to be better than several other implementations of parallel Warshall-derived transitive closure algorithms that are also based on boolean matrices: see Figure 14.17 and Zurek et al. (1993) for details.

5 SOME PERFORMANCE RESULTS

In sections 2.2 and 3 we identified several parameters that influence the performance of query processing. In this section we will give performance results obtained by some sequences of experiments on a Connection Machine CM-200. In these experiments we concentrated on investigating the performance dependency with respect to one single parameter, namely the length L of the longest path in the underlying graph of a database relation. For the experiments we used the most simple linear recursive query that computes the transitive closure of a relation Q:

$$P(X, Z) = Q(X, Z) \qquad (9)$$
$$P(X, Z) = P(X, Y) \qquad Q(Y, Z) \qquad (10)$$

In each experiment Q holds 1000 tuples.

We give results for two different types of structures for the graph[11] that is defined by relation Q:

- directed acyclic graphs (DAGs), and
- trees.

Such graphs can be found, for example, in relations holding data about company hierarchies or part-subpart relationships.

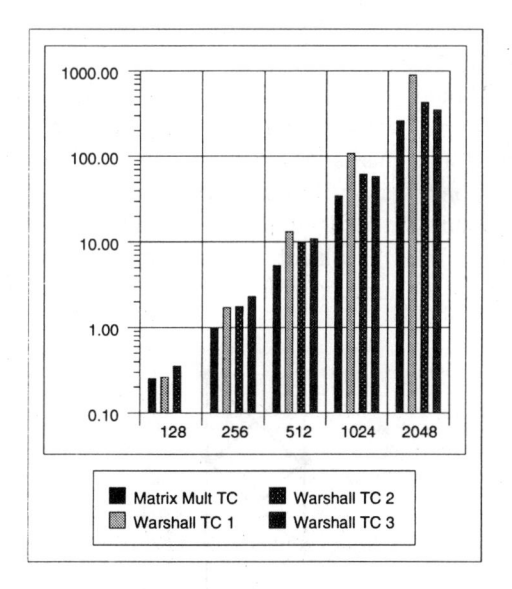

FIGURE 14.17. Performance results of transitive closure algorithms on a CM-200 with 16384 processors for graphs with n = 128, 256, 512, 1024, 2048 nodes. Times are seconds of CM busy time.

---

[11]A relation $Q(X, Z)$ can be considered as the set of edges of the graph, i.e. a tuple (a,b) $\in Q$ denotes that there is an edge from node a to node b. The values for attributes X and Y define the set of nodes of the graph.

232 Parallel Information Processing

For each type of graph a sequence of experiments was set up. In each sequence the length L of the longest path in Q (respectively in the underlying graph of Q) was varied over $\{1, 2, \ldots, 10\}$.

The times given in the experiments are CM elapsed times, i.e. they include also the time spent on the non-parallel front-end computer and not only the time when the CM was busy. This is important because we want to consider also the parts of the code that do, for example, data structure transformations (before calling the actual database operation) or interaction with secondary storage. Using only the CM busy times would give misleading results in these cases.

5.1 Performance results for DAGs

Figure 14.18 shows the type of DAG that was used in the experiments of Figure 14.19. Each such DAG has $4 \cdot L$ edges and therefore represents $4 \cdot L$ tuples of Q. The relation Q was built up by several such DAGs[12] each with a longest path no longer than L.

Figure 14.19 shows the performance of the bottom-up and the transitive closure strategies on a CM-200. The bottom-up strategy performs better for $L \leq 5$, whereas the transitive closure strategy is better on larger values of L. Clearly this value should no be considered as 'naturally given' as it may vary depending on the implementation, but we can conclude that there is such a threshold value for L that marks the crossing point in which a query optimizer should switch from one strategy to the other.

Another important aspect is that the evaluation time of the bottom-up strategy is increasing linearly with the longest path as the number of joins is equal to the length of the longest path.

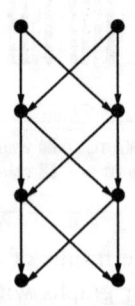

FIGURE 14.18. A DAG structure with $L=3$ used for the experiments.

---

[12]The exact number D of DAGs is computed by $D = 999/(4 \cdot L) + 1$.

The times for the transitive closure strategy increase according to the number of matrix multiplications that have to be performed. This number is given by [$\log_2 L$] which causes the 'stair'-effect for the transitive closure times in Figure 14.19.

5.2 Performance results for trees

Figure 14.20 shows the type of binary tree graphs that was used in the experiments of Figure 14.21. Q was built of several such trees each one having a longest path not longer than L.

Naturally the number of trees in Q is higher for small values of L because small L values imply that each tree has only a small number of edges which represent the tuples of Q. Therefore a larger number of trees is required in these cases. But a higher number of trees implies a higher number n of nodes, i.e. attribute values in Q. This is an important fact as the size of the adjacency matrix of the graph is determined by n. In the experiments n varied from 1500 for $L = 1$ to 1000 for $L = 10$. An important switch is between $n = 1034$ for $L = 4$ and $n = 1017$ for $L = 5$ because the CM operating system requires matrix sizes to be powers of 2 as the matrix represents a set of virtual processors to be mapped to the set of physical processors. For $1 \leq L \leq 4$ matrices of size 2048 × 2048 were used which represents a ratio of 256 virtual processors per physical processor whereas for $L \geq 5$ matrices of size 1024 × 1024 were used with a ratio of 64 virtual processors per physical processor. This marginal effect given by the hardware and the operating system software can be seen in Figure 14.21, which shows the performance results of the experiments.

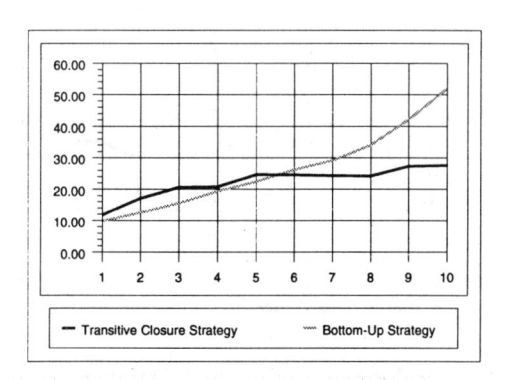

FIGURE 14.19. Performance of the two strategies on DAG-structure database relations with the longest path L varying over 1, 2, ..., 10 uing 16384 processors. Times are CM elapsed times in seconds.

234 Parallel Information Processing

Figure 14.21 shows that the transitive closure strategy performs better for $L \geq 6$. As in the DAG experiments the existence of such a threshold value should be noted.

To make the contrast between the two strategies more evident we give also performance results for $L = 11, 12, ..., 20$ in Figure 14.22. The bottom-up strategy increases linearly as the number of joins – which is the dominant operation of the strategy – is equal to L. The transitive closure strategy performs – apart from the effects implied by the virtual/physical processor ratio that we have discussed above – according to the number of matrix multiplications which is $[\log_2 L]$ (see section 5.1).

6   SUMMARY AND CONCLUSIONS

In section 2 we have presented the generation matrix model which offers several possibilities of processing a query. Two possibilities are the bottom-up and the transitive closure strategies.

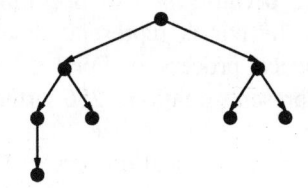

FIGURE 14.20.   A binary tree with $L = 3$ and 8 nodes.

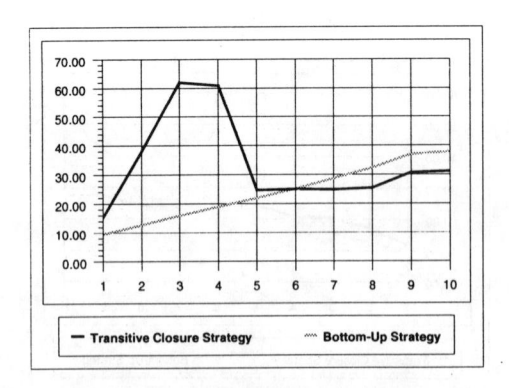

FIGURE 14.21.   Performance of the two strategies on tree-structured database relations with the longest path L varying over $1, 2, ..., 10$ using 16384 processors. Times are CM elapsed times in seconds.

Section 3 gave several parameters that influence the performance of these strategies and the join and transitive closure operations have been identified to be the most crucial. Therefore section 4 analysed two implementations of parallel join and transitive closure algorithms and showed their performance behaviour.

Finally, section 5 presented some performance results for two types of graph structures: DAGs and trees. In the experiments we concentrated on varying only one of several parameters that influence the performance, namely the length of the longest path of the relational graph structure. The analysis and the performance results show that the behaviour of linear recursive query processing strategies is quite sensitive to several factors. An optimal strategy can only be found by analysing the characteristics of the query, the data and the algorithms for the database operations involving factors of the hardware and software systems as the virtual/physical processor ratio.

The transitive closure strategy has proved to be better if the length of the longest path passes a certain threshold value whereas the bottom-up strategy performed better on small values. An optimizer can therefore choose the appropriate strategy if the length of the longest path or at least an upper bound is known in advance or provided by the statistical information in the database catalogue.

The Connection Machine system architecture has also proved to be worth being considered as a platform for database query processing. We have shown that there are several data-parallel aspects than can be exploited naturally by spreading the data over a large number of processors and processing each portion of data independently by using the same database operations. This holds

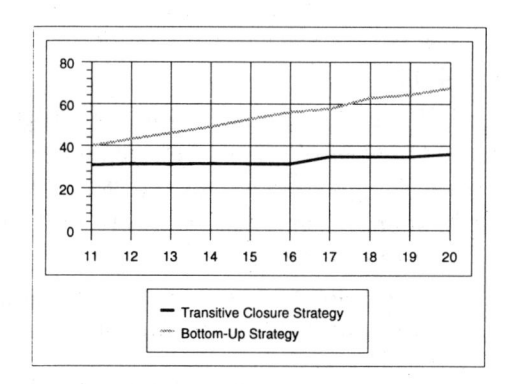

FIGURE 14.22. Performance of the two strategies on tree-structured database relations with the longest path L varying over 11, 12, ..., 20 using 16384 processors. Times are CM elapsed times in seconds.

for the several database operations as the join, but also for the overlying query processing model as the generation matrix where several 'moves' can be executed simultaneously on different portions of data.

7 ACKNOWLEDGEMENTS

The work presented in this chapter was done at the Department of Computer Science of Edinburgh University. The programs were implemented and run on the Connection Machine CM-200 of the Edinburgh Parallel Computing Centre (EPCC). Parts of the work were funded by TRACS, an EC-funded project on high performance computing.

REFERENCES

Agrawal, R., Dar, S. and Jagadish, H. V. (1990) Direct Transitive Closure Algorithms: Design and Performance Evaluation, *ACM Transactions on Database Systems*, September, pp. 427–458.

Akl, S. (1989) *The Design and Analysis of Parallel Algorithms*, Prentice Hall.

Boral, H. and DeWitt, D. (1983) Database Machines: An Idea Whose Time Has Passed? A critique of the future of database machines, in H. O. Leilich and M. Missikoff (editors), *Proceedings of the Workshop on Database Machines*, Springer Verlag.

Cannon, L. E. (1969) A Cellular Computer to Implement the Kalman Filter Algorithm, PhD thesis, Montana State University.

DeWitt, D. J. and Gray, J. (1990) Parallel Database Systems: The Future of Database Processing or a Passing Fad, *ACM SIGMOD RECORD*, 19(4), December, pp. 104–112.

Ioannidis, Y. E. and Wong, E. (1991) Towards an Algebraic Theory of Recursion, *Journal of the ACM*, 38(2), April, pp. 329–381.

Jagadish, H. V., Agrawal, R. and Ness, L. (1987) A Study of Transitive Closure As a Recursion Mechanism, in: *Proceedings ACM SIGMOD 1987 Conference on Management of Data*, pp. 331–344.

Johnsson, S. L. (1987) Communication Efficient Basic Linear Algebra Computations on Hypercube Architectures, *Journal of Parallel and Distributed Computing*, April, pp. 133–172.

Johnsson, S. L. and Ching-Tien Ho (1989) Multiplication of Arbitrarily Shaped Matrices on Boolean Cubes Using the Full Communications Bandwith,

Technical Report TR 721, Yale University, Department of Computer Science.

Kitsuregawa, M. and Matsumoto, K. (1991) Massively Parallel Relational Database Processing on the Connection Machine CM-2, Annual Report of Kitsuregawa Lab, University of Tokyo.

Kitsuregawa, M. and Ogawa, Y. (1990) Bucket Spreading Parallel Hash: A New, Robust, Parallel Hash Join Method for Data Skew in the Super Database Computer (SDC), in D. McLeoad, R. Sacks-Davis and H. Schek (editors), *Proceedings of the 16th International Conference on Very Large DataBases*, pp. 210–221, Morgan Kaufmann.

Lanzelotte, R. S. G., Valduriez, P., Zaït, M. and Ziane, M. (1994) Industrial-Strength Parallel Query Optimization: Issues and Lessons, *Information Systems*, 19(4), pp. 311–330.

Minty, E. M. (1993) An Algorithm for a Data Parallel Hash Join on the Connection Machine, Technical Note EPCC-TN93-02, Edinburgh Parallel Computing Centre (EPCC), March.

Thinking Machines Corporation (1991) *Connection Machine CM-200 Series Technical Summary*, June.

Ullman, J. D. (1988) *Database and Knowledge-Base Systems*, Volume 1, Computer Science Press.

Ullman, J. D. (1989) *Database and Knowledge-Base Systems*, Volume 2, Computer Science Press.

Walton, C. B. and Dale, A. G. (1991) Data Skew and the Scalability of Parallel Joins, *Proceedings of the 3rd IEEE Symposium on Parallel and Distributed Processing*, pp. 44–51, IEEE Comput. Soc. Press.

Walton, C. B., Dale, A. G. and Jenevein, R. M. (1991) A Taxonomy and Performance Model of Data Skew Effects in Parallel Joins, in G. M. Lohman, A. Sernadas, and R. Camps (editors), *Proceedings of the 17th International Conference on Very Large Data Bases*, pp. 537–548, Morgan Kaufman, San Mateo.

Wolf, J. L., Dias, D. M. and Yu, P. S. (1993) A Parallel Sort Merge Join Algorithm for Managing Data Skew, *IEEE Transactions on Parallel and Distributed Processing*, 4(1), January, pp. 70–86.

Zurek, Th. and Thanisch, P. (1993) Processing Linear Recursive Database Queries on the Connection Machine, Technical Report EPCC-TR93-05, Edinburgh Parallel Computing Centre (EPCC).

Zhou, X., Zhang, Y. and Orlowska, M. E. (1993) A Parallel Transitive Closure Algorithm for SIMD Meshes, *Australian Computer Science Communication*, 15(1), pp. 143–151.

15 Processing Databases of Chemical and Biological Structures on the Distributed Array Processor

P. *Willett*
Department of Information Studies
University of Sheffield

1 INTRODUCTION

The Distributed Array Processor, or DAP, is an SIMD array processor, in which there is a 2-D synchronous array of bit-serial processing elements, or PEs, and a master control unit, or MCU, that broadcasts instructions for parallel execution in the processor array (Parkinson and Litt, 1990). The DAP, and machines with similar architectures such as the MasPar-MP1 and the Connection Machine, are potentially well suited to data processing applications, where a relatively simple sequence of operations needs to be executed on very many records in a database.

There are two main ways in which a database algorithm can be implemented on an array processor. The simpler of the two approaches is to exploit what is variously referred to as *database parallelism* or *outer-loop parallelism*. This involves the application of the basic sequential algorithm to different database records at the same time, i.e. the database is distributed across the available PEs. A search is then effected by loading the query record into the array processor's MCU and broadcasting the attributes that have been specified in the query for comparison with the sets of attributes characterizing the records stored in each of the PEs. The alternative approach, which is referred to as *algorithm parallelism* or *inner-loop parallelism*, involves the identification of any inherent parallelism in the algorithm that is to be implemented, so that different parts of it can be executed concurrently. On an SIMD machine, this involves applying the same operations to (subsets of) the data structures involved in the algorithm. Both types of approach have been used in previous work at Sheffield on the use of the DAP for database processing (Willett and Rasmussen, 1990). For example, we have exploited outer-loop parallelism for the scanning of text signatures (Pogue and Willett, 1987) and for hierarchic agglomerative clustering of numeric databases (Rasmussen and Willett, 1989), and inner-loop parallelism for string searching in text databases (Carroll *et al.*, 1988).

In this chapter, we discuss the use of the DAP for the processing of databases of 2-D and 3-D chemical structures; further details of these studies are reported by Artymiuk *et al.* (1992), Rasmussen *et al.* (1988), Rasmussen *et al.* (1993) and Willett *et al.* (1991). Most of our experiments have used a DAP 610 at the Centre for Parallel Computing, Queen Mary and Westfield College, University of London; this machine is hosted by a VAX and contains a 64 × 64 array of PEs, each of which has 8 Kbytes of local storage, giving 32 Mbytes overall. The clustering experiments described in section 3 used an earlier, and slower, first-generation DAP hosted by an ICL 2980 mainframe. Our DAP programs are all in Fortran Plus, and are compared with sequential programs in Fortran 77; these were all implemented on an IBM 3083 BX mainframe, with the exception of the similarity searching experiments in section 4, which used an Evans and Sutherland ESV-3 UNIX workstation. The performance measure used is the speed-up: if a parallel implementation of an algorithm requires T(P) units of time and the most efficient sequential algorithm requires T(S) units, then the speed-up is defined to be T(S)/T(P) (Parkinson and Liddell, 1983).

2 SUBSTRUCTURE SEARCHING IN DATABASES OF 2-D STRUCTURES

The primary function of research and development in the fine chemicals industry is to identify structurally-novel molecules that exhibit useful biological properties, e.g. a pharmaceutical company might be interested in a compound with analgesic activity as a potential painkiller. To this end, fine chemicals companies make very extensive use of sophisticated information systems that contain structural and activity data for tens, or hundreds, of thousands of molecules that have been synthesized in-house by their chemists or that are available from public database hosts (Ash *et al.*, 1991).

Chemists normally refer to molecules by means of 2-D chemical structure diagrams. These may be represented in machine-readable form by graphs, called *connection tables*, in which the nodes and edges of a graph represent the atoms and bonds, respectively, of a chemical compound (Ash *et al.*, 1991). Searching operations hence typically involve the use of isomorphism algorithms from graph theory. The most important such operation is *substructure searching*, which identifies all of those molecules in a database that contain a user-defined query substructure and which is implemented by means of a subgraph isomorphism algorithm.

Substructure searching involves a backtracking tree search, in which database atoms are tentatively assigned to query atoms and the match extended in a depth-first manner until a complete match is obtained or until a mis-match is identified; in the latter case, the search backtracks, i.e. moves one level back up the search tree, to the previous correct assignment. The speed of searching is maximized by using procedures that minimize the numbers of database atoms that can be mapped to each of the query atoms. The most effective of these procedures is the algorithm described by Ullmann (1976), which uses a *refinement procedure* to minimize the number of levels of the search tree that have to be investigated before a mis-match is identified. The refinement is based on the following heuristic: if some query atom Q(X) is bonded to another atom Q(W), and if some structure atom S(Z) matches with Q(W), then there must also be some atom S(Y) bonded to S(Z) which matches with Q(X) and which uses the same types of bond. This is a necessary, but not sufficient, condition for a subgraph isomorphism to be present (except in the limiting case of all of the query atoms having been matched, when the condition is both necessary and sufficient). The refinement procedure is called before each possible assignment of a database atom to a query atom; and the matched substructure is increased by one atom if, and only if, the condition holds for all atoms W, X, Y and Z. Although originally developed for the processing of random graphs, this heuristic seems to be particularly well-suited to the processing of the graphs representing chemical structures and the Ullmann algorithm is hence used in several operational substructure searching systems.

The main data structures for the Ullmann algorithm are the connection tables for the query substructure and the database structure that are being matched, and a binary match matrix that contains all of the possible equivalences between atoms from the query substructure and atoms from the database structure. This matrix is initialized by setting to one all elements that correspond to pairs of atoms that are of the same atomic type and that have sets of connected atoms and bonds such that the set surrounding the query atom is identical to, or is a subset of, that surrounding the database atom. Elements of the matrix that are initially set to one are systematically checked using the heuristic described previously, and the search continued until all of the query atoms have been matched to database atoms or until an atom is identified for which there are no possible matches (which correspond to the presence or absence, respectively, of a subgraph isomorphism).

The Ullmann algorithm consists of two main parts, these being the depth-first, backtracking tree search and the refinement procedure that is called at each node of this search tree. Much of the tree search is inherently sequential in character and thus not suited to an SIMD implementation. However, the great bulk of the processing on a sequential processor takes place during the refinement procedure, which involves large number of logical operations that can be mapped onto the DAP with great efficiency. Specifically, one bit in each of the 64×64 array of bit-serial PEs can be used to represent one element in each of the logical matrices that represent the two connection tables and the match matrix that lie at the heart of the Ullmann algorithm: the DAP allows the simultaneous processing of an entire matrix, whereas a conventional processor requires that each matrix element must be processed in sequence. This algorithm, Algorithm I, is thus an example of an inner-loop algorithm, since the matching operations for a single database record are distributed across the processor array.

Algorithm II, conversely, utilizes outer-loop parallelism, which is much simpler in concept and involves executing the same basic sequential algorithm on the different database structures that are allocated to each of the PEs. This has the great advantage that up to 4096 database structures can be processed in parallel; however, the SIMD nature of the DAP means that rapid searching will be achieved if, and only if, it is possible to prevent most of the PEs being idle for most of the time. When the Ullmann algorithm is implemented on a sequential machine, there are very many paths that can be followed, depending on the characteristics of the particular query substructure and database structures that are being processed. For example, with one database structure, a complete mis-match may be identified after the very first call of the refinement procedure; another database structure, conversely, may not identify an incorrect assignment of a query atom to a database atom until all but one of the query atoms have been mapped, so that backtracking will be required to consider alternative mappings for several of the query atoms. This is not a problem when only a single structure is being processed but is an important issue when many structures are being processed in parallel, since each structure may require a different path to be followed in the search tree. In an SIMD machine, there is, necessarily, only a single control unit, and it is thus necessary to identify a path that will ensure a high level of processor utilization, i.e. that will ensure that as many of the PEs as possible are engaged in useful computation for as much of the time as possible. The identification of the best, or least worse, such path is discussed by Willett et al. (1991).

Both algorithms have some inherent limitations. Algorithm I involves extensive use of control, shifting and matrix operations, which are much slower on a DAP than the basic Boolean operations that underlie Ullmann's original algorithm; in addition, some, or many, of the PEs may not be utilized with small query substructures and/or database structures. These factors mean that the speed-up that can be achieved in practice is rather less than might have been expected from a simple analysis of the refinement procedure. In addition, even though the execution of the refinement is now much faster, there is nothing that can be done to the wholly-sequential, backtracking component of Ullmann's algorithm, which thus plays a larger part in determining the overall execution time than it does on a sequential processor. Algorithm II has two main limitations. The first of these is the overhead occasioned by the need to identify the best path. The second is that it requires much more local memory in each PE than Algorithm I, having a storage complexity of order $O(NQ^2 \times ND)$ for a query substructure and a database structure having NQ and ND atoms, respectively. Indeed, the memory available in the DAP-610 used for our experiments meant that we could use only query substructures (and database structures) having not more than 16 (and 64) atoms.

The experiments used seven different sets of 4096 structures from the *Fine Chemicals Database*, together with 57 substructure queries taken from the journal literature on substructure searching. Algorithm I was generally about 2–3 times faster than Algorithm II, the median speed-ups being 1.15 and 0.58, respectively, when averaged over all of the data sets and all of the query substructures, i.e. many of the Algorithm II runs were slower than the corresponding sequential runs. The problem with Algorithm II is that the overall run time is determined by the time for the slowest match: thus, even if a large fraction of the structures has been completed, a small number of long-running matches, or even a single match, can result in this algorithm having a very low processor utilization and giving an extended run-time for a particular query. The problems occasioned by a few, long-running database structures may be much reduced by means of a combined algorithm, Algorithm III. Here, Algorithm II is executed until some user-defined number, N, of the matches have been completed, and Algorithm I is then invoked for the remaining 4096-N long-running structures. Values for N in the range 3300–3900 were always found to result in a better level (and sometimes a substantially better level) of performance than either of the two individual algorithms, the median speed-up for Algorithm III being 3.19.

Willett *et al.* (1991) present evidence to suggest that rather larger speed-ups might be obtained in an operational system that included an initial screening system (see section 3 below) and that did not put restrictions on NQ and ND. A reasonable conclusion would be that speed-ups in the range of 5–8 should be achievable in practice: this degree of speed-up is rather less than had been expected when the work commenced.

3   CLUSTERING OF 2-D CHEMICAL STRUCTURES

Even though the Ullmann algorithm is highly efficient, the NP-complete character of subgraph isomorphism means that substructure searching is very demanding of computer resources. Operational substructure searching systems hence make use of an additional *screening search*, which is carried out prior to the detailed atom-by-atom search. A screen is a substructural fragment, the presence of which is necessary but not sufficient for a molecule to contain the query substructure. The fragments used are small, atom-centred, bond-centred or ring-centred substructures that are algorithmically generated from a connection table, and the screening search involves checking each of the database structures for the presence of those screens that are present in the query substructure; if a database structure does not contain all of the screens that are present in the query, then it cannot possibly contain the full substructure and can thus be eliminated from further consideration.

Substructure searching is the main retrieval mechanism that is available in a chemical information system, but the availability of the screen records for a file of molecules provides an alternative way of searching a chemical database. This is *similarity searching*, in which those molecules are retrieved that are most similar to an input query molecule and in which the similarity between a pair of molecules is based on the fragment substructures that they have in common (Willett, 1987). A similarity search involves the user inputting a target molecule, e.g. a lead compound that has been shown to exhibit some beneficial chemical or biological property. The similarity is calculated between the target and each compound in the database by comparing the corresponding fragment bit-strings to identify the bits (and hence substructural fragments) that they have in common; this information is then used to calculate a similarity coefficient for each structure in the database, which is finally sorted into order of decreasing similarity with the target. Interesting compounds from near the top of this ranking can then be used as the basis for subsequent searches.

Cluster analysis, or automatic classification, is a natural extension of similarity searching and involves the identification of groups of similar objects in multi-dimensional datasets (Dubes and Jain, 1980; Gordon, 1981). It is being used increasingly in chemical information systems to organize files of chemical structures, primarily as an aid to compound selection in biological screening programmes (Johnson and Maggiora, 1990). Previous work in Sheffield with text databases had demonstrated that the DAP was well suited to the implementation of similarity searching and it hence seemed possible that it could also be used for large-scale clustering applications. We accordingly carried out an evaluation of the use of the DAP with a range of clustering methods and types of data (Willett and Rasmussen, 1990) and now summarize the results of some of these experiments that involved the clustering of fragment bit strings.

The clustering method used here is that due to Jarvis and Patrick (1973), which has been shown to have wide applicability in chemical information systems (Willett, 1987). The Jarvis-Patrick method is based on the concept of shared nearest neighbours. Given a set of N objects, each of which is associated with its k nearest neighbours, a pair of objects, I and J, are assigned to the same cluster if all three of the following criteria are met: at least k(T), a user-specified threshold, of the k nearest neighbours associated with each object are common to both of the objects, if I is one of the k nearest neighbours of J, and if J is one of the k nearest neighbours of I. Both k and k(T) can be varied until clusters acceptable to the user are produced. In the chemical structure context, the inter-molecular similarities are calculated by comparing the fragment bit strings characterizing each of a pair of molecules to identify the fragment substructures, i.e. bit locations, in common; this information is then used to calculate an association measure, the Tanimoto similarity coefficient.

The computation required for the Jarvis-Patrick method is in two separate stages, these being the creation of the nearest-neighbour lists and then the processing of these lists to create the clusters; of these, the former is much the more demanding in computational terms. On a serial processor, the nearest neighbours are identified most efficiently using an inverted-file algorithm, which involves storing the fragment bit strings so as to provide rapid access to the postings lists corresponding to the fragments that characterize each of the molecules in the dataset that is to be clustered (Rasmussen et al., 1988). Once the sets of nearest neighbours have been identified, the clusters are generated using the standard procedure described by Jarvis and Patrick (1973). The nearest-neighbour searching algorithm that is used on the DAP involves the bit strings representing each of 4096 compounds being matched in parallel against the bit string representing the current query molecule, Q. Each of the non-zero elements in the bit string representing Q is broadcast, each such broadcast resulting in the identification of all of the other members of the dataset that have this fragment in common with Q. Once this common-fragment information is available, it is simple to identify the k nearest neighbours and hence to construct the nearest-neighbour table that forms the input to the actual clustering stage. However, the clustering criteria used in the Jarvis-Patrick method are not overly well suited to parallel processing as only k of the 4096 structures need to be considered for clustering with the current structure, i.e. those corresponding to the k nearest neighbours stored for each molecule; the detailed implementation of this stage is described by Rasmussen et al. (1988).

The experiments used sets of 4096 and 8192 molecules from the *Fine Chemicals Database*, with each molecule being represented by a 1123-member fragment bit-string. The resulting bit map was used as the basis for the DAP processing. In the case of the serial processing, the bit map was inverted and the non-zero elements eliminated to create the inverted file. The speed-up that is achieved depends on the dataset size, on k and on k(T): in our experiments, the speed-ups for the nearest neighbour searching and the clustering stages were in the ranges 5.4–7.9 and 0.7–3.1, respectively. A detailed analysis of the operation of the serial and parallel algorithms shows that the time taken for the serial processing is highly dependent on the threshold, k(T), which is chosen, while the parallel processing is affected very little by this factor; conversely, the DAP processing is much more susceptible to the length of the nearest neighbour lists that must be processed in the clustering stage. These points are discussed in detail by Rasmussen et al. (1988) who demonstrate that in clustering from the nearest neighbour tables, the DAP performs best for a large number of records and short nearest neighbour lists, whereas the serial algorithm is better for a small number of records and long nearest neighbour lists. The results for the two stages of the Jarvis-Patrick clustering method can be consolidated to show the overall time requirements for our parallel implementation of the method. The overall speed-up is in the range 1.5–5.0 for 4096 structures and in the range 1.9–6.7 for 8192 structures. The speed-up for the larger dataset is always greater than the corresponding speed-up for the smaller dataset for all values of k and k(T) that were tested; this suggests that the use of the DAP would become still more attractive as larger and larger structure databases need to be clustered.

4   SIMILARITY SEARCHING IN DATABASES OF 3-D STRUCTURES

Recent developments in molecular modelling (Cohen et al., 1990) mean that it is now relatively easy to generate the 3-D atomic coordinates for a small molecule from its 2-D connection table, thus allowing the creation of databases of 3-D structures from the corresponding databases of 2-D structures. A structure in such a database is represented by a graph, with the geometrical arrangement of the atoms in a molecule (or in a query substructure) being described by a labelled graph in which the nodes again represent the atoms but in which the edges describe the inter-atomic distances (Willett, 1991). Several software systems have subsequently been developed for substructure searching in these 3-D databases (Martin, 1992).

The success of 2-D similarity searching systems suggests that 3-D similarity searching might also prove to be an effective way of identifying database structures that are structurally related to an input target structure. Pepperrell and Willett (1991) have reported a comparison of four different ways of quantifying the geometric similarity between pairs of 3-D structures, and have suggested that a procedure called *atom mapping* is the most effective of those that they tested. The atom mapping method provides a quantitative measure of the similarity between a pair of 3-D molecules, A and B, that are represented by their inter-atomic distance matrices. The measure is calculated in two stages.

The first stage involves calculating the geometric similarity between each possible pair of atoms. This is done by taking each of the atoms in A in turn, and then comparing the distances associated with this atom with all of the distances associated with each of the atoms in B. In this way, we can identify the number of distances in common between each atom in A and each atom in B. The numbers of common distances are used to produce the corresponding Tanimoto similarity coefficients, and these coefficients are stored in a similarity matrix, the *atom-match matrix*. In the second stage, the similarities in this matrix are used to identify pairs of atoms, one from A and one from B, that are geometrically equivalent to each other. The overall, inter-molecular similarity is then calculated from the inter-atomic similarities for the pairs of atoms that have been judged to be geometrically equivalent.

A complexity analysis of the atom mapping method shows that the time requirement is dominated by the calculation of the atom-match matrix, which has a time requirement of order $O(ND^3)$, where ND is the number of atoms in an average-sized database molecule (Pepperrell et al., 1990). It is thus clear that extremely efficient algorithms are required if atom mapping is to be used to search large databases of 3-D structures, and we have recently investigated DAP implementations of atom mapping (Artymiuk et al., 1992). The calculation of the inter-atomic similarities is the most time-consuming part of atom mapping, and our attempts at parallelization have thus focused on this part of the method (although we have also been able to make some improvements in the sorting procedures that are used to identify the matching pairs of atoms in the second part of the method).

It is possible to visualize three levels at which the similarity calculation can be parallelized. The Distributed Molecules algorithm is a simple outer-loop implementation in which each PE is assigned one of the database structures, and the similarity calculation is done sequentially on large numbers of database structures in parallel. The remaining two approaches are examples of inner-loop implementations, in which the calculation of the Tanimoto coefficient is carried out in parallel. In the Distributed Atoms algorithm, each PE is assigned one atom, so that each database structure is distributed over several PEs. The similarity is calculated for each atom in the target structure in turn, with each such atom being matched against all of the atoms in a database structure in parallel. Finally, the Distributed Distances algorithm involves assigning one distance to each PE, so that the distances associated with each atom are distributed over several PEs (and thus a single database structure over many PEs). The similarity is calculated for each distance in the target structure in turn, with it being matched against all of the database distances in parallel. Full details of these three approaches are presented by Artymiuk et al. (1992).

It must be emphasized that these three levels of parallelism (molecules, atoms and distances) are not completely distinct, since it is possible to exploit molecular parallelism in the Distributed Atoms algorithm by processing the atoms from several database structures together (since there are generally significantly more PEs available than atoms in a single database structure). In a similar way, we can exploit both molecular and atomic parallelism in the Distributed Distances algorithm, with the distances for several (or all) of the atoms in one molecule (and the distances of further molecules) being processed in parallel.

The three algorithms were tested on a file of structures provided by ICI Agrochemicals, with several different target molecules containing between 6 and 31 non-hydrogen atoms. Unfortunately, it was not possible to implement the Distributed Molecules algorithm. This was because the PEs on the DAP-610 that was available to us were too small to store the inter-atomic distance information associated with each of the 4096 molecules that were to be processed in parallel; and there were also problems associated with the packing of this information to allow it to be transferred into the DAP from the VAX 11/750 host. The mean speed-up values obtained in our initial experiments for the Distributed Distances and Distributed Atoms algorithms were 7.4 and 39.6, respectively, where the speed-up is defined in terms of an Evans and Sutherland ESV~3 UNIX workstation running the upperbound sequential algorithm described by Pepperrell *et al.* (1990). The Distributed Atoms algorithm is thus much the faster; indeed, the speed-up here is comparable with the best that have been obtained in any of our previous studies of the use of the DAP for database processing applications (Willett and Rasmussen, 1990).

5 RANKING OF PROTEIN STRUCTURES

Thus far, we have considered databases of chemical small molecules. There is also much interest in techniques for searching databases of biological macromolecules (Thornton and Gardner, 1989). We have developed an approach to protein searching that is based on graph-matching and that involves the representation and searching of proteins at the secondary structure level. The search program, called POSSUM (Protein Online Substructure Searching – Ullmann Method), allows substructure searches to be carried out for user-defined motifs, i.e. patterns of secondary structure elements in 3-D space, in the protein structures in the Protein Data Bank, the primary source of 3-D data for macromolecules (Mitchell *et al.*, 1990).

POSSUM makes use of the fact that the common helix and strand secondary structure elements are approximately linear repeating structures and that such an element can hence be described by a vector drawn along its linear axis. The set of vectors corresponding to the secondary structure elements in a protein or a query motif can then be used to describe the structure of that protein in 3-D space, with the relative orientation of the helix and strand elements being defined by the inter-line angles and distances. Proteins and motifs may be regarded as labelled graphs, with the nodes of the graph corresponding to the linear representation of the helices and strands, and the edges to the inter-line angles or distances. It is accordingly possible to use subgraph isomorphism algorithms for the detection of motifs in protein structures; that used in POSSUM is a suitably-modified version of the Ullmann algorithm which is described in section 2. Matches to the query motif are output for display on a molecular graphics system. Searches using a range of typical motifs have demonstrated the effectiveness of POSSUM for detecting both known and previously unknown occurrences of these motifs in the Protein Data Bank and the program is now being distributed commercially by Tripos Associates.

It is possible to rank the output from a POSSUM search so that the structures at the top of the ranking are those which contain motifs that are structurally most similar to the query motif. The basic idea of the ranking algorithm is to approximate the overall shape of a motif, either in a query or in a database structure, by the distribution of inter-line distances between the component secondary structure elements. Whereas the basic substructure searching algorithm in POSSUM utilizes only a single inter-line distance, either the midpoint distance or the distance of closest approach, the ranking procedure utilizes large numbers of distances between each pair of lines. Specifically, each linear secondary structure element is automatically assigned a series of NPOINTS points, located at equal distances along the major axis representing the secondary structure element. Distances are then calculated between each distinct pair of points for each distinct pair of lines and the frequency distribution of these distances calculated. The degree of geometric similarity between a query motif and a database motif resulting from the initial search is then measured by the extent of the agreement between the two frequency distributions.

The ranking algorithm requires the user to specify values for two real variables, T and R, once an initial search has been carried out to identify the potential query-motif to database-motif matches. T defines the size of segments along the lines representing the secondary structure elements; the smaller the value of T, the greater the number of points there are along the lines. R defines the width of the range categories in the frequency distributions that are used for the subsequent ranking calculation. The values of these two parameters control the precise form of the distribution that is calculated.

Rasmussen *et al.* (1993) discuss the use of this algorithm on typical secondary structure motifs and demonstrate that it provides an effective way of relaxing the rather stringent and arbitrary distance constraints that need to be used in POSSUM, while ensuring that the best matches to the query are those that are displayed first to the user. The algorithm is, however, time-consuming in execution owing to the very large numbers of inter-point distances that need to be calculated. Specifically, if it is assumed that the database motif being searched contains NLINES secondary structures and that each of these lines contains NPOINTS points, then the computation for each structure has a running time of order $O(NLINES^2 \times NPOINTS^2)$.

The algorithm may be implemented on the DAP by storing one set of coordinate points in each of the PEs. An individual point is then selected and its coordinates broadcast from the MCU, thus allowing the parallel calculation of the distances between this distinguished point and all of the other points in the motif. The computation for each structure has a running time of order $O(NLINES \times NPOINTS)$, i.e. the square root of that for the serial algorithm, and it would thus be expected that the advantage of the DAP should increase with an increase in the number of points in each line (since NLINES is fixed for a given query motif). There are, however, two other factors that need to be considered in the DAP processing but that can be neglected in the case of a serial processor. The first of these is the updating of the frequency distribution that is used to cumulate the distances as they are calculated. The number of times that this updating operation needs to be carried out on the DAP is determined by the value of R, the distance range for each element of the frequency distribution. When R is small, there will be very large numbers of elements and very large numbers of updating operations required, whereas a large value for R implies fewer updates and faster overall DAP processing. On a serial machine, conversely, the update time is independent of R. The second factor is the number of points that need to be processed. The DAP that we have used contains 4096 PEs. Hence, any dataset that contains less than 4096 points will not make full use of the parallelism that is available. The use of a small value of T, i.e. of a large number of points per line, will help to maximize the number of points; even so, none of the motifs used in this work could make use of more than a small fraction of the available PEs. However, a strategy has been devised that allows several motifs to be inspected at the same time by shifting the coordinates of their constituent points to a single coordinate system, thus permitting full utilization of the array of PEs (Rasmussen *et al.*, 1993).

The efficiencies of the parallel and serial versions of the similarity algorithm were studied using three well-known secondary structure motifs, these being the calcium-binding fold, the eight-stranded beta barrel, and the NAD-binding fold (Mitchell *et al.*, 1990). The speed-ups for these three motifs were in the ranges 1.0–6.7, 0.9–10.1 and 3.1–11.3, respectively. The performance of the DAP, relative to an IBM 3083, increases in line with decreases in T and/or with increases in R; this behaviour is entirely in agreement with the discussion above.

6 CONCLUSIONS

In this chapter, we have reviewed several studies of the use of the DAP for the processing of files of chemical and biological structures. Use of the DAP invariably results in at least some improvement in run-time when compared with efficient serial algorithms for the same application; typically, we can expect about a two-fold to ten-fold improvement in performance. The precise degree of speed-up depends in part on the particular application, and upon the amount of inherently-sequential processing (see, for example, the tree search in the Ullmann algorithm and the updating stage in the protein ranking procedure). However, it also depends on the precise characteristics of the data that is being processed, with small variations in the experimental parameters sometimes resulting in several-fold variations in the speed-up. Similar conclusions have been reached in analogous investigations of textual and numerical database processing (Rasmussen and Willett, 1990).

It must be emphasized that we have considered only the matching operations that are required for each of our chosen applications, and have assumed that all of the necessary data is stored within the array of PEs. An operational implementation would require the rapid re-filling of the DAP with new data as each sub-set of a database needed to be processed (e.g. matched against the target structure in a similarity search); unfortunately, while such high-speed disk units are available for the DAP, the machines that we have been using have only limited communication links to backing storage and to the host processor, making it impossible for us to evaluate a full system at present. Even so, we believe that the DAP provides an appropriate architecture for the implementation of a range of database searching applications, and we are now hoping to test this conclusion on other types of SIMD array processor.

7 ACKNOWLEDGEMENTS

My thanks are due to Helen M. Grindley, Edie M. Rasmussen, Stewart F. Reddaway, David J. Wild and Terence Wilson for their contributions to the work reported here; to Active Memory Technology Limited, the British Library Research and Development Department, the Department of Education and Science, ICI Agrochemicals, the Science and Engineering Research Council and Tripos Associates for funding; and to the Centre for Parallel Computing at Queen Mary and Westfield College, University of London for the provision of DAP facilities.

REFERENCES

Artymiuk, P. J., Bath, P. A., Grindley, H. M., Pepperrell, C. A., Poirrette, A. R., Rice, D. W., Thorner, D. A., Wild, D.J., Willett, P., Allen, F. H. and Taylor, R. (1992) Similarity Searching in Databases Of Three-Dimensional Molecules And Macromolecules, *Journal of Chemical Information and Computer Sciences*, 32, pp. 617–630.

Ash, J. E., Warr, W. A. and Willett, P. (Eds.) (1991) *Chemical Structure Systems*, Ellis Horwood, Chichester.

Carroll, D. M., Pogue, C. A. and Willett, P. (1988) Bibliographic Pattern Matching Using the ICL Distributed Array Processor, *Journal of the American Society for Information Science*, 39, pp. 390–399.

Cohen, N. C., Blaney, J. M., Humblet, C., Gund, P. and Barry, D. C. (1990) Molecular Modeling Software and Methods for Medicinal Chemistry. *Journal of Medicinal Chemistry*, 33, pp. 883–894.

Dubes and Jain, A. K. (1980) Clustering Methodologies in Exploratory Data Analysis, *Advances in Computers*, 19, pp. 113–228.

Gordon, A. D. (1981) *Classification*, Chapman and Hall, London.

Jarvis, R. A. and Patrick, E. A. (1973) Clustering Using a Similarity Measure Based on Shared Nearest Neighbours, *IEEE Transactions on Computers*, C-22, pp. 1025–1034.

Johnson, M. A. and Maggiora, G. M. (Eds.) (1990) *Concepts and Applications of Molecular Similarity*, Wiley, New York.

Martin, Y. C. (1992) 3D Database Searching in Drug Design, *Journal of Medicinal Chemistry*, 35, pp. 2145–2154.

Mitchell, E. M., Artymiuk, P. J., Rice, D. W. and Willett, P. (1990) Use of Techniques Derived from Graph Theory to Compare Secondary Structure Motifs in Proteins, *Journal of Molecular Biology*, 212, pp. 151–166.

Parkinson, D. and Liddell, H. M. (1983) The Measurement of Performance on a Highly Parallel System, *IEEE Transactions on Computers*, C-32, pp. 32–37.

Parkinson, D. and Litt, J. (Eds.) (1990) *Massively Parallel Computing with the DAP*, Pitman, London.

Pepperrell, C. A. and Willett, P. (1991) Techniques for the Calculation of Three-Dimensional Structural Similarity Using Inter-Atomic Distances, *Journal of Computer-Aided Molecular Design*, 5, pp. 455–474.

Pepperrell, C. A., Willett, P. and Taylor, R. (1990) Implementation and Use of an Atom-Mapping Procedure for Similarity Searching in Databases of 3-D Chemical Structures, *Tetrahedron Computer Methodology*, 3, pp. 575–593.

Pogue, C. A. and Willett, P. (1987) Use of Text Signatures for Document Retrieval in a Highly Parallel Environment, *Parallel Computing*, 4, pp. 259–268.

Rasmussen, E. M., Downs, G. M. and Willett, P. (1988) Automatic Classification of Chemical Structure Databases Using a Highly Parallel Array Processor, *Journal of Computational Chemistry*, 9, pp. 378–386.

Rasmussen, E. M. and Willett, P. (1989) Efficiency of Hierarchic Agglomerative Clustering using the ICL Distributed Array Processor, *Journal of Documentation*, 45, pp. 1–24.

Rasmussen, E. M., Willett, P. and Wilson, T. (1993) Chemical Structure Handling Using the Distributed Array Processor, in W. A. Warr (editor), *Chemical Structures 2, The International Language of Chemistry*, Springer-Verlag, Berlin, pp. 327–341.

Thornton, J. M. and Gardner, S. P. (1989) Protein Motifs and Database Searching, *Trends in Biochemical Sciences*, 14, pp. 300–304.

Ullmann, J. R. (1976) An Algorithm for Subgraph Isomorphism, *Journal of the ACM*, 23, pp. 31–42.

Willett, P. (1987) *Similarity and Clustering in Chemical Information Systems*, Research Studies Press, Letchworth.

Willett, P. (1991) *Three-Dimensional Chemical Structure Handling*, Research Studies Press, Taunton.

Willett, P. and Rasmussen, E. M. (1990) *Parallel Database Processing: Text Retrieval and Cluster Analysis Using the DAP*, Pitman, London.

Willett, P., Wilson, T. and Reddaway, S. F. (1991) Atom-by-Atom Searching Using Massive Parallelism Implementation of the Ullmann Subgraph Isomorphism Algorithm on the Distributed Array Processor, *Journal of Chemical Information and Computer Sciences*, 31, pp. 225–233.

16 Exploitation of Parallelism in Commercial Systems

J. A. Keane[+] and X. Ye[*]

[+] *Department of Computation*
UMIST, Manchester

[*] *Department of Computer Science*
University of Auckland

1 INTRODUCTION

In recent years, parallel machines have been targeted at the commercial market place. At the same time there has been a recognition by commercial users that parallel systems offer potential improvements over existing mainframe systems in the areas of higher performance, larger memory size, more disks, higher levels of availability, open systems, better price/performance and scalability.

In this chapter, three parallel systems aimed at the commercial marketplace will be considered. The three systems will be described briefly and contrasted. The implementation of two commercial applications on the programming models provided by these systems will be considered. Finally, issues that impact on the spread of parallel systems will be discussed.

2 TRENDS IN PARALLEL SYSTEMS

In the last five years parallel systems with physically distributed memory have been aimed at the commercial marketplace. This type of physical architecture offers the potential for scalability beyond the 30 processor limit that has proven a bottleneck for physically shared memory architectures.

The three systems discussed in this chapter are a Kendall Square Research KSR1, a Meiko CS-2 and an Esprit European Declarative System (EDS). Both the KSR1 and the CS-2 are commercially available and targeted at both scientific and commercial applications. The EDS machine is a prototype system designed solely for the commercial marketplace. It was built by a consortium led by ICL, UK; Bull, France and Siemens, Germany. At least one commercial derivative, the ICL Goldrush machine, is now available.

Each of the machines is physically a set of nodes connected by a high-speed communication mechanism. Each of the nodes contain a processor and a store unit. All of the machines are share-nothing architectures, i.e. there is no physically shared memory in the system.

The provision of a virtual shared memory programming model on top of such scalable parallel hardware has been an interesting development of the last few years. The intention of such systems is to ally the programming convenience of the virtual shared memory model with the scalability of a physically distributed memory architecture. All three of the systems under consideration offer some variant of virtual shared memory.

The programming model for the three systems is relatively similar. KSR and EDS have adopted a lightweight thread approach for their parallel programming model, where a thread is a single, sequential flow of execution, i.e. a 'lightweight process' executing serially on a single processor. Each thread operates within a task – where a task corresponds to a conventional 'heavyweight' Unix-like process but does not have its 'own' control flow. The address space of the task is shared by all threads within the task – each thread is a flow of control. Because both EDS and KSR support virtual shared memory, threads of a task can be associated with different processors; each thread sees the same address space. Coherency of the task address space across multiple processors is handled by the underlying system, whether in hardware or software. The CS-2 is the newest machine and it is not yet clear what its programming model will provide. The model is discussed further in section 4.1.

3   KENDALL SQUARE RESEARCH: KSR1

Each node in the KSR1 (Frank, Burkhardt and Rothnie, 1993) has a custom-built superscalar 64-bit processor with a 0.5 Mbyte sub-cache. Each node also has a store unit, which is a local cache, of 32 Mbytes.

The KSR1 provides a virtual shared memory programming model, with all its processors connected to the logically shared, but physically distributed, memory. The physical memory is composed of the local caches of the nodes and the machine has no separate 'main' memory. When data is referenced by a node and it is not present in the local cache, a request is issued to a 'search engine' which causes the data to be found and brought to the local cache. The local caches are interconnected by the search engine which provides a routing and directory system for memory management. The local caches therefore behave logically as a single, shared address space.

The search engine is a two-level hierarchy of uni-directional rings. The lower level ring is termed a *search engine:0* and contains two types of cell:

- ALLCACHE Processor, Router, and Directory (APRD) cells include a processor, subcache, local cache, local cache directory and a portion of the Search engine:0 routing interconnect.

- ALLCACHE Router and Directory (ARD) cells include a directory of the entire Search engine:0 and a portion of the routing interconnect. The ARD directory comprises all the entries in all APRD local-cache directories in the Search engine:0

In the upper level ring, termed *search engine:1*, routing interconnect operates in a similar manner to a search engine:0 but it contains only ARD cells. A search engine:1 manages the routing and directory requirements of between two and 34 search engine:0s to which it is connected.

The memory system of the KSR thus comprises a number of levels which may be summarized as follows (ordered by increasing latency): sub-cache, local cache, on-search engine:0, off-search engine:0. Data is moved around these levels in 128 bytes chunks.

The KSR1 has a *symmetric* operating system (Almasi and Gottlieb, 1989). KSR O/S is a Unix-based OSF/1 operating system. Details of database software on the KSR1 can be found in Reiner, Miller and Wheat (1993). In that paper a query decomposer is described. In the general case, the KSR database model will make use of the underlying hardware model of moving data to the node where it is requested, i.e. a data sharing model.

The maximum envisaged configuration is 1088 nodes. A 256 node system has already been sold.

4   MEIKO: CS-2

Each node on the CS-2 (Meiko, 1993) can contain one or more processors. Each node has a store unit of between 32 and 512 Mbytes.

Each node has at least one computational processor: a super-scalar SPARC. Two on-chip caches are provided: a 20 Kbytes instruction cache and a 16 Kbytes data cache. An optional second level cache is available. For problems that require vector processing capability, two vector processors can be on a node, in addition to the SPARC processor.

Each node also contains a custom-built communication processor. The communication processor manages all remote data access without the need for data copying, kernel intervention or main processor interrupts. The use of remote store access primitives removes the synchronization overheads associated with message passing. The communication processor supports remote read and write operations specified by virtual processor number and virtual address.

The CS-2 data network is a multi-switch network; a fat tree with constant bandwidth per stage. The intention of the machine is to provide constant time for remote access from any node to any other node. This has been an important design consideration for the network. As the number of nodes grows, network stages are added to preserve bandwith.

Each node in the CS-2 runs a Unix operating system based on Solaris. It appears likely that certain extensions may be added to take advantage of the remote access primitives of the communications processor. This type of structure is termed separate supervisors (Almasi and Gottlieb, 1989). For a discussion of database implementation on the Meiko SPARC-based CS-1, the precursor to the CS-2, see Holman (1992).

The maximum configuration envisaged is 1024 nodes. A 256 node system has already been sold.

4.1 Programming model

The parallel programming model for the CS-2 is an extension to the CSTools model (Meiko 1990) that was available with earlier Meiko machines.

CSTools provides a message passing model of parallelism, with processes communicating and synchronizing by message passing. The processes do not share address space, i.e. the model is based on the traditional distributed memory model. The process model tends to be more coarse-grained than the virtual shared memory thread model. The hardware support for remote store access in the CS-2 can be exploited to implement this message passing model very efficiently.

At the present time the message passing model will be concentrated upon. However, extensions to the model are envisaged to allow processes in the same application to share address space across nodes by mapping common address spaces and providing efficient access between nodes by making use of the communication processor.

5   EUROPEAN DECLARATIVE SYSTEM: EDS

The EDS machine (Skelton, Hammer, Lopez *et al.*, 1992) has been specifically designed as a relational database engine that can also efficiently support declarative languages, e.g. functional and logic languages. It is intended, for the present, to act as a back-end database engine hosted by a mainframe.

By being very focused in its design EDS is different to the KSR1 and the CS-2 which have been targeted as general-purpose systems. EDS is also somewhat different in that what is described here is a prototype machine rather than a commercial product.

The system is a set of processing element nodes, and one each of:

- a *diagnostic element*, which collects run-time statistics, does initial program load, and handles PE failure,
- a *host element*, which interfaces the EDS system to a mainframe,

- an *I/O element*, which provides secondary disk storage. Disks are optional in the system because EDS is a back-end machine, and is seen as a main memory database system, i.e. the active part of the database is always memory resident. Disks are thus only for backup and recovery.

The functionality of a processing element node has been split into four units, which are connected by a standard high-speed internal M-bus:

- a *processing unit*, which in turn is made up of a SPARC processor, a floating point unit and an MMU which is coupled to a 64 Kbytes cache,
- a *system support unit*, which is responsible for low level message passing and remote store copying,
- a *network interface unit*, which is a custom-built chip for low-level inter-PE communication,
- a *store unit*, which is dynamic random access memory and can provide between 64 Mbytes to 2 Gbytes of main storage.

The EDS operating system is a Unix-based *symmetric* operating system (Almasi and Gottlieb, 1989), supporting:

- a light-weight process model which implements the concepts of threads, teams and tasks. A team is all threads of a task on a single node,
- message-passing inter/intra process communications coupled with efficient buffer management, and
- a memory model which employs a virtual address scheme that can spread across an arbitrary number of nodes.

The EDS virtual shared memory model is somewhat different to the KSR model. The EDS model is implemented in software at the operating system level. Hardware support for the software level is available to copy store between nodes in 128 byte chunks. However, because of the overhead in providing software coherency various relaxations of 'strong' coherency (i.e. every read 'sees' the most recent write) have been proposed. Such a 'weak' coherency model appears useful for declarative language implementation, however, the formal definition of the model is somewhat complex (Hussak and Keane, 1993).

The maximum envisaged configuration is 256 nodes. The performance target for this configuration was 12,000 transactions per second (TPS) at 30% utilization for OLTP applications. Simulation figures suggest 19200 TPS would be possible for a 256 node system at 30% utilization (Wong and Paci, 1992). For a description of the database implementation on the EDS machine, see Watson and Townsend (1990). The EDS database model is one of function shipping rather than data sharing (Haworth, 1992). The approach being to move functions that require data access to the node containing that data.

6 COMPARISON OF SYSTEMS

All three machines appear well suited to exploiting parallelism in commercial systems. This topic will be addressed more fully in section 7. In this section, the different emphasis of the systems will be discussed. Systems design is very much a compromise exercise. Important features are identified and emphasized within the design. Necessarily this involves less focus on what are, from the view of the designers, less important features.

The major emphasis of the KSR machine is the provision of virtual shared memory with hardware support. Thus very important elements of the system are the search engines and their functionality. The other systems have gone some of the way to providing virtual shared memory but not to the extent that KSR has. Overall, the KSR system is an extremely interesting experiment in parallel machine architecture. The KSR approach removes most of the considerations of data location that are necessary to program distributed memory model systems. The success of this feature will be determined by the frequency that commercial systems make use of strongly coherent shared store.

The major emphasis of the Meiko CS-2 system is the desire to make off-node access very efficient and of a uniform time throughout the system. The communications processor is highly innovative and appears to offer a highly scalable system. This uniform-access time contrasts both with the KSR memory latency levels, and the EDS delta network approach. At the present time the message passing model will be used to exploit the underlying remote access primitives. The remote store primitives also suggest that a virtual shared memory programming model will be provided at some stage.

The EDS system has been deigned specifically as a database engine and thus has not had to make design compromises to support different types of applications. The decision not to make use of disks but run as a main memory database engine is based on a view that disk speed and capacity are increasing more slowly than main memory, and disk costs are dropping less slowly than main memory costs. Thus main memory will be cheaper and much faster than disks. A consequence is that the local store size can be as large as 2 Gbytes, much larger than on either the Meiko or KSR. The approach to virtual shared memory lies somewhere between KSR and Meiko: the model is provided but mainly through a software implementation.

7 PARALLELIZING COMMERCIAL SYSTEMS

The parallelization of scientific and engineering codes to achieve high performance have proven to be extremely complicated tasks. Nonetheless, such systems have a number of advantages over commercial systems in respect to parallelization:

- Science and engineering systems are computation-intensive rather than data-intensive and, generally, are rather static in nature. Commercial, particularly symbolic systems, tend to be highly data dependent and thus dynamic in nature (Halstead, 1986). The consequence is that purely static analysis of commercial systems, whilst important and beneficial, is unlikely to be sufficient. Some dynamic analysis of commercial systems is likely to be necessary.
- Most scientific systems are written in Fortran. Fortran has 'parallelizing' compilers, which identify independent activity within a program that could be performed in parallel. In addition, some scientific problems exhibit vector-style parallelism that can be automatically detected.

    In contrast, commercial systems tend to be written in Cobol, or occasionally in C. Neither of these languages have commercially available tools for 'automatic' parallelism. With data partitioning there is much opportunity for parallelism within Cobol programs, and yet there appears to be little serious investigation in this area. Some Cobol programs access data via database software, and thus can exploit parallelism, but this does not apply in all cases.
- Commercial systems have rarely been parallelized, consequently there are few 'rules of thumb' available for programmers addressing the problem for the first time. Some of the techniques from the scientific world translate to the commercial world, but, as mentioned above, commercial systems address a different type of problem domain.

Generally, experience with parallelizing commercial systems suggests there is no short cut: often the problem needs to be revisited and a parallel structure devised which can take advantage of data distribution. Following this, implementation on a parallel programming model is necessary. This type of expertise is not usually available within commercial DP departments; the expertise present is normally application-specific, not parallel programming model-specific.

When there is application-specific expertise allied to parallel programming knowledge, the parallelization of a complex commercial application remains a difficult task. Even with a well-structured sequential system it is likely that the design structure of the system will have to be revisited. Commercial systems do tend to involve database software and it in this area that automatic parallelism will be most readily available. Already systems are available that offer both inter-query and intra-query parallelism. Even in this respect it is not apparent that it is easy to port to the new Unix-based database platforms. As yet there is little experience of 'complex' commercial systems on large-scale parallel machines.

In the next two sub-sections, two commercial systems are discussed that have been investigated for their parallelism. One is an application-level system, the other is more a system-software level system. For a comparison of distributed memory and virtual shared memory across a number of applications, see Keane, Grant and Xu (1995).

7.1 Actuarial system

In this section, a parallel design for an actuarial system is discussed (Keane, 1993). Implementations for this system have been considered for both message passing and virtual shared memory programming models.

The purpose of an actuarial system is to evaluate the liabilities of a pension scheme by calculating for each member their expected cost to the system in the future. The *calculation* part of an actuarial system is computationally intensive, made up of integer and floating-point operations. As a result, for pension schemes involving hundreds of thousands of members, the run-time on a Sun SPARC 330 is in terms of number of days. Thus the commercial value of parallelizing the system to achieve speedup to make such large schemes more tractable is considerable.

The main processing activity involves the application of a function to every member of a set:

$\forall m \in$ *pension-scheme*
map-update *(liabilities, m, process-member (map-lookup(member-data, m)))*

This model corresponds to a set of tasks, a task being the processing of a member, that can be implemented in a master-worker structure. The master is responsible for co-ordinating the work and collecting the results; the worker processes are identical and carry out work under direction of the master. This structure usually provides a good load balance as work is transferred dynamically as the worker processes become idle. This type of problem is representative of applications that suit a master-worker paradigm and problems that require a large amount of data to be passed to the worker before processing begins.

When implemented on a distributed memory model a master process passes approximately a megabyte of data (primarily the actuarial tables) to each of the worker processes at system set-up time. Subsequently the master passes down the data associated with a member (approximately 250 bytes). The worker process calculates the liability for this member and then passes the result back to the master to update the results list. The master then passes another member to the worker for processing, and so on.

In the actuarial system model, using virtual shared memory, the master process and each worker process would be associated with a thread. All such threads would belong to the same task, and thus share the same address space. The task address space would consist of both the actuarial table data and all the data for the members. This shared address space for the master and the workers would remove the need to explicitly pass the actuarial table data and the individual member data to each of the worker processes. In addition, the worker processes would not need to explicitly pass back results to the master: the workers need only update the shared address space.

Any data that is only to be read by the workers, e.g. the actuarial table data and the member data, would be passed to the appropriate processor by the underlying shared memory system. However, when updating shared memory, for example the task queue when a worker removes a task and the result list when a worker adds a result, there is a need to introduce locking and, thereby, introducing implied communication between the workers.

The initial set-up data is, in the virtual shared memory model, passed to each worker by the underlying mechanism as it is accessed. The only programmer instruction to pass this data from one processor to another is implicit in the logic of the thread code.

The virtual shared memory model is more convenient for the programmer as there is less 'housekeeping' activity, such as moving data, to be explicitly expressed, and the programmer can be more concerned with the logical structure of the program. At the same time the unit of transfer on both the KSR1 and the EDS machines is 128 bytes so if the 1 Mbyte initial set-up data is accessed densely in the worker then overall transfer rate of the data required for the worker to process members will be very slow. If the initial data is to be accessed sparsely then the EDS/KSR approach fits very well.

7.2 Database implementation

In this sub-section, issues that affect the scalability of database implementation on parallel systems are discussed. The provision of database software on parallel systems is perhaps the primary consideration for commercial users. In particular, an important aspect is the scalability of the database implementation. This is a different issue to how fast a single processor can run: although this is of importance, scalability is of more importance when systems of up to 10^3 nodes are being considered.

A crucial aspect to parallel database systems is how lock management is handled. Lock management is crucial because it ensures the consistency of data.

Such management is logically a centralized activity. When implemented this way on shared memory systems, lock management can often cause bottlenecks for database systems. This is an interesting problem because as a logically shared resource, the lock manager is used more and more as the number of processors increase because the frequency of lock requests increases. If the lock manager is centralized then there are severe consequences for scalability above a relatively small number of processors.

It appears likely that even on a virtual shared memory model (physically distributed memory machines), lock management is liable to be a bottleneck if implemented as a centralized resource because the network traffic will increase with increasing numbers of processors, thus once again impacting on scalability.

The solution that is forced upon a distributed memory system without a shared memory programming model is to design a parallel or distributed lock manager that runs on each node in the system in such a way that requests can be mapped to local lock managers, ensuring that there is no need for broadcasting information each time a lock is taken. This type of algorithm will, of course, work on virtual shared memory machines, but rather obviates the need for the model.

A related, important aspect for database systems is detecting deadlock. Once again, this is a logically centralized problem. It appears slightly harder to deal with than lock management because it cannot be purely localized to a node. However, once again algorithms have been designed that carry out as much detection as possible on a localized basis and only as much detection as is necessary in a non-local or global fashion.

It appears easier to handle the necessarily non-local or global aspects of deadlock detection on a virtual shared memory machine than on a distributed memory machine.

8 DISCUSSION

The spread of large-scale machines into the commercial marketplace has begun and will grow significantly in the next five years. In this time-frame a number of issues will become clearer.

- **Locality**: despite the hardware developments that have enabled virtual shared memory systems, locality remains crucial in all parallel systems, i.e. for high performance it is necessary that most references from activity on a node are to its closely-coupled store unit. This is likely to remain so despite virtual shared memory or uniform remote access time.
- **Virtual shared memory**: if virtual shared memory is used extensively in commercial systems then a hardware-supported implementation will be much faster than a software implementation. At this stage it appears

that there is increased programmer convenience with the virtual shared memory model. It is not yet clear how essential the model will prove.

It is clear that there is a trend towards providing hardware support for virtual shared memory, but there appears to be no obvious agreement yet on what the programming model will look like.

- **Commodity items**: the provision of hardware support for virtual shared memory, at present, involves proprietary hardware of some sort. It is obviously easier and faster in development time to design systems that include commodity items throughout. This allows interception of specialist development, rather than requiring in-house expertise on all fronts. The trade-off is that it is extraordinarily difficult to get peak performance from processors anyway, so that having a system design involving custom hardware can be an advantage if it enables users to achieve higher absolute performance.

  It appears likely that networks will become commodity items in the next five years. The style of network is not yet obvious though. If this occurs then parallel systems will become almost identical at the hardware level and the value-adding aspect will be the software implementations, i.e. operating systems, compilers and database implementations.

- **Availability and recovery**: a very important and much neglected aspect of commercial systems requirements is ensuring availability and recovery (Keane, Franklin, Grant *et al.*, 1993). It is not acceptable that parallel systems still have single points of failure in their design, that, for example, force a re-boot when a processor fails. With database systems particularly, recovery from a crash can be a very long task.

  It is also unacceptable that even if processor failure can be handled the work being run on that processor is lost. The user is normally sent a message to say **restart job**. In the case of either a large MIS query, perhaps being run overnight, or a time-critical OLTP transaction worth millions or billions of pounds this is inadequate. To ensure that such failure recovery is handled transparently to the user it appears necessary to introduce duplication into the system software level.

  Parallel systems provide the opportunity to provide very high, perhaps continuous, levels of availability, and it is expected that this issue will be of most significance in the next few years.

In conclusion, the three systems described in this chapter represent interesting developments in parallel systems design. Certain design emphases have been identified in this chapter: time will determine which is deemed the most suitable for commercial applications.

REFERENCES

Almasi, G. S. and Gottlieb, A. (1989) *Highly Parallel Computing*, Benjamin/Cummings Publishing Co.

Frank, S., Burkhardt, H. and Rothnie, J. (1993) The KSR1: Bridging the Gap Between Shared Memory and MPPs, in: *Proceedings of Compcon'93*, San Francisco, USA, February, IEEE Press, pp. 285–294.

Halstead, R. (1986) Parallel Symbolic Computing, *IEEE Computer*, August, pp. 35–43.

Haworth, G. (1992) *Information Servers, Present and Future,* in: (Ed. P. Valduriez) *Parallel Processing and Data Management*, UNICOM Applied Information Technology 13, Chapman & Hall, pp. 261–274.

Holman, A. (1992) The Computing Surface: A Parallel & Scalable Open Systems Platform for ORACLE, Meiko Ltd, 650 Aztec West, Almondsbury, Bristol, BS12 4SD, UK.

Hussak W. and Keane J. A. (1993) Representation of Coherency Classes, in Parallel Systems, in: *Proceedings of SPDP 93*, Dallas, USA, October, IEEE Press, pp. 391–398.

Keane, J. A. (1993) Parallelizing a Financial System, *Future Generation Computer Systems*, 9(1), May, pp. 41–51.

Keane, J. A., Franklin, T. J., Grant, A. J., Sumner, R. and Xu, M. Q. (1993) Commercial Users' Requirements for Parallel Systems, in: *Proceedings of 1993 DAGS Parallel Computation Symposium*, New Hampshire, USA, June, pp. 15–25.

Keane J. A., Grant, A. J. and Xu, M. Q. (1995) Comparing Distributed Memory and Virtual Shared Memory Parallel Programming Models, *Future Generation Computer Systems*, 11(1), January (to appear).

Meiko Ltd. (1990) CSTools Tutorial for C Programmers, 650 Aztec West, Almondsbury, Bristol, BS12 4SD, UK.

Meiko Ltd. (1993) CS-2 Product Description, 650 Aztec West, Almondsbury, Bristol, BS12 4SD, UK.

Reiner, D., Miller, J. and Wheat, D. (1993) The Kendall Square Query Decomposer, in: *Proceedings of COMPCON '93*, San Francisco, USA, February, IEEE Press, pp. 300–302.

Skelton, C. J., Hammer, C., Lopez, M., Reeve, M. J., Townsend, P. and Wong K. F. (1992) EDS: A Parallel Computer System for Advanced Information Processing, in: *PARLE'92* (Eds. D. Etiemble and J. C. Syre), Lecture Notes in Computer Science Volume 605, Springer-Verlag, pp. 3–18.

Valduriez, P. (Ed.) (1992) *Parallel Processing and Data Management*, UNICOM Applied Information Technology 13, Chapman & Hall.

Watson, P. and Townsend, P. (1990) The EDS Parallel Relational Database System, in: *Parallel Database Systems* (Ed. P. America), Lecture Notes in Computer Science Volume 503, Springer-Verlag, pp. 149–166.

Wong, K. F. and Paci, M. (1992) *Performance Evaluation of an OLTP Application,* in: (Ed. P. Valduriez) *Parallel Processing and Data Management*, UNICOM Applied Information Technology 13, Chapman & Hall, pp. 317–350.